PUBLICATION NUMBER 8
Duke University Commonwealth-Studies Center

Commonwealth Perspectives

Duke University Commonwealth-Studies Center Publications

Commonwealth

Perspectives

Nicholas Mansergh, Robert R. Wilson,
Joseph J. Spengler, James L. Godfrey,
B. U. Ratchford, Brinley Thomas

PUBLISHED FOR THE

Duke University Commonwealth-Studies Center

DUKE UNIVERSITY PRESS, DURHAM, N. C.

CAMBRIDGE UNIVERSITY PRESS, LONDON

1958

PRINTED IN THE UNITED STATES OF AMERICA

BY THE SEEMAN PRINTERY, INC., DURHAM, N. C.

PREFACE

"IF IT DID NOT exist, you could not invent it." This use of a neat aphorism was Professor K. C. Wheare's way of calling attention in 1953 to the peculiar structure of the British Commonwealth, a structure marked by a shifting equilibrium between forces making for both unity and separateness. It is therefore appropriate that this volume, the eighth in the Commonwealth-Studies series, should consist of essays which throw light on some of the factors which affect this evolving relationship.

These essays represent revised versions of faculty contributions to a Joint Seminar conducted at Duke University in the spring of 1957. The broad purpose of the Seminar was to provide for a group of graduate students in economics, history, and political science an introduction to Commonwealth problems and to the possibilities for advanced research therein. The faculty participants—economists, historians, political scientists—contributed to the objectives of the Seminar through a series of papers in which they brought to bear the research and analytical techniques of their respective disciplines.

The opening essay on "Commonwealth Membership," by Professor Nicholas Mansergh, traces the formulation of the Commonwealth concept, the translation of Commonwealth status into positive law, and the enlargement of the Commonwealth by the addition of Asian and other members in the post Second World War years. It is this development that has added to the diversity of the types of membership. The emergence of the multiracial Commonwealth has, as Professor Mansergh shows, snapped one of the original bonds of Commonwealth unity, that of common allegiance, and placed certain other bonds under added stress. The second essay, "Commonwealth Foreign Policies 1945-56: A Perspective View," also by Professor Mansergh, further illustrates the interplay between centripetal and centrifugal forces. The events leading up to the Second World War and the crises resulting from the East-West split afterwards have perhaps served to indicate the circumstances under which the members of the Commonwealth, or at least most of them, are prepared to act in unison. They have also pointed up the conditions under which Commonwealth countries have gone their separate ways in their foreign policies. Not to be ignored, as Professor Mansergh points out, is the gravitational pull exerted by the United States on certain Commonwealth members.

The third essay, "The Commonwealth and the Law of Nations," by Professor Robert R. Wilson, investigates the nature of the rules of public law applicable between members of the Commonwealth. Professor Wilson considers particularly the rules and practices pertaining to nationality, settlement of disputes, and international organizations. In these areas and in others, the *inter se* legal relationships differ in some respects from those which under international law would normally obtain as between independent states. But, as Professor Wilson indicates, the prophecy made twenty years ago that these *inter se* relationships were likely "to approximate more and more closely to the analogy of international law" has indeed been borne out.

In his study "The Commonwealth: Demographic Dimensions —Implications," Professor Joseph J. Spengler is concerned, *inter alia*, with the problem of whether the demographic forces in the Commonwealth are "essentially centrifugal or centripetal." His survey of the demographic situation in the many areas of the Commonwealth leads to the conclusion that continued Commonwealth unity must rest on bonds other than those of common ethnic origin, together with the associated common values and sentiments. Professor Spengler suggests that under given conditions such bonds, including those of economic advantage and defense security, may be existent.

The next two essays in this volume do not deal with the Commonwealth as a whole. However, they provide case studies which focus attention on two countries, the internal developments of which affect their ties as Commonwealth members. "The Emergence of Ghana," by Professor James L. Godfrey, sketches the constitutional evolution of the first genuinely African member. The very newness of Ghana as an independent political entity places in bold relief certain problems faced not only by it but also by other members of the "new" Commonwealth. Among these are the underdeveloped economy, the changing features of the bureaucracy, and the unresolved constitutional conflicts. Professor B. U. Ratchford's essay, "The Development of Health and Welfare Programs in Australia: A Case Study," serves to turn attention to the "old" Commonwealth and what is likely to be a persistent domestic problem in all of the "older" members. It is the balancing of resource expenditures as between welfare needs and the requirements of capital expansion. While this balancing is determined largely by the domestic situation, it affects trade policy and, above all, the capacity of older members as suppliers of capital for the undeveloped economies of the "new" Commonwealth members.

The last essay is by Professor Brinley Thomas and it analyzes "The Evolution of the Sterling Area and Its Prospects." Among the economic factors which will determine the future of the Sterling Area are the need for investment capital, the repayment of debts to non-Sterling Bloc creditors, and the urge for trade with countries outside the Bloc. The "towering stature and bewildering dynamism of the American economy" must be considered in assaying the prospects. Professor Thomas finds some grounds for optimistic prediction as to the future of the Sterling Area.

And now it is appropriate to introduce the contributors more formally. They are: Nicholas Mansergh, Smuts Professor of the

History of the British Commonwealth, Cambridge University;
Robert R. Wilson, Professor of Political Science, Duke University; Joseph J. Spengler, Professor of Economics, Duke University; James L. Godfrey, Professor of History and Dean of
the Faculty, University of North Carolina; B. U. Ratchford,
Professor of Economics, Duke University; and Brinley Thomas,
Professor of Economics, University College, Cardiff, Wales.

The interpretations and conclusions presented in this volume
are those of the several contributors and are not to be considered
as the views of the Commonwealth-Studies Center or of the
Carnegie Corporation, whose assistance has made possible the work
of the Center.

DAVID R. DEENER

R. TAYLOR COLE

CONTENTS

Commonwealth Perspectives

Commonwealth Membership

Nicholas Mansergh

1. Dominion Status: The Demand for Definition

In the debate on the Anglo-Irish Treaty of 1921 Mr. Lloyd
George posed the question: "What does dominion status mean?"
He did not attempt to answer it. He spoke instead of the dangers
of definition. He recalled that the Dominion delegates to the
Imperial Conference in 1921 had agreed that there should not
be "any rigid definitions" of imperial relations. "That is not
the way of the British Constitution," he said. And he continued,
"We realize the danger of rigidity and the danger of limiting
our constitution by too many finalities."[1] The question at issue
was not, however, whether there should be "too many finalities"
but rather whether some measure of definition was not due, indeed, overdue. Conservative opinion in Britain, in Australia,
and in New Zealand discounted the need almost altogether.
Its viewpoint was eloquently stated by Australia's ever forthright
Mr. W. M. Hughes at the 1921 Imperial Conference:

The difference between the status of the dominions now and twenty five
years ago is very great. We were Colonies, we became Dominions. We
have been accorded the status of nations. Our progress in material great-
ness has kept pace with our constitutional development. Let us leave well
alone. That is my advice . . . . We, the representatives of the Dominions,
are met together to formulate a foreign policy for the Empire. What
greater advance is conceivable? What remains to us? We are like so
many Alexanders. What other worlds have we to conquer?[2]

[1] *Parl. Deb.*, 5th ser., Commons, vol. 149, cols. 27-28 (Dec. 14, 1921).
[2] Cmd. 1474; reprinted in Arthur B. Keith, *Speeches and Documents on the
British Dominions 1918-1931* (London, 1932), 56.

But others, including General Smuts, to whom Mr. Hughes's argument was immediately addressed, did not, and indeed could not, agree.

At the Imperial War Conference in 1917 General Smuts had already urged that in intra-imperial relations constitutional forms and political realities should be brought in conformity. As things were there was the practice of equality, but the theory of subordination. That theory was embodied in convention and in law. Above all the supremacy of the United Kingdom Parliament remained unimpaired. Even if its overriding authority was rarely exercised in respect of the self-governing Dominions, it continued to possess full statutory sanction. This was clearly inconsistent with notions of equality as between the United Kingdom and the Dominions. General Smuts felt indeed that the unique character of the British Empire, "the only successful experiment in international government that has ever been made,"[3] was disguised to its own disadvantage by such outworn constitutional apparel and that the continued existence of what Mr. W. M. Hughes lightly dismissed as "a figment, a few ancient forms" in sober fact constituted a barrier to the uninhibited membership of a British Commonwealth of free and equal nations by peoples of non-British extraction. General Smuts, as his faithful companion in many a bitter electoral contest Denys Reitz later recalled, knew from experience that many Afrikaners, filled with memories of Boer War imperialism and moved by strong racial sentiment,[4] were not easily to be convinced either that practical equality was consistent with legal inequality or that the forms of Dominion subordination to Britain were merely "figments."

A few years later in a memorandum entitled "The Constitution of the British Commonwealth," which sums up a whole phase of Commonwealth history, General Smuts pointed out that

[3] Speech at the Imperial War Conference 1917; reprinted in Arthur B. Keith, *Selected Speeches and Documents on British Colonial Policy 1763-1917* (London, 1948), part II, 393.
[4] Denys Reitz, *No Outspan* (London, 1943), 26-27.

unless dominion status was quickly solved in a way that would satisfy the aspirations of these young nations [the Dominions], separatist movements were to be expected in the Commonwealth . . . . The only way to meet such movements is not to wait until they are fully developed and perhaps irresistible in their impetus, but to anticipate them and to make them impossible by the most generous concession of the dominion nationhood and existence as a state. The warning against always being too late with a proper solution, of which Ireland is an example to the whole Commonwealth, is one which we can ignore only at our own peril.[5]

It was not in fact ignored. The addition of the nationalist Irish Free State to the number of the Dominions in 1921 in itself strengthened the case and reinforced the demand for definition while in the immediately succeeding years experience in foreign policy and especially in treaty making suggested that intra-Commonwealth misunderstanding and friction would almost certainly be a consequence of continuing failure to do so. The accession of General Hertzog to office in South Africa in 1924 and Mr. Mackenzie King's conviction, crystallized by the judgment of the Judicial Committee of the Privy Council in *Nadan's Case*[6] and by his controversy with the Governor-General Lord Byng (following the rejection of his advice to dissolve the Canadian House of Commons), that subordination was more than a theory were of decisive importance in respect of timing. By 1926 the risks of inaction were acknowledged to be greater than the risks of definition even by those temperamentally allergic to such an exercise.

The demand for the definition of intra-Commonwealth relations was in essence a demand for full equality of status as between the United Kingdom and the self-governing Dominions. It was inspired by a belief that continuing subordination in form implied an essential subordination in fact and that such subordination, appropriate in the days of Empire, was altogether inconsistent with the nature of the British Commonwealth as it emerged

---

[5] Reprinted in C. M. Van den Heever, *General J. B. M. Hertzog* (trans., and abridged by the author; Johannesburg, 1946), 212.

[6] Reprinted in Frederick Madden, *Imperial Constitutional Documents 1765-1952* (Oxford, 1953), 47-54.

after the First World War. "I think, Sir, it will be generally agreed," General Hertzog observed in 1926, "that the corner stone of the Empire is the will, the goodwill of those who compose it . . . . If therefore, the Empire is to be maintained . . . we must see that the will to live in the Empire, as a Commonwealth of free nations, will in future, as it is to-day, be present with everyone of its constituent elements."[7] This could be assured, as he rightly contended, only if there were full equality in form and in fact between the member nations which composed it. This was something more easily achieved than many Dominion nationalists, including General Hertzog, supposed.

In 1926 General Hertzog believed there were strong forces in Britain prepared to challenge Dominion claims to equality. He came to London for the Imperial Conference of that year therefore resolved either to secure equality or to advocate the secession of South Africa from the Commonwealth. But the predominant British interest, as Mr. Amery's record amply confirms,[8] was the continued unity of the Empire and assuredly that would not have been well served by resistance to Dominion views. The Government of the United Kingdom, in fact, neither opposed nor contemplated opposition to them so long as they were not inconsistent with that aim. There were, however, many doubts in London about the practical possibility of satisfactory definition. General Hertzog's first draft seemed to confirm them. It spoke of the Dominions as "independent" states—a phrase whose American overtones Mackenzie King disliked—as being "equal in status and separately entitled to international recognition" and "freely associated as members of the British Commonwealth of Nations." Then there followed some sentences saying that "whatever surviving forms of inequality or subordination may exist in the mutual relations of one to another of the aforesaid states, either in regard to the legislative, executive or judicial

[7] Quoted in W. K. Hancock, *Survey of British Commonwealth Affairs* (London, 1937), I, 161.
[8] L. S. Amery, *Thoughts on the Constitution* (London, 1953), 128-132; and *My Political Life* (3 vols.; London, 1953-55), II, chap. 12.

power, such inequality and insubordination are attributable to, and dependent upon, the voluntary agreement of the associated state concerned" and that steps should be taken to make the essential equality of status known to all the world.[9] This was rather painfully pedantic drafting which does something to explain why even the Irish, Hertzog's natural allies in 1926, found him something of a bore—Kevin O'Higgins allowed that "Hertzog was a very decent and likeable sort of man" but he also complained that he talked "a lot and none too clearly"[10]—but it was also instructive inasmuch as it provided a statement of the principal aims of Dominion nationalists at this time.

There were many succeeding drafts and suggestions, in the course of which Mr. Amery reintroduced the term British Empire while the Irish ejected "common bond of allegiance" and the South Africans "common citizenship of the Empire." Ultimately the definition, the work of the Committee on Inter-Imperial Relations of which all the Prime Ministers were members and over which Lord Balfour presided "with a smile like moonlight on a tombstone,"[11] produced the Report which bears his name. It is a document to be considered as a whole with particular attention to, but without undue emphasis upon, that section of it which was italicized because of a typist's misunderstanding and which describes the relations of the United Kingdom and the Dominions in phrases as well known as any in British constitutional history.[12]

The Balfour Report stated the Committee on Inter-Imperial Relations were of the opinion that nothing would be gained by attempting to lay down a constitution for the whole Empire, but there was in it one important element which from a constitutional viewpoint had reached full development. This element was composed of the United Kingdom and the overseas Dominions. Their position and mutual relations might therefore be "readily

[9] Van den Heever, op. cit., 213-217.
[10] T. de v. White, Kevin O'Higgins (London, 1948), 221.
[11] Ibid., 222.
[12] The Summary of Proceedings of the Imperial Conference of 1926, Cmd. 2768, contains the Report of the Committee. It is reprinted in Keith, Speeches and Documents, 161-170.

defined." "They are autonomous communities within the British Empire, equal in status, in no way subordinate one to another in any aspect of their domestic or external affairs, though united by a common allegiance to the Crown, and freely associated as members of the British Commonwealth of Nations." In this sentence four important characteristics of membership of the British Commonwealth, which comprised the United Kingdom as well as the Dominions, were identified. The Dominions were (1) autonomous communities (2) within the British Empire (3) freely associated as members of the British Commonwealth of Nations, (4) and united by a common allegiance to the Crown. There was also some ambiguity which enabled New Zealanders for example to place most emphasis on their being within the British Empire and South African nationalists by contrast on "autonomous" communities, but it was of secondary importance. So too, were the questions of interpretation that arose about the meaning of "freely associated"—did it or did it not imply that a Dominion was free to dissociate if it so desired?—and "common allegiance." Henceforward at least these were questions that could be debated within an accepted context. That is what made the 1926 Report so significant. It identified the things of fundamental importance in a new and experimental interstate relationship and in so doing suggested the pattern of future development.

The setting in which the 1926 italicized definition was placed was written by Lord Balfour.[13] It observed that a foreigner attempting to understand the true character of the British Empire by the aid of this formula "would be tempted to think that it was devised rather to make mutual interference impossible than to make mutual co-operation easy."[14] But he would be mistaken. The rapid evolution of Dominions, it continued, demanded an adjustment to changing conditions. "The tendency towards equality of status was both right and inevitable." "Geographical

[13] Blanche E. C. Dugdale, *Arthur James Balfour* (2 vols.; New York, 1930), II, 281-282.

[14] This is very questionably true. The belief that Britain retained control is implicit, for example, in the published German Foreign Office documents on the origins of the Second World War.

and other conditions" made federation "impossible" and the only alternative was autonomy. Every Dominion in 1926 was in fact, if not always in form, master of its own destiny and subject to no compulsion whatever. But the British Empire "is not founded upon negations." It depends upon positive ideals. Free institutions are its life blood. Free co-operation is its instrument. And while each Dominion is now and must always remain the sole judge of the nature and extent of its co-operation "no common cause will, in our opinion, be thereby imperilled." Equality of status, the Report continued, is thus the root-principle governing inter-imperial relations, not, be it noted, either common allegiance or free association. But principles of equality do not extend to function. Diplomacy and defense required more flexible machinery and for a long time the United Kingdom would remain the predominant partner. This was certainly true. It was also a distinction which imperialists emphasized, nationalists discounted. It existed markedly in the transitional period[15] and it made relations psychologically difficult in the years before the Second World War. There was equality in principle but dependence in some fields of practice.

2. Dominion Status: Its Realization in Law and Convention

The Balfour Report was "first and foremost purely accurate description." It described "not merely the form but the motion of a community."[16] Professor Wheare, in the authoritative study on the Statute of Westminster and Dominion status, has noted that the importance of the Balfour Report was underestimated in 1926 and in consequence that of the Statute of Westminster overestimated in 1931 because the full implications of the definitions included in it were not realized until the attempt was made to translate some of them into strict law five years later[17]—

[15] See Nicholas Mansergh, Survey of British Commonwealth Affairs: Problems of External Policy 1931-1939 (London, 1953), 73-79, 429-432, for some assessment of this.
[16] Hancock, op. cit., 263.
[17] K. C. Wheare, The Statute of Westminster and Dominion Status (4th ed.; London, 1949), 28-29.

or to put the matter rather differently, the Balfour Report had made explicit the principles on which the British Commonwealth rested and what remained to be done thereafter was the important but lesser task of giving them effect where necessary in law. Since equality was the "root-principle," this involved first the removal of inequalities. They included the power of reservation whether obligatory or discretionary, the power of disallowance, the sections of the Colonial Laws Validity Act of 1865 which declared that "an Act of Parliament or any provision thereof shall be said to extend to any colony when it is made applicable to such colony by the express words or necessary intendment of such Act . . ." and that such colonial legislation (section 2) as was repugnant to any provisions of an act of the Imperial Parliament "shall be to the extent of such repugnancy . . . void and inoperative." Even if it was at the time of enactment "an enabling Act not a restrictive or disabling Act,"[18] its provisions were clearly inconsistent with equality of status. There were also limitations on the power of Dominions to enact extraterritorial legislation implying inequality and causing practical inconvenience. All these were matters on which detailed and expert inquiry was necessary. It was carried out in 1929-30 by the Operation of Dominion Legislation and Merchant Shipping Legislation Committee[19] and the Imperial Conference of 1930.[20] Where appropriate their recommendations were embodied in the Statute of Westminster.

The Imperial Conference of 1926 in enunciating the root-principle of equality had itself either reinterpreted certain of the conventions of intra-Commonwealth relations or made recommendations to ensure the full application of this principle. Thus the Conference had recommended a small amendment of the King's title to take account of the status of the Irish Free State. This amendment contemplated the substitution of a comma for an "and" between Great Britain and Ireland so that the title would read, "George V by the Grace of God of Great Britain,

[18] See *ibid.*, 79.   [19] Cmd. 3479.
[20] Cmd. 3717 and 3718.

Ireland and the British Dominions beyond the Seas King, Defender of the Faith, Emperor of India." King George V acquiesced with reluctance in this modification, for in such matters, we are told, he disliked change.[21] In respect of the office of Governor-General the Conference recommended that the Governor-General in a Dominion should in all essential respects hold the same position in relation to the administration of public affairs as the King in the United Kingdom. This satisfied Mr. Mackenzie King, mindful of his controversy with General Byng about the discretionary authority of Governors-General but did not define what the King's position was. In conformity with this recommendation the Governor-General was no longer to act in any way as the representative or agent of the United Kingdom Government. The Imperial Conference of 1930 carried this reinterpretation of the role and functions of Governors-General to its logical conclusion by stating that "the parties interested in the appointment of a Governor-General of a Dominion are H. M. the King whose representative he is and the Dominion concerned. . . . The Ministers who tender and are responsible for such advice are H. M. ministers in the Dominion concerned."[22] Mr. Scullin in the exercise of this authority overbore the King's wishes in pressing the appointment of Sir Isaac Isaacs as first Australian-born Governor-General of Australia.[23] The royally representative character of the office declined in succeeding years.

Equality in the relationship of the Dominions and the United Kingdom to the Crown was most significantly recognized by according to them an equal responsibility in determining the succession to it. "In as much as the Crown is the symbol of the free association of the members of the British Commonwealth of Nations, and as they are united by a common allegiance to the Crown, it would be in accord with the established constitutional position of all the members of the Commonwealth in relation to one another that any alteration in the law touching the Succession to the Throne or the Royal Style and Titles shall hereafter re-

[21] See Harold Nicolson, *King George V* (London, 1952), 483-484.
[22] Cmd. 3717.   [23] Nicolson, *op. cit.*, 477-482.

quire the assent as well of the Parliaments of all the Dominions as of the Parliament of the United Kingdom."[24]   This definition of Dominion responsibilities in respect of the royal succession set out in 1929, was reproduced in the preamble to the Statute of Westminster.   Mr. Amery entertained misgivings about its possible implication of a Dominion relationship to the monarchy that amounted to no more than a purely personal union.   General Hertzog on the other hand and for precisely the same reason was well contented until General Smuts argued that the new relationship precluded secession without agreement.   Hertzog responded by moving an amendment in the House of Assembly adopting the Report of the 1929 Conference subject to the condition that the relevant section should not be taken as "derogating from the right of any member of the British Commonwealth of Nations to withdraw therefrom."   This was duly noted by the Imperial Conference in 1930.

The Preamble of the Statute of Westminster 1931,[25] which has not force of law, described the conventions already agreed in respect of status and of succession to the Crown and declared that in accordance with the established constitutional position no law made by Parliament of the United Kingdom "shall extend to a dominion save at its request and consent."   The Act itself clarified the powers of Dominion Parliaments in accordance with the principles of the 1926 Imperial Conference by giving them power to legislate on matters of Dominion concern hitherto within the competence of Imperial Parliament, to repeal legislation on such matters and to legislate with extraterritorial effect coupled with the assurance that the United Kingdom Parliament would legislate only at their request and with their consent in matters affecting them.   In this way the root-principle of equality was expressed in a statutory form.

It was at the request of some of the Dominions that some continuing restrictions were placed upon their powers.   At Canada's request section 7 expressly excluded the British North

---

[24] Cmd. 3479, sec. 60; reprinted in Keith, *Speeches and Documents*, 189.
[25] 22 Geo. 5, c. 4.

America Acts, 1867-1930 from the operation of the statute; at the request of Pacific Dominions section 8 likewise excluded the Constitutions of Australia and New Zealand; section 10, inserted again at the request of the Dominion Governments concerned, stipulated that the Statute should not apply to New Zealand, Australia, and Newfoundland unless and until it was adopted by their respective Parliaments. In 1931 they did not want to exercise the powers conferred by the Statute whilst Canada, subject to the reservation in respect of its Constitution, South Africa, and the Irish Free State accepted them wholeheartedly, though neither South Africa nor the Irish Free State altogether relished the notion of an act of the British Parliament as the charter of their freedom. For this reason South Africa embodied the substance of the Statute of Westminster in its own Status of the Union Act, 1934, whilst the militant wing of Irish nationalism which came to office in 1932 under Mr. de Valera moved towards the goal of a new constitution deriving its authority directly from the people. Let us consider these varied reactions more closely.[26]

The Statute of Westminster was not adopted in Australia and New Zealand until 1942 and 1947 respectively. In 1931 there was even protracted delay in taking the steps necessary to complete its drafting. The reasons were those elaborated by Mr. Menzies in 1942. "I think that the business of devising the Balfour Declaration in 1926, and the business of devising and drafting the Preamble to the Statute of Westminster . . . were both open to grave criticism." The 1926 declaration was "a grave disservice"; the 1926-31 process "a misguided attempt" to reduce to written terms something which "was a matter of the spirit and not of the letter."[27] Mr. W. M. Hughes at the same vantage point in time spoke of the 1926 Report as a "wonderful document." "It took stock of everything. Nothing escaped it . . . . Every Prime Minister went away perfectly satisfied—

---

[26] The text of the Statute and source of material on Dominion reaction to it are to be found in Nicholas Mansergh, *Documents and Speeches on British Commonwealth Affairs 1931-1952* (2 vols.; London, 1953), I, secs. I and II.

[27] *Ibid.*, 21.

Mr. Bruce because it altered nothing that affected Australia, Mr. Mackenzie King because it taught Lord Byng where he got off, and General Hertzog because he was able to assure the burghers that the King of England was no longer King of South Africa, although it was true that the King of South Africa was also King of England."[28]   But to Hughes it was all a mistaken attempt to appease the unappeasable.   The predominant Pacific view was summed up by the New Zealand Attorney-General in a letter to an Australian colleague on a matter which bore no relation to the Statute—"it is all the fault of that damned Statute of Westminster."   In Britain there was a lack of enthusiasm in Conservative circles, *The Times*, for example, writing of the Statute of Westminster as a piece of "mere pedantry" for which there was and could be no enthusiasm but about which also there would be no great apprehension.[29]

The influence of the Canadian Government had probably been decisive in securing the passage of the Statute of Westminster, and steps were taken shortly after its enactment to abolish Canadian appeals to the Judicial Committee of the Privy Council in criminal cases, *Nadan's Case* being much in mind.   In South Africa the Statute was of crucial political importance.   In the halcyon days of late 1926 even Dr. Malan had said that "instead of looking upon Great Britain as the conqueror we look upon her as the mother of our freedom."   Full independence, he felt, was attained with the Balfour Report.   But Hertzog's liberal interpretation of the Report was challenged by English-speaking imperialists, and controversy was revived.   For Nationalists the aim was equality.   They deemed the assertion of a South African as distinct from a United Kingdom source, as hitherto, for the fundamental law of the Union to be a condition of such equality.   Accordingly they concluded that the substance of the Statute of Westminster should be enacted by the South African Parliament as a South African law.   This was not without its complications, chief among them being the existence of the entrenched

[28] *Ibid.*, 26-27.
[29] *The History of the Times* (4 vols.; London, 1952), IV, part II, 879-890.

clauses in the South Africa Act of 1909. These clauses, safe-
guarding existing voting rights in the Cape and equality of the
English and Dutch languages, had been a condition of Union.
Mindful of this Generals Smuts and Hertzog in requesting the
enactment of the Statute of Westminster placed on record that
this was done on the understanding that the Act would not
derogate from the entrenched clauses of the South Africa Act.
Their statement was morally but not legally binding. Later
agreement between the two generals resulting in a Coalition and
then in a Fusion government made possible the enactment of the
Status of the Union Act in 1934.[30] Section 2 indicated its principal purpose. "The Parliament of the Union shall be the sovereign
legislative power in and over the Union." As a corollary the
position of the King as King of South Africa was emphasized and
by implication there was enunciated the doctrine of a divisible
crown. In all this Afrikaner legalism was seeking to find a
way by which a separatist policy could be legally carried through.
But the bearing of the Statute of Westminster upon the entrenched clauses of the South Africa Act was unresolved in law
and was to be the occasion of a major constitutional crisis some
twenty years later.

Irish emphasis after 1932 was rather different. A party of
revolution was in office, republican by conviction, and its members
did not want the King in their constitution but out of it. Mr.
de Valera customarily referred to him as "an alien monarch."
There was also the question of the Treaty recognized in the Constitution of 1922 as constituting the fundamental law of the state.
Amendments to the Statute designed to distinguish the Irish position from other Dominions enlisted little support at Westminster
but in constitutional disputes following de Valera's accession to
office the United Kingdom Government contended that since the
Treaty constituted the fundamental law of the state it froze the
Irish constitutional position to the extent that change was conditional on United Kingdom agreement even when permissible for

[30] No. 69 of 1934.

other Dominions. This view, although accepted by the Irish courts, paradoxically enough was deemed untenable on appeal by the Judicial Committee of the Privy Council.

The abdication of King Edward VIII in 1936 was the first major test of the new constitutional arrangements. All the self-governing members of the Commonwealth were concerned with the succession to the Crown. In the early stages of the crisis, however, Mr. Baldwin alone advised the King as "counsellor and friend." The King himself first suggested consultation with Dominion Governments on the question of a possible morganatic marriage with Mrs. Simpson. Consultation followed between Governments and not, as might have been expected, between the King and his Governors-General.[31] Dominion Governments were united in opposition to it. Mr. Lyons spoke of "widespread condemnation" if Mrs. Simpson became Queen and of a morganatic marriage as "running counter to the best traditions of the Monarchy."[32] Mr. Mackenzie King said that Canada would not approve whether Mrs. Simpson became Queen or not; General Hertzog that abdication would be a lesser evil than marriage. "The one would be a great shock, the other a permanent wound." The King abdicated. Because Australia and New Zealand had not adopted the Statute of Westminster, the Abdication Act merely records their assent thereto. Canada requested and consented to its enactment. The South African Government maintained no legislation was necessary in the Union, whereupon King George VI succeeded under the relevant provisions of Status of Union Act on the signature of the Instrument of Abdication by King Edward VIII on December 10. This interpretation of the constitutional position served further to underline the separate position of the King as King of South Africa. The Irish Free State took the opportunity of removing

[31] Lord Beaverbrook, when he learned of the procedure adopted, commented to the King, "You have put your head upon the execution block. All Mr. Baldwin has to do is to swing the axe." Edward Duke of Windsor, *A King's Story* (London, 1951), 330.

[32] The relevant legislation and speeches on the abdication are reprinted in Mansergh, *Documents and Speeches*, I, sec. V.

all reference to the Crown in the Constitution and of enacting the External Relations Act. This took two days, so that between December 10-12 there were, as Professor Wheare has noted, two Kings in the Commonwealth.[33] This is a matter of much interest to constitutional historians but of incidental importance. What was at once important and impressive was the measure of agreement among Commonwealth Governments throughout the crisis. Because Mr. Baldwin's opinion that the Crown was the "Last link of Empire that is left" was generally agreed to, all who were anxious to preserve its unity exercised their responsibilities with due regard to the magnitude of the issues at stake.

3. Commonwealth Membership Enlarged

In the discussion at the Imperial War Conference in 1917 on the readjustment "of the constitutional relations of the component parts of the Empire"—which was, as we have seen, carried through between 1926 and 1931—Sir Robert Borden took the occasion to observe "that the greatest intellects of the Empire in the past have miscalculated the conditions that would develop in the Dominions, and have failed to foresee the relations of the Empire under the policy of developing full powers of self-government which was supposed to have the effect of weakening, if not severing, the ties which unite the Dominions to the Mother Country."[34] But the policy "which was supposed to weaken the Empire," he continued, "has really strengthened it"; the action of the Dominions "in this war has made the spirit of nationhood splendidly manifest" and further progress along the line of past development and towards "an increasingly equal status" would help to realize "the ideal of an Imperial Commonwealth of United Nations." Even now, he claimed, "the nations of the Empire are really bound together by the tie of a common allegiance, by like institutions and ideals of democracy, and by like purposes." In all this the Canadian Prime Minister dis-

[33] Wheare, op. cit., 288-289. See generally, chap. 11.
[34] Cmd. 8566. Sir Robert Borden's speech is reprinted in Keith, Selected Speeches, part II, 376-381.

played insight and foresight. But while he foreshadowed with remarkable accuracy the character of the Commonwealth that was to emerge, he refrained from speculation about its future membership.

The Imperial War Conference contemplated the increasing association of India with the Dominions. Yet despite this and the more explicit assurances of the Montagu Declaration of 1917, many in Britain and in the Dominions continued to entertain the view, expressed by the Liberal Lord Crewe in 1909, that the enactment of the South African Act of Union that year placed the self-governing Dominions of the King in something like their final form.[35] And in fact the Dominions whose status was defined in the Balfour Report and whose names were listed in section 1 of the Statute of Westminster were, with the one addition of the Irish Free State, those conventionally described as Dominions in 1909 and in 1917. They were predominantly European in respect of their population and wholly European in respect of their government, for while there were minorities of non-European origin in Australia, in Canada, and in New Zealand and a large non-European majority in the Union of South Africa, neither minorities nor majority were in a position to exert a decisive influence upon government. Yet, even apart from the promise of responsible government as the goal of British rule in India, the composition of the British Empire in itself posed the problem of non-European membership of the British Commonwealth of Nations, unless indeed non-European states were to be excluded permanently from this privileged, self-governing circle.

The association between self-government and the equal partnership of the Dominions with the United Kingdom in the Imperial Commonwealth which Sir Robert Borden contemplated is the principal foundation on which the contemporary Commonwealth rests. In the past radical imperialists like Joseph Chamberlain, great proconsuls like Lord Curzon had been at one in empha-

[35] Keith, *ibid.*, 46-47.

sizing excellence in the art of government as the outstanding contribution of the British people to the world. That British settlers in Canada or Australia or New Zealand should believe that they, too, inheriting the traditions were entitled to practice the art of responsible parliamentary government was an occasion neither for surprise nor for concern. When other Europeans, non-British in extraction, claimed corresponding privileges there was more reserve. Neither Afrikaners nor Irish were considered to be equally well fitted to enjoy them, the former largely because they were too paternalist in their notions of government and too hostile to the British connection, the latter ostensibly because they were thought too volatile. Representative institutions and responsible self-government for non-Europeans for long seemed altogether inconceivable, even in India, the greatest of all Britain's overseas dependencies.

It is one of the curiosities of Commonwealth history that it was the Indian National Congress that from the day of its first session in Bombay in 1885 demanded the extension of representative institutions to India and that it was the British exponents of what they themselves described as "the best form of government" who expressed continuing doubts about the wisdom of acceding to the Congress demand. The oblique introduction of the representative principle in India in 1892, its extension in 1909, were widely regarded in Britain, and not only by conservative opinion, as a "sop to impossible ambitions." "The notion," said Lord Kimberley, a former Liberal Secretary of State for India in 1892, "of a parliamentary representation of so vast a country—almost as large as Europe—containing so large a number of different races is one of the wildest imaginations that ever entered the minds of men!"[36] Lord Morley in 1909 thought it neither desirable nor possible nor even conceivable that English political institutions should be extended to India,[37]—a conclusion which later elicited from an Asian historian the tart observation

[36] *Parl. Deb.*, 3rd ser., Lords, vol. 342, col. 93 (March 6, 1890); quoted in Sir Reginald Coupland, *India: A Restatement* (London, 1945), 103.
[37] *Recollections* (2 vols.; London, 1917), II, 172-173.

that in respect of Asian self-government there was little to choose between an "advanced thinker" like Lord Morley and " 'old China hands,' sun-dried Anglo-Indians and French colonials."[38] The Simon Commission in 1929 exuded the depressing sort of wisdom that springs from doubt and misgivings. "The British parliamentary system . . . has been fitted like a well-worn garment to the figure of the wearer, but it does not follow that it will suit everybody." "British parliamentarism in India is a translation, and in even the best translations the essential meaning is apt to be lost."[39] But while the Simon Commission talked somewhat spaciously of forms of responsible government other than the British, it is extremely doubtful whether the British rulers of India, or indeed Indians trained under the Brititsh system, would have been well qualified to apply them. What is certain is that the British system is what self-conscious Indian opinion wanted and it was also the system to which by a gesture of faith rather than by reasoned conviction Britain was pledged by the Montagu Declaration of 1917.

Representative institutions carried another implication once more best illustrated from Indian experience but by no means confined to it. In countries comprising more than one culture or community they placed ultimate control in the hands of the majority grouping should it in fact wish to exert the power which under such a system numbers placed in its hands. No safeguards, whether in the form of separate electorates, of weightage, of a federal constitution with a weak center and residuary powers vested in the states, could alter the fact that under representative government the will of the majority was ultimately likely to prevail. In India both the British and the Hindus, preferring strong central government, were slow to understand the implications of this fact. Yet as India advanced by leisurely stages towards the promised goal of Dominion status the Muslims became increasingly restive at the prospect of their subjection to the

[38] K. M. Panikkar, *Asia and Western Dominance* (London, 1953), 220.
[39] *Report of the Indian Statutory Commission*, vol. II: *Recommendations*, pp. 6-7, Cmd. 3569.

Hindu majority, and experience of Congress rule in the provinces between 1937 and 1939 convinced them that in the last resort "Hindustan" would be "for Hindus." Here, their leaders maintained, was the Hindu raj almost in being and they deemed it intolerable for Muslims to be subject to it. Provincial autonomy no longer seemed a sufficient safeguard, and federation—no matter how weak the center—accordingly appeared as a snare and delusion. Separation alone would suffice. So it was that in March, 1940, at Lahore, Pakistan was proclaimed to be the goal of the Muslim League. "No constitutional plan would be acceptable" unless it grouped the Muslim majority areas together to constitute a sovereign state or states. Jinnah in a memorable speech declared, "Pakistan is our goal for which Muslims of India will live and, if necessary, die." No compromise, he said, was possible, for the differences between Muslims and Hindus were not between two communities but between two different civilizations. British conceptions of Indian unity were a misreading of history. The problem of India was not intercommunal but international, separate homelands for separate nations. Islam and Hinduism were not religions in the strict sense but different and distinct social orders with different religious philosophies, social customs, literatures. Hindus and Muslims "neither intermarry, nor even interdine."[40] It would be a disaster to compel them to live together under a democratic constitution. This conclusion, whether warranted or unwarranted, proved to be final.

The Cabinet Mission sent out by Mr. Attlee's postwar Labor Administration in 1946 suggested an elaborate and ingenious solution based upon the assumption that in however loose a form the unity of India, the principal achievement of British rule, would survive its passing.[41] But it was not to be. On February 20, 1947, the British Government announced its "definite intention to take the necessary steps to effect the transference of power into Indian hands by a date not later than June 1948" and the appointment of Lord Louis Mountbatten (later Earl Mount-

[40] Reprinted in Mansergh, *Documents and Speeches*, II, 609-612.
[41] Their report, Cmd. 6821, is reprinted in *ibid.*, 644-652.

batten) as Viceroy. Implicit in the declaration was the assumption that India would be partitioned and that power would be transferred not to one but to two successor states. Any attempt to maintain Indian unity on the basis of majority Hindu rule would lead, so Mr. Jinnah warned the new Viceroy, to the bloodiest civil war in the history of Asia. Communal tension and outrage gave ample evidence that this warning could not be lightly disregarded, and in fact by early June even the Congress leaders reluctantly agreed—Gandhi at the last acquiescing silently in the vivisection of Mother India[42]—to a settlement which involved the creation of two successor states to whom power was transferred on August 15, 1947, almost a year earlier than had been contemplated in the Declaration of February 20. Both were to have Dominion status, but it was made abundantly clear that the final decision about continuing membership in the British Commonwealth was for them and them alone to take.

The principal aims of Indian and of Pakistani external policies on the morrow of independence were, as very largely they continue to be, national freedom for colonial peoples and the ending of racial discrimination.[43] In themselves these aims implied antagonism to European imperialisms. And however clearly informed Asian opinion might distinguish between Britain's liberal policies, as applied in Asia and as epitomized in Mr. Attlee's assertion that the Commonwealth desired to have no unwilling members, and the attitudes of the "reactionary imperialisms" of the Netherlands and France, it did not overlook the fact that Britain's vast colonial Empire in Africa had not reached the goal of self-government and, more important, that in South Africa, a member of the Commonwealth, racial discrimination was enforced as a matter of political principle. Indeed, in 1947 the fact that South Africa was a member of the Commonwealth seemed to many Congress leaders sufficient reason why India

[42] Alan Campbell-Johnson, *Mission with Mountbatten* (London, 1953), 101-102.
[43] Much interesting light was thrown on this at the Asian Relations Conference in Delhi in 1941. A report, under the title *Asian Relations* (New Delhi, 1948), was published by the Asian Relations Organization.

should not be, and if easy justification for negative policies had been wanted, it lay there ready to hand.

In late 1947 and in 1948, however, there was a gradual and discernible trend in Indian opinion away from isolationism and towards the maintenance of friendly associations which would not commit India to explicit policies but would enhance her influence in world affairs and contribute to international understanding in a wider field. In particular it was increasingly felt that association with the Commonwealth might act as a steadying influence at a time when revolutionary forces were challenging newly established national authority in many parts of South and South East Asia. Thus in February, 1949, Pandit Nehru spoke of the policy of the Communist party in India as one "of open hostility bordering on open revolt." And, however firmly resolved the Indian Government might be to remain aloof from the grouping of the powers, events in South East Asia and the advance of communism in China suggested that the Commonwealth connection might serve as a worthwhile reinsurance of newly acquired independence. Yet even if a cool appreciation of the international scene underlined certain advantages in continued association with the Commonwealth, external factors were not in themselves decisive. In the last resort it was the nature of the Commonwealth and more especially of the Indo-British relationship that determined the issue.

While the older Dominions were largely British and almost wholly European in origin and outlook, India was a mother country with memories and traditions that went back to the dawn of history and with a cultural influence that had at one time or another spread over much of Asia. Could this India, never more mindful of the glories of her past, find a satisfying sense of fulfilment in her membership of a Commonwealth formally united by a symbolism deriving from another's history not her own? Dominion status as a practical expedient by which a threatened deadlock over the transfer of power in 1947 might be resolved was one thing; as a permanent element in India's

Constitution, it was quite another. To many, both within India and without, the Constituent Assembly's resolution of January 22, 1947, declaring that India would become a sovereign, independent republic, seemed to dispose of all prospect of Indian membership of the Commonwealth. Admittedly, republican sentiment in India had not acquired the doctrinaire, uncompromising character of Irish republicanism after the Easter Rising of 1916. But in a sense that distinction was irrelevant. The Indian leaders felt beyond question that republicanism was the only form of government appropriate to the circumstances of their country. It was also the only form of government which seemed to them to make clear beyond question that India was an independent nation. It could be, and was, argued that Dominion status, too, conferred full autonomy, but these arguments carried only partial conviction in South Asia. Long, and at times somewhat acidulous, prewar debates about the right of a Dominion to secede or to remain neutral in a war in which the United Kingdom was engaged had sown doubts and reservations, not easily to be removed, about the fulness of the autonomy which Dominion status conferred.

The question of continued Commonwealth membership concerned two of the smaller Asian countries as well as India and Pakistan. Burma, which had been separated from India in the Government of India Act of 1935, had experienced the full rigors of war and of enemy occupation between 1941 and 1945. But Japanese propaganda on the theme of "Asia for the Asiatics" had made an impact little qualified by the harshness of Japanese military rule,[44] and with the return of peacetime conditions younger men, impatient of the old order, came to power in Burma. Outstanding among them was U Aung San, who early in 1947 led a Burmese delegation to London. The outcome of discussions with the United Kingdom Government was an agreement to set up a Constituent Assembly in Burma, for which

[44] Cf. Thakin Nu, *Burma under the Japanese* (edited and translated, with an Introduction by J. S. Furnivall; London, 1954); and Maung Maung, *Burma in the Family of Nations* (Amsterdam, 1956), chap. 8.

elections were held in April of that year. They resulted in an overwhelming victory of the Anti-Fascist People's Freedom League, of which U Aung San was the leader, and on June 16 of that year he moved a resolution in the Assembly declaring that the constitution should be that of "an independent, sovereign republic to be known as the Union of Burma." His assassination with four of his colleagues in the executive council a month later did not qualify the attitude of Constituent Assembly towards Commonwealth membership, and when the draft constitution was approved in September all that remained to complete the process of separation was the enactment of the necessary legislation by the United Kingdom Parliament. For this purpose the Burma Independence Bill was introduced and duly passed.[45] It declared that Burma was henceforward to be regarded "neither as forming part of His Majesty's dominions nor entitled to His Majesty's protection." Of the former association all that survived was a treaty which came into force on January 4, 1948, and provided for the settlement of outstanding financial questions, for the making of a commercial agreement and for the reception by the Burmese Government of a naval, military, and air force mission from the United Kingdom Government. The Burmese leaders somewhat lightly assumed that India would follow the precedent they had set. In this they were mistaken.

The secession of Burma was paralleled by the steady progress of another Asian country, Ceylon, towards Dominion status. Since 1931 the island had enjoyed representative, though not responsible, cabinet government under the Donoughmore Constitution.[46] During the war its great strategic importance was underlined and its political leaders, influenced by the rising tide of nationalism in Asia pressed, with gentlemanly moderation be it said, for self-government. The response in London, though at first hesitant, became more forthcoming by 1945, and the United

---

[45] 11 Geo. 6, c. 3; reprinted in Mansergh, *Documents and Speeches*, II, 779-784.

[46] It was based on the Report of the Special (Donoughmore) Commission on the Constitution. Cmd. 3131 (1928).

Kingdom Government then declared its willingness to co-operate with the Ceylonese in their advance to self-government. Under the Soulbury Constitution of 1946 (which was based largely on the recommendations of a Commission[47] of which Lord Soulbury had been chairman) the island attained full self-government in all matters of internal administration. Then in June, 1947, the Colonial Secretary, Mr. A. Creech-Jones, stated in the House of Commons that the United Kingdom Government was preparing to negotiate with the Government of Ceylon for the amendment of the Soulbury Constitution so as to give to Ceylon full self-government in external as well as in internal affairs. Accordingly in November, 1947, the Ceylon Independence Bill was introduced in Parliament and it came into force on February 4, 1948. It was supplemented by agreements on defense and external affairs, which were signed on November 11, 1947.[48] The agreement on defense between the two Governments, terminated in 1956, made provision for such "military assistance for the security of their territories, for defence against external aggression and for the protection of essential communications as may be in their mutual interest to provide," and also permitted the United Kingdom to base naval and air forces and to maintain such land forces in Ceylon as might be mutually agreed as being necessary for the island's security. In the agreement on external affairs the Government of Ceylon undertook to adopt and follow the resolutions of past Imperial Conferences and to observe the accepted principles and practice of Commonwealth consultation. For its part the United Kingdom Government undertook to support Ceylon's application for membership of the United Nations, which was not in fact secured till 1956.

The significance of Ceylon's advance from colonial to Dominion status was thought to be far-reaching. "This is the first occasion in our history," said Lord Addison, the Lord Privy Seal and a former Dominions Secretary, in introducing the second reading of the Ceylon Independence Bill in the House of Lords

[47] Cmd. 6677.
[48] See Mansergh, *Documents and Speeches*, II, 749-751.

on December 4, 1947, "upon which a Colony, developing this system of self-government of its own accord, has deliberately sought to become a Dominion State in our Commonwealth . . . but we hope and expect it will not be the last."[49] Encouraging however though the implications of Ceylonese membership might be, it was on the decision of India and Pakistan that the future of the Commonwealth in Asia ultimately depended. Would they follow the precedent set by Burma or the example of Ceylon?

The conference of Commonwealth Prime Ministers in London in October, 1948, was a landmark in the history of the Commonwealth because then, for the first time, the three new Dominions of Asia were represented.[50] But if this meeting was the outward sign of the new phase in Commonwealth relations, a phase in which non-British and non-European peoples were to contribute as equals to the framing of Commonwealth policies, the form of their membership or relationship was not discussed in full session at all. On the contrary, this conference concerned itself with severely practical questions of defense, security, and economic development, and though discussions about the Irish repeal of the External Relations Act were proceeding at the time that the Prime Ministers were meeting in London, the tacit agreement of all parties to leave constitutional questions affecting the Asian Dominions on one side remained unaltered. These Fabian tactics enabled the Prime Ministers of the Asian Dominions to see at first hand how the Commonwealth worked before taking any final decisions about their own position, for it was felt that only by participation in the councils of the Commonwealth at the highest level might a full understanding of its working be acquired. Since India, Pakistan, and Ceylon "have come into the Commonwealth," said Mr. Liaqat Ali Khan, the Prime Minister of Pakistan, after the conference, "its complexion has changed—now it is a Commonwealth of free nations who believe in the same way of life and in the same democracy. To my mind,

---

[49] *Parl. Deb.*, 5th ser., Lords, vol. 152, cols. 1204-1207, at col. 1205 (Dec. 4, 1947); reprinted in Mansergh, *Documents and Speeches*, II, 756-758, at 756-757.
[50] All three by graduates of the University of Cambridge.

these ideas are even stronger than racial ties." These words suggested a growing feeling evidently shared by the other Asian Prime Ministers after the conference had concluded that their countries might find an enduring place in the Commonwealth and in so doing modify its character to suit their particular needs and outlook. More explicitly on December 18 that year the Congress, meeting at Jaipur, foreshadowed the coming rapprochement between India and the Commonwealth. It there resolved that

in view of the attainment of complete independence and the establishment of the Republic of India which will symbolise Independence and give to India the status among the nations of the world that is her rightful due, her present association with the United Kingdom and the Commonwealth of Nations will necessarily have to change. India, however, desires to maintain all such links with other countries as do not come in the way of her freedom of action and independence and the Congress would welcome her free association with the independent nations of the Commonwealth for their common weal and the promotion of world peace.[51]

The Jaipur Resolution posed the problem with which Commonwealth statesmen were squarely confronted in April, 1949. It was a republican India that contemplated continued association with the Commonwealth. There was no suggestion from any quarter that India could or should renounce republicanism for membership. The question was, could the two be reconciled? A quarter of a century earlier the Sinn Fein leaders in Ireland had been told with emphasis backed by the threat of force that they could not. Time, however, had brought many changes. The problem was, moreover, distinct in certain important respects from that which had been raised by Irish nationalists in 1921. India was a dominion, as Ireland had not been, which was about to become a republic and which expressed a positive wish to co-operate as a full member with the other countries of the Commonwealth. Nonetheless, the Indian desire to reconcile

[51] Significantly it was quoted by Pandit Nehru in the Indian Constituent Assembly on May 16, 1949, in the debate on the subsequent London Agreement. See Mansergh, *Documents and Speeches*, II, 850.

republicanism with full membership could be met only by a modification, even if for her case alone, of one of the conventional characteristics of membership as set out in the Balfour Report and restated in the Preamble to the Statute of Westminster.

The Commonwealth Prime Ministers, including those of the three new Dominions in Asia, met again in London in April, 1949, to determine the issue. Agreement was reached in the short period of six days. Making due allowance for preliminary discussions by emissaries sent from Downing Street to the Dominion capitals, this was a considerable achievement brought about, be it noted, not by open but by secret diplomacy. The text of the communiqué issued at the conclusion of the meeting tells best its own story:

During the past week the Prime Ministers of the United Kingdom, Australia, New Zealand, South Africa, India, Pakistan and Ceylon, and the Canadian Secretary of State for External Affairs have met in London to exchange views upon the important constitutional issues arising from India's decision to adopt a republican form of constitution and her desire to continue her membership of the Commonwealth.

The discussions have been concerned with the effects of such a development upon the existing structure of the Commonwealth and the constitutional relations between its members. They have been conducted in an atmosphere of goodwill and mutual understanding, and have had as their historical background the traditional capacity of the Commonwealth to strengthen its unity of purpose, while adapting its organization and procedures to changing circumstances.

After full discussion the representatives of the Governments of all the Commonwealth countries have agreed that the conclusions reached should be placed on record in the following declaration:—

The Governments of the United Kingdom, Canada, Australia, New Zealand, South Africa, India, Pakistan and Ceylon, whose countries are united as Members of the British Commonwealth of Nations and owe a common allegiance to the Crown, which is also the symbol of their free association, have considered the impending constitutional changes in India.

The Government of India have informed the other Governments of the Commonwealth of the intention of the Indian people that under the new constitution which is about to be adopted India shall become a sovereign independent republic. The Government of India have, however, declared and affirmed India's desire to continue her full membership of the Commonwealth of Nations and her acceptance of The King as the symbol of the free association of its independent member nations, and as such the Head of the Commonwealth.

The Governments of the other countries of the Commonwealth, the basis of whose membership of the Commonwealth is not hereby changed, accept and recognise India's continuing membership in accordance with the terms of this declaration.

Accordingly the United Kingdom, Canada, Australia, New Zealand, South Africa, India, Pakistan and Ceylon hereby declare that they remain united as free and equal members of the Commonwealth of Nations, freely co-operating in the pursuit of peace, liberty and progress.

These constitutional questions have been the sole subject of discussion at the full meetings of the Prime Ministers.

The settlement reached, it will be observed, was specific, not general, in application. There was no decision that a republic, as such, could be a full member of the Commonwealth. The conference simply recorded that when India, under her new constitution, became a sovereign, independent republic, she would remain, in accordance with her own wishes, a full member of the Commonwealth and would acknowledge the King as a symbol of the free association of its independent member nations, and, as such, the Head of the Commonwealth. The Indian Republic, therefore, owes no allegiance to the Crown, and the King has no place in its government. It is in this respect that the settlement involved a notable departure from the doctrine embodied in the Preamble to the Statute of Westminster in which the members of the Commonwealth were declared to be "united by a common allegiance to the Crown." At the time it was maintained that this compatibility extended only to the case of India, and that one exception did not constitute a category and did not modify the general conditions of Commonwealth membership. In 1955 and 1956 it was, however, agreed that Pakistan and Ceylon should continue their membership on the same basis. Republicanism, which in the past both in Ireland and in South

Africa had been regarded as synonymous with seccession, was thereby accepted as compatible with membership.

At first sight the Indian constitutional settlement seemed almost metaphysical in its refinement. It had, however, the merit of going a long way towards reconciling constitutional forms with political realities. In the Dominions and particularly in the older Dominions, which are predominantly British in extraction, loyalty to the Crown was a unifying force of the highest value. For them all, the constitutional position remained unchanged. The King remained King of Canada, King of Australia, King of New Zealand, as much as King of the United Kingdom. But the different traditions, the very different history, of India (as later of other Asian members), suggested that she should have another symbolism, which, with the agreement of all of her partners, was accepted in April, 1949, as compatible with membership of the Commonwealth.

Of the broad political advantages of the solution reached, there could be little question. The Commonwealth, as a result of it, became an international democracy in a fuller sense than in the past, and the successful outcome of the historic conference of April, 1949, made it likely that the association of Asian peoples with the older Dominions, predominantly European in stock, was to be, not an episode, but a continuing factor in its history. Here was at the least impressive evidence of the continuing vitality of the Commonwealth idea which was duly weighed by political leaders in British colonial territories in Africa and elsewhere aspiring to national independence.

In India the Constituent Assembly endorsed the settlement reached in London with only one dissentient voice. No doubt this did not fairly reflect the balance of opinion within India, for it was severely criticized by Socialists as well as by Communists both then and later when India's first general election was held in 1951-52. Yet the general satisfaction with the solution reached was unmistakable. "We join the Commonwealth," Pandit Nehru told the Constituent Assembly, "obviously because we think it is beneficial to us and to certain causes in the world that we wish to advance. The other countries of the Commonwealth want us to remain, because they think it is beneficial to them . . . . In the world today where there are so many disruptive forces at work, where we are often on the verge of war, I think it is not a safe thing to encourage the breaking up of any association that one has . . . . it is better to keep a co-operative association going which may do good in this world rather than break it."[52] He admitted that he was "a bad bargainer," that he was not used "to the ways of the market place" and that he had thought it, in London, "far more precious to come to a decision in friendship and good will than to gain a word here or there at the cost of ill will." Here in view of past history and personal experiences was magnanimity as well as statesmanship, and the Prime Ministers of the Commonwealth had responded to it with imaginative understanding. At critical moments in succeeding years Pandit Nehru never wavered in his view that the decision had been the right one to take.

Multiracial membership of the Commonwealth in the strict sense, meaning the full self-governing membership of peoples of different racial origin, dates from 1947. For that reason in March, 1954, at the Commonwealth Relations Conference at Lahore the Prime Minister of Pakistan spoke of 1947 as a date in Commonwealth history as important as 1926 or 1867. It was from the British North America Act that the conception of Dominion self-government derived; from the definition of Dominion status in the Balfour Report that the contemporary Commonwealth might be dated. But, while in Asia, in the opinion of Mr. Mohammed Ali, "the pace of constitutional evolution was slow, painfully slow," in 1947 Asian states were accorded self-government and Commonwealth membership at last. The London Declaration of April, 1949 further and impressively demonstrated that once they had attained their goal the root-

---

[52] Constituent Assembly of India, *Debates*, vol. 8, 2-10; reprinted in Mansergh, *Documents and Speeches*, II, 847-857, at 853, 854.

principle of equality of which the Balfour Report had spoken applied to them in full measure.

In 1917 Sir Robert Borden had spoken of common allegiance, like institutions and ideals of democracy and like purpose as bonds of a decentralized Commonwealth. Common allegiance to the Crown was no longer a condition of membership after 1949, and the importance of like political institutions and like purposes was thereby enhanced. The extent to which members of the enlarged postwar Commonwealth entertained "like purposes" may fittingly be examined later in considering the aims and objectives of their several foreign policies, but here something may be said in conclusion about like political institutions. Liaquat Ali Khan in 1948, as has been noted, spoke of the common practice of responsible self-government as the strongest bond of Commonwealth unity, and on this point his conviction was emphatically reaffirmed at the Commonwealth Relations Conference at Lahore in 1954.[53] Some recent history, not least in Pakistan, gives somewhat ironic significance to these assertions and invites critical re-examination of their implications. Nonetheless the Commonwealth remains an experiment in co-operation between states of varied races and cultures, and the common practice (with variations to suit local circumstances) of the parliamentary system of government would seem to be an unwritten condition of membership. Or to put the point more exactly and in less positive form, it is doubtful whether states adopting other forms of government would continue to find membership congenial. This is something to be kept in mind both in assessing the nature and permanence of the existing enlarged membership of the Commonwealth, and in considering future membership. In respect of the latter, it has also to be remembered that representative institutions impose, as John Stuart Mill foresaw and as Indian experience amply confirmed, a great strain upon

[53] A report of its proceedings has been published as *The Multi-Racial Commonwealth* (London, 1955) by the author of this paper.

the unity of multicommunal societies. Their path to Commonwealth membership through the traditional gateway of responsible
parliamentary government is thus beset with exceptional difficulties and even dangers.

2

Commonwealth Foreign Policies
1945-56: A Perspective View

Nicholas Mansergh

1. Prewar Experience

THE DEFINING of Dominion status between 1926 and 1931 left the Dominions with full responsibility for the determination of their external policies. Their Governments, however, had still to create machinery for the execution of policy and a tradition of policy itself. As a result the period 1926-39 was for them a period of trial and experiment. To the uncertainties inseparable from the working out of a new Commonwealth relationship there were added in consequence uncertainties about Dominion intentions. Both combined to encourage an attitude of caution in London, greater no doubt than the facts themselves warranted. Nonetheless the root-principle of equality which proved so effective a solvent of intra-Commonwealth tensions was not well calculated in this early phase of its application to produce a strong Commonwealth foreign policy in time of nominal peace.

The drafters of the Balfour Report in stating that each Dominion was to be the sole judge of the nature and the extent of its co-operation expressed its conviction that no common cause would be thereby imperiled. Their faith in fact was substantially vindicated in 1939 but nonetheless the formal abandonment of all attempts to frame a common foreign policy—for such in effect it was—earlier posed questions of the most far-reaching importance for the United Kingdom Government. Their practical significance was heightened by the then clearly asserted intention of the Dominions not to commit themselves by treaty obligation to a particular course of action in particular eventualities. Under what circumstances then could the United Kingdom count on Dominion co-operation in war? Was it certain that collectively they would fight in a war for the enforcement of the authority of the League? In a war for maintenance of the peace treaties? In a war for the Empire's survival? Only experience in the years 1931-39 sufficed to elicit answers to these questions.

By the close of 1935 it was apparent that a united Commonwealth would not fight to enforce the authority of the League; by March, 1936, that it would not fight to uphold the peace treaties; by 1937 that it would fight to resist aggression which threatened its own survival and that of the United Kingdom on certain conditions. From the point of view of the United Kingdom therefore it was important to ensure that those conditions were fulfilled. That was a principal aim of its foreign policy in the last years of peace and at a price it was substantially achieved.[1]

After the Second World War there was a resolve that the price of divided counsel and uncertain intention not only among Commonwealth but among all peace-loving states should not be paid again. The lessons of the thirties were deeply impressed on the minds of those who led the United Nations in war and who were responsible in its later phases for the foundation of a new international organization intended above all to avoid the errors of the old. But even among Commonwealth statesmen there was no agreement about how this might be done.

2. The United Nations and the Peace Treaties

In April, 1945, there was a meeting of Commonwealth statesmen in London to consider the Dumbarton Oaks proposals for the Charter for the United Nations, prior to the meeting of the

---

[1] The evidence from which these conclusions derive is set out in the author's *Survey of British Commonwealth Affairs: Problems of External Policy 1931-1939* (London, 1952). See especially chap. 11.

Conference of the United Nations due to take place at San Francisco later that month. The aim of the London meeting was, to judge by the observations of Dominion leaders, emphatically not to produce a common policy, or uniformity of view, but to exchange opinions and to frame individual policies in the light of discussions with Commonwealth colleagues. Their purpose, said Lord Cranborne at the opening session, was "not to 'gang up' against other nations or to obtain any sectional advantages" for themselves,[2] but to contribute as best they might to the creation of the new world organization. It was possible to be a member of a family and citizen of the world and it was as members of a family that they were deliberating together.

The United Kingdom Government did not expect that Dominion Governments would all subscribe to the agreements they had made with the other sponsoring powers at Yalta and Dumbarton Oaks. This expectation was well founded. The San Francisco Conference in 1945, like the Paris Peace Conference a year later, made plain to all the world that the Dominions were little disposed to acquiesce in arrangements distasteful to them merely because they carried the *imprimatur* of United Kingdom sponsorship. To anyone who entertained the notion that there was a Commonwealth bloc the debates on the United Nations Charter must have proved a sharply disillusioning experience. Among Commonwealth countries there was a clear-cut division of opinion between the United Kingdom with South African backing on the one hand and Australia and New Zealand with qualified Canadian support on the other, on the place to be given to the Great Powers in the United Nations Charter. The United Kingdom as a sponsoring power defended the exceptional authority vested in a Security Council certain to be dominated by its permanent Great Power members and expressed its conviction that such concentration was necessary in the interests of universality and the preservation of peace; it was not prepared to yield, even in respect of the veto, to demands strongly and at times vehemently

[2] *The Times*, April 6, 1945.

expressed[3] by the middle powers, with the Dominions other than South Africa chief among them, for a more democratic organization. With the resulting Dominion failure to secure concessions of more than very limited significance in respect of the political provisions of the Charter, their representatives sought at the least to safeguard their own position under the Charter. If powers, other than the greatest, were to be deprived of an effective voice in the making of decisions, the Dominions and especially Canada and Australia were anxious to ensure that they should not be committed to responsibilities or actions over which they exercised little or no control. Responsibility, in their view, should be related to power and privileged position. Their first aim—of democratizing the Charter—therefore, was positive, and failing its achievement their second, broadly speaking, was self-protective and negative. In the pursuit of this second aim they secured some important concessions.

The Commonwealth contribution at San Francisco was most considerable in the setting up of the Trusteeship Council and in extending the functions of the Economic and Social Council. But the Conference itself was for most Commonwealth delegations a disillusioning experience. There they were brought face to face with the widening rift between the U.S.S.R. and the Western World, a rift which was to render otiose for years to come much of the detailed work that was done at San Francisco. The rift was soon destined to widen into an open breach, the drafting of the peace treaties being the immediate occasion. In respect of one matter of principle Dominion Governments—again other than that of South Africa where General Smuts accepted the notion of Great Power predominance as a distasteful political necessity—felt themselves to be directly concerned. They had conceived that peace-making would be a matter for those who had played an active part in securing the defeat of the Axis powers.

[3] So vehemently that Mr. Fraser, for example, found it necessary to reassure the New Zealand House of Representatives "that no differences of opinion on the wording of the principles of the Charter between any of the dominions, or between any of the dominions and the Mother-country in any way has loosened our close ties." *Parl. Deb.*, July 24, 1945; vol. 268, 575.

"We consistently maintain," said Dr. Evatt, "the right of all active belligerents to a full share in the framing of the peace. Those who have contributed substantially to victory are entitled to make a corresponding contribution to the peace. This is the only fair and democratic method of making the peace; and a just method of making a peace settlement is as important as the settlement itself."[4] "We in Canada," said Mr. Mackenzie King at the Paris Peace Conference in 1946,[5] "felt that the measure of our participation in the war against aggression would have warranted a similar measure of participation in the making of peace." But the Soviet Union was inexorably resolved on a Great Power peace, if indeed there was to be a peace at all, and not all the violent indignation of Dr. Evatt nor the pained remonstrances of Mr. Mackenzie King sufficed to qualify by one iota their hard resolve. "We were fighting," said the Canadian Prime Minister, "to prevent two countries from dominating the world, and we do not now wish to see any one, two, three or four countries dominate the peace."[6] When, however, he did see it the Canadian Prime Minister felt constrained to remark that he feared greatly as a consequence the drying up of the springs of chivalry and of generosity in many nations.[7]

In the United Nations Charter the Dominions signed not grouped together under the general heading British Empire, as they had signed the League of Nations Covenant and the peace treaties in 1919, but separately according to the alphabetic order among the nations. This has been regarded as symbolic of the advancement of their Commonwealth and international status in the intervening years. On a shorter view, however, Yalta, Potsdam, Paris, and Moscow marked a significant and depressing depreciation of their ability to influence international politics and a

---

[4] Dr. Evatt's speech to the Australian House of Representatives (*Parl. Deb.*, March 13, 1946; vol. 186, 187-192) sets out Australian demands in respect of peacemaking in Europe and in the Far East. He believed he had secured important concessions but with the breakdown of the Foreign Ministers' Conference in Moscow their value disappeared.

[5] Department of External Affairs, *Canadian Weekly Bulletin* (Aug., 1946).

[6] Canada, *Parl. Deb.*, Commons, vol. 1, 57 (Feb. 3, 1947).

[7] *Ibid.*, 58.

sorry reward for those who had fought so gallantly from first to last against what Mr. Mackenzie King had once called the "forces of evil."

3. The Commonwealth and Western European Union

It was evident by 1943 that the Second World War would leave a vacuum in power, and therefore a lack of balance, in Central and Western Europe. Field-Marshal Smuts was the first Commonwealth statesman to suggest how it might best be filled. This he did in his speech to the Empire Parliamentary Association in November, 1943. He was concerned on the one hand to consolidate the Commonwealth by associating the self-governing Dominions with the government of colonial territories falling within their area of regional interest, and on the other to extend its stabilizing influence to Europe by linking it with the free peoples on its western seaboard. What he said on this score is worth recalling.[8]

We have evolved a system in the Commonwealth which opens the door for developments of this kind. Today in the Commonwealth we have a group of sovereign States working together, living together in peace and in war, under a system that has stood the greatest strain to which any nations could be subjected. They are all sovereign States, they retain all the attributes and functions and symbols of sovereignty. Other neighbouring nations, therefore, living the same way of life, and with the same outlook, can with perfect safety say: "That is our group; why are we not there? With full retention and maintenance of our sovereign status, we choose that grand company for our future in this dangerous world."

The emphasis he placed on the retention and maintenance of full sovereign status is especially noteworthy. What Field-Marshal Smuts contemplated in 1943, and what the Dominions naturally contemplated, was a union in Western Europe which would leave each member state within that union master in its own house. If there were to be co-ordinating authorities, Dominion opinion welcomed them without misgiving so long as they

[8] Reprinted in Nicholas Mansergh, *Documents and Speeches on British Commonwealth Affairs 1931-1952* (London, 1953), I, 568-575, at 571.

did not infringe fundamentally upon national sovereignty. That was the sort of relationship which a decentralized Commonwealth understood, and the extension of it to Western Europe raised no particular problems, for it would leave the United Kingdom with a freedom of action sufficient to enable her to undertake and discharge obligations in other parts of the world.[9]

Field-Marshal Smuts's emphasis on national sovereignty was not to be found in the pronouncements on Western Union made by United Kingdom statesmen and particularly by Mr. Bevin, who on January 22, 1948 launched the concept as the principal aim of Britain's foreign policy in Europe to a welcoming Western World.[10] On the contrary, so far as national sovereignty was concerned Mr. Bevin's words left an impression of judiciously considered imprecision. There was no doubting his deep conviction that "the free nations of Western Europe must now draw closely together." That had been rendered necessary by the scale of Russia's expansion and her ruthless communization of Eastern Europe, by the emergence once again of the police state, by the breakdown of the Four-Power discussions on Germany, and finally by the naked hostility of the Soviet Union to the European Recovery Program. All this made the closing of "the breach between East and West" the task for another day. What was imperative now, urged the Foreign Secretary, was the drawing together of "the kindred souls" of the West to preserve at least in one part of Europe the liberties of men and nations. He spoke of federal union as a distant goal, and for the immediate future he confined himself to emphasizing the need for taking one step at the time. "If," he said on January 22,[11] "we are to have an organism in the West it must be a spiritual union.

[9] The misuse of the word "union" was a source of misunderstanding. By any definition union means something more than alliance or association; more than economic and political consolidation. In English history it applied to two formal acts of state (the Acts of Union with Scotland and Ireland) by which countries previously separate and distinct entered into—or were inveigled into as some few Scots and most Irishmen would say—a wider community, in which their separate identities were to be merged.

[10] *Parl. Deb.*, 5th ser., Commons, vol. 446, cols. 383-409 (Jan. 22, 1948).

[11] *Ibid.*, cols. 407-408.

While, no doubt, there must be treaties or, at least, understandings, the union must primarily be a fusion derived from the basic freedoms and ethical principles for which we all stand . . . . It is more of a brotherhood and less of a rigid system."

But if Britain's approach to Western Union was empirical and its aim very largely undefined, that made the more important the consultations with the partner-states in the Commonwealth which culminated in the Commonwealth Prime Ministers meeting in October, 1948. It is clear that their concern throughout was not with distant prospects, but with actual problems. They judged Western Union not by what it might one day become but by what it was at any given moment. Nor is it to be overlooked that their opportunities for influencing policy were many. When the Commonwealth Prime Ministers assembled they were presented not with a *fait accompli* but with an evolving policy whose direction they could influence, perhaps even determine. On this point the evidence is clear. The Prime Minister, on May 5, 1948, asserted in the House of Commons that "in all these matters we keep in the closest touch with the other Commonwealth countries . . . we have kept in very, very close touch, and we take very full account of their views." In the same debate[12] the Prime Minister remarked that he "was disturbed by the suggestion . . . that we might somehow get closer to Europe than to our Commonwealth. The Commonwealth nations are our closest friends. While I want to get as close as we can with the other nations, we have to bear in mind that we are not solely a European Power but a member of a great Commonwealth and Empire." Through Britain, and at one remove, the Dominions were thus in a position to influence developments in Western Europe. And because of the Commonwealth association one possibility at least was seemingly excluded, namely Britain's membership of a European federation which would by its very character undermine the foundations of the Commonwealth system.

[12] *Ibid.*, vol. 450, cols.1316-1319 (May 5, 1948).

4. The North Atlantic Treaty

As late as May, 1948, Field-Marshal Smuts still conceived Western Union with British membership as constituting a third or middle power group at least equal to the other two, so that the security of the world "will rest on the triangle of Power, and will not continue to be precariously poised between two great Powers facing each other across a broken Europe."[13] But neither the United Kingdom, nor still less the Canadian Government envisaged such a possibility. Their endeavors were directed towards the expansion of the Western defensive grouping so as to include within its framework two of these great powers. For the idea of a balance of power they substituted, with almost missionary zeal in the case of Canada, with some apparent reluctance and on grounds of expediency in the case of the United Kingdom, that of a preponderance on the side of the peace-loving nations.

The policy of the Canadian Government in this period is of particular interest to students of Commonwealth history. Before 1939 no Dominion Government had been more consistent in its opposition to specific commitments which would limit the freedom of the Canadian Parliament to decide on Canadian participation in war; and no Dominion Government had expressed greater devotion to the United Nations and to the principle of universalism on which it was founded after 1945. How then is one to account for the transformation in policy which is symbolized by Canada's sponsorship of the North Atlantic Treaty? There were many reasons but chief among them were the lessons of recent experience. The world was once again threatened with aggression by a totalitarian military state. Even at San Francisco Mr. Mackenzie King was filled at times with the deepest forebodings of what the future might bring and of the inability of the new international organization then being shaped to provide security for peace-loving peoples.[14] Those fears, voiced inter-

---

[13] Broadcast, May 23, 1948; reprinted in Mansergh, *Documents and Speeches*, II, 1133-1135, at 1135.

[14] Bruce Hutchison, *The Incredible Canadian* (Toronto, 1953), p. 410.

mittently in succeeding months by Mr. Mackenzie King, received outspoken expression from his Minister of External Affairs, Mr. St. Laurent, on September 18, 1947. Alarmed especially by Russia's exercise of the veto power in the Security Council, he told the General Assembly that it "would be folly" not to admit that the United Nations Organization had been weakened, and that "this veto privilege . . . if it continues to be abused, may well destroy the United Nations." "Nations, in their search for peace and cooperation," he warned the Assembly, "will not, and cannot, accept indefinitely an unaltered Council which was set up to ensure their security and which . . . has become frozen in futility and divided by dissension. If forced, they may seek greater safety in an association of democratic and peace-loving states willing to accept more specific international obligations in return for a greater measure of national security."[15] By their failure to offer united resistance to Nazi demands the democracies had earlier enabled Hitler to destroy his victims singly. That lesson at least remained deeply graven on the mind of the Western World. "We must," said Mr. St. Laurent in the Canadian House of Commons, "at all costs avoid the fatal repetition of the history of the pre-war years when the nazi aggressor picked off its victims one by one. Such a process does not end at the Atlantic."[16] But effective resistance was conditional in Canadian eyes upon United States participation in an organized defensive system. That was lacking before 1939; it was forthcoming after 1945. In the earlier period the Western World without United States support could hope at best to establish a balance of power; in the later, with United States participation, the peace-loving states could reasonably expect to possess a decisive preponderance.

United States association with the United Kingdom in the western alliance further fulfilled one of the principal aims of Canadian policy by bringing together her greater North American

[15] Department of External Affairs, *Canada at the United Nations 1947* (Ottawa, 1948), 178-180.
[16] Canada, *Parl. Deb.*, Commons, vol. 4, 3449 (April 29, 1948); reprinted in Mansergh, *Documents and Speeches*, II, 1128-1129. The speech as a whole is a clear guide to Canadian thinking at that time.

neighbor and her principal Commonwealth partner in a common association for a common aim. That aim was to deter, if necessary by force, further Soviet expansion in Europe. "The formation of such a defensive group of free states," said Mr. St. Laurent, "would not be a counsel of despair but a measure of hope. It would not mean that we regarded the third world war as inevitable; but that the free democracies had decided that to prevent such a war they would organize so as to confront the forces of communist expansionism with an overwhelming preponderance of moral, economic and military forces and with sufficient degree of unity to ensure that this preponderance of force is so used that the free nations cannot be defeated one by one."[17] The aim was one that commended itself particularly to Catholic and traditionally isolationist Quebec. The Nazi-Soviet alliance of August, 1939, had contributed notably to French-Canadian support for Canada's entry into the Second World War, while the revelations of Soviet espionage in 1945[18] confirmed a rooted conviction that, despite wartime co-operation, Russian communism was at all times the most deadly menace to the Catholic Church and to the way of life it enjoined.[19] Finally, the retreat from universalism which regional alliances of necessity involved was thought of as a temporary refuge provided for in the Charter of the United Nations, not in itself prejudicing the ultimate prospects for realization of the larger aim. The provisions of the Charter, explained Mr. St. Laurent, were a floor under rather than a ceiling over the responsibilities of member states. If some preferred to go even below that floor, others need not be prevented from moving upwards.[20]

The signing of the North Atlantic Treaty in April, 1949,

[17] *Idem.*

[18] *The Report of the Royal Commission to Investigate the Facts Relating to and the Circumstances Surrounding the Communication, by Public Officials and Other Persons in Positions of Trust of Secret and Confidential Information to Agents of the Foreign Power* (Ottawa, 1946).

[19] This point is usefully illustrated in W. E. C. Harrison, *Canada in World Affairs 1949 to 1950* (Toronto, 1957), 23-24. See generally 18-37.

[20] Speech, Sept. 18, 1947, reprinted in *Canada at the United Nations 1947*, 180.

was an oblique recognition on the part of the United States that Britain and Canada were right, in September, 1939, in deciding that resistance must be offered to aggression, and that there was no lasting safety to be found in detachment and isolation even for the greatest or geographically most favored powers. But more than this it embodied the conviction, born of common experience in the Second World War, that those who thought alike should work together to preserve the things they cherished in peace as in war. The North Atlantic Treaty, to Canadian statesmen especially, was not a reversion to the past but a step forward into the future. Mr. Mackenzie King had welcomed the Brussels Pact "as far more than an alliance of the old kind."[21] The North Atlantic Treaty even more emphatically was not "an old fashioned military alliance," to quote the phrase used by Mr. St. Laurent, but an association of democratic and like-minded peoples resolved to strengthen and preserve their way of life and ultimately to bring into existence a true community of North Atlantic peoples. It had an economic, social, and above all a moral purpose. It was, said Mr. St. Laurent, "based on the common belief of the North Atlantic nations in the values and virtues of our Christian civilization."[22] If, therefore, the non-military clauses of the alliance were largely Canadian in inspiration and in drafting, that was because the Canadian Government attached from the outset so much importance to them. It hoped that the need for the military provisions of the treaty might in time disappear with a strengthening of the United Nations Organization, but that the conception of a North Atlantic community would remain.

5. *The Pacific Security Agreement*

The negotiation of the North Atlantic Treaty inevitably suggested that to balance the Atlantic Pact in the West there should be a Pacific Pact in the East. Yet the needs and the circum-

---

[21] Canada, *Parl. Deb.*, Commons, vol. 3, 2303 (March 17, 1948).
[22] *Ibid.*, vol. 3, 2063 (March 28, 1949).

stances of the two areas were very different. The Atlantic Pact was a superstructure. It followed upon various defensive agreements in Western Europe—the Dunkirk Treaty, the Brussels Pact, and the working out of plans for future economic and political co-operation. It did not precede them. No such developments however had taken place on the continent of Asia. There was indeed no suggestion that any state (with the possible exception of Japan), other than the original signatories, the United States, Australia, and New Zealand, should participate in the Pacific Security Agreement. The Pacific Agreement stood by itself; it was the foundation.

In one respect the Pacific Security Agreement had more important implications for the Commonwealth than the North Atlantic Treaty. It was the first treaty signed by Australia and New Zealand with a foreign country and it signified the military dependence of two members of the Commonwealth outside North America upon the United States. Canada on any reckoning lay within the American defensive system; Australia and New Zealand did not. They came within it because of the acknowledged inability of the United Kingdom to underwrite the security of these two states after the Second World War. In that respect it was a departure the significance of which was heightened by the fact that, contrary to the belief widely entertained in the United Kingdom, it was not the United States that sought by means of the treaty to seduce Australia and New Zealand from their allegiance to the Commonwealth but rather two conservative and traditionally imperialist governments in Australia and New Zealand that persuaded the United States to underwrite their security in return for their acquiescence in United States ideas of an appropriate peace treaty with Japan. It was indeed the hope of the two Dominions that their traditional association with Britain could at all times be reconciled with their new treaty relationship with the United States and thus remain unimpaired. "Where Britain stands we stand: where she goes we go." So Mr. Holland declared on a visit to London early in 1951. Within a few weeks in Washington he asserted that New Zealand would "stand by the United States through thick and thin, right or wrong." Opposition critics at home found in these two assertions much scope for diverting criticism.[23] But in effect what Mr. Holland was saying was that, like Canada, New Zealand could no longer contemplate with equanimity any serious divergence between United States and United Kingdom policies.

In the United Kingdom there were divided opinions on the implications for the Commonwealth of the Pacific Security Agreement. Mr. Casey assured the Australian and Mr. Doidge assured the New Zealand House of Representatives that there had been the closest consultation with the Government of the United Kingdom throughout the negotiation of the Agreement and that the same consultation and close association would be continued in the working of a treaty which recognized in its preamble the defense obligations of the two Dominions outside as well as inside the Pacific area because of their membership of the British Commonwealth of Nations.[24] But while Mr. Attlee's Labor Government was prepared to acquiesce in the negotiation of a Pacific Treaty to which Britain was not a party, Mr. Churchill was not. On the return of the Conservative party to office Mr. Churchill felt his freedom of action to have been impaired while his sense of dissatisfaction had been in no way diminished. "It is one thing," he told Mr. Morrison on October 14, 1952, "to do harm and another thing to get it undone."[25] Mr. Menzies continued to offer courteous but incomplete explanations.[26] Mr. Casey at the first meeting of the Anzus Council spoke in general

---

[23] Cf. New Zealand, *Standard*, Feb., 1951. There was some dispute as to whether Mr. Holland had said that New Zealand would follow the United States "through right and wrong" or "through right or wrong." Some of the criticism was skilfully deflected from the substance of Mr. Holland's remarks to this rather fine textual distinction.

[24] Australia, *Parl. Deb.*, vol. 213, 1708-1709 (July 13, 1951); New Zealand *Parl. Deb.*, vol. 294, pp. 318-319 (July 13, 1951); both reprinted in Mansergh, *Documents and Speeches*, II, 1173-1177.

[25] *Parl. Deb.*, 5th ser., Commons, vol. 505, col. 28 (Oct. 14, 1952). See generally cols. 26-28.

[26] Australia, *Parl. Deb.*, Senate, vol. 220, 2951 (Oct. 14, 1952).

terms of possible future expansion of the treaty organization.[27] But the United Kingdom remained without. In a treaty negotiated by three states, one of which was among the greatest of world powers, it was, in this as in other matters, the will of the one that prevailed.

6. Indian Repudiation of Regional Defense Agreements

While the older members of the Commonwealth, other than South Africa, sought refuge in regional defense agreements extended by 1954 to cover the Middle East and South East Asia, the newer Asian members in the early years of their independence placed their faith—and India and Ceylon, though not Pakistan, continued to repose it—in a policy of nonalignment. This policy was not thought of as tantamount to neutrality but as signifying a refusal to identify foreign policy with those of either of the Great Power groupings in the cold war.[28] Principle, preconception, and calculation all played their part in its formulation; and its appeal to the sentiments of the peoples of South Asia and especially of India was very great. Public opinion in India, noted the Governor of Bombay, G. S. Bajpai, in 1952, would not have approved any Indian commitment in the cold war and he attributed the victory of the Congress Party in the Indian general election of that year as "preeminently an endorsement" of Mr. Nehru's foreign policy.[29]

Despite the policy of nonalignment India, Pakistan, and Ceylon inclined perceptibly towards the West in the early years of independence. Ceylon, barred from membership of the United Nations, was closely associated with Britain not only through her membership of the Commonwealth but also by the terms of the 1947 Defense Agreement. Pakistan, struggling for survival, had one overriding external preoccupation—Kashmir—to

[27] Australia, Dept. of External Affairs, *Current Notes*, vol. 23, no. 8 (Aug., 1952).
[28] On this point see a short but illuminating article by G. S. Bajpai entitled "India and the Balance of Power" in *The Indian Year Book of International Affairs* (Madras, 1952), I, 4.
[29] *Idem.*

which all else was subordinated and despite early disappointment continued, with occasional and deliberately provocative glances towards Moscow, to place her hopes of a favorable outcome upon the support of the Western powers. The Indian Government, threatened by communist subversion at home,[30] sought strength and stability in association with Asian neighbors and Commonwealth partners. If India was either in open conflict with or estranged from Pakistan over Kashmir throughout this period, and bitterly critical of South Africa's racial policies at the United Nations, she found understanding with Labor Governments in the United Kingdom, Australia, and New Zealand and the Liberal Government in Canada. Australia and New Zealand were represented at the Delhi Conferences on Indonesia[31] and their Governments showed themselves, as did that of the United Kingdom, to be sympathetic to Asian nationalist aspirations. Nationalism and Commonwealth membership, it appeared, were not contradictory but compatible, and even complementary, concepts. But after 1950, the year in which India exercised her greatest influence on United Kingdom policy and the Commonwealth, perhaps its greatest influence in Washington, Indian policy, while remaining unchanged in principle, was no longer colored by a pro-Western bias, no longer vigorously condemned by Moscow for that very reason and became by 1955-56 one of independence so regarded by East and West alike.[32]

The reasons for this adjustment in India's attitude to the Western powers deserve especial attention, partly because India is a major power in Asia and partly because therein are to be found the principal causes of difference in Commonwealth external policies. These reasons would seem to have been not general

[30] The Indian Prime Minister has been at all times outspoken in his denunciations of the Indian Communist party and its members, chiefly on the ground that they are not a national party but one which accepts orders from without.

[31] The report of the Conference on Indonesia held in Delhi in January, 1949, is reprinted in Mansergh, *Speeches and Documents*, II, 1177-1179.

[32] Cf. J. C. Kundra, *Indian Foreign Policy 1947-1954: A Study of Relations with the Western Bloc* (Groningen, 1955), which has much useful and detailed material on this point and broadly speaking reaches this conclusion. See also for a more detailed review of a shorter period, K. P. Karunakaran, *India in World Affairs August 1947-January 1950* (London, 1952).

but particular, though certainly they had deep roots in history, psychology, and experience. In Asia the Western powers at this time decided to pursue policies against the advice and in conflict with the known views of the Indian Government. Thus in 1950 India advised most strongly against the crossing of the 38th parallel in Korea, Pandit Nehru observing on September 30 of that year that the Indian Government believed every effort should be made to bring the Korean war to a conclusion, that in the circumstances it would be wrong to carry on military operations and that therefore the U.N. Forces should not go beyond the 38th parallel till "all other means of settlement have been explored."[33] India's advice was disregarded. With Pakistan she pressed for the recognition of the People's Government in Peking. The United Kingdom, much influenced by Asian views, did so;[34] neither the United States nor any of the older members of the Commonwealth followed her example. There were sharply expressed differences with the United States over the peace treaty with Japan in 1951. The Indian Government advised against recognition of the French puppet Emperor Bao Dai in Indo-China. Such recognition, however, was accorded by the United Kingdom, the United States, Australia, and New Zealand. It was followed by Soviet and Chinese recognition of Ho Chi Minh. India, in the words of her Prime Minister, was not ready "to jump into the fray,"[35] though unquestionably her Government believed that continuing attempts to maintain a French-sponsored regime involved greater risks to peace than the possible extension of communist influence. This was at variance with the views of the Western bloc. Finally, the Indian Government, though no longer with the support of Pakistan, argued against an exten-

[33] *The Times*, Oct. 2, 1950.
[34] The Lord Chancellor, Lord Jowitt, stated (*Parl. Deb.*, 5th ser., Lords, vol. 166, col. 88; March 7, 1950) that there had never been a matter with regard to which closer or more continuous and more direct consultation between the United Kingdom and members of the Commonwealth had taken place. He was replying to criticisms by Lord Salisbury, who felt that the Labor Government's decision to recognize the People's Government "bears all the signs of a panic-stricken haste." *Ibid.*, col. 42.
[35] Quoted in Kundra, *op. cit.*, 206.

sion of defense agreements to the Middle East and South East Asia and against Western aid to Pakistan which in her view could only serve to bring the cold war to the Indian subcontinent and to alter the balance of power there to India's disadvantage. The setting up of the South East Asia Treaty Organization with Pakistan as a member in particular angered Mr. Nehru. Why, he enquired, should the Western powers seek to set up military bases in parts of the world whose chief desire was to keep out of war, to protect countries which for the most part have not asked for their protection, or to elaborate military plans with lesser Asian nations when the stronger and often more democratic Asian governments were outspokenly opposed to them? "Asian problems, Asian security and Asian peace," he complained[36] in September, 1954, "are not only discussed but actions are taken and treaties are made in regard to them chiefly by non-Asian countries." Military alliances were familiar but here Pandit Nehru detected something new and "rather extraordinary." What was emerging was not simply alliances for regional defense but interlocking alliances both on the part of the communist and Western powers. This, in his opinion, increased the prospect of war on a world scale and was something, therefore, undesirable in principle.

The chief aim of Indian foreign policy was to preserve South and South East Asia as an area of no war, and it was because it was thought that military pacts extending to the area would prejudice the prospect of its fulfilment that there was such outspoken opposition to them.[37] There were also, however, other factors. There was resentment at what was thought to be the indifference of the Western World to the opinions and even at times to the sufferings of Asian peoples. The use of the atom bomb against Japan, statements in Washington of its possible further employment against North Korea or Communist China,

[36] Sept. 9, 1954, to Delhi Press Association. See *Times of India*, Sept. 10, 1954.
[37] On this point, see the discussions at the Fifth Commonwealth Relations Conference at Lahore in 1954, as reported in Nicholas Mansergh, *The Multi-Racial Commonwealth* (London, 1955).

threats of "massive retaliation," and the awful destruction in
Korea itself[38] suggested that Asia might become itself the battle
field of rival imperialist groups neither of whom had the interests
of Asian peoples themselves as their first thought. There was resentment, too, at Asia's underrepresentation, or misrepresentation,
in the Security Council where at one critical moment in its history
the spokesmen of this continent peopled by some three-fifths
of the human race were the Lebanon—"an excellent but small
power," as Pandit Nehru observed—and Chiang Kai Shek's exiled
Government in Formosa. "I am not a great admirer of President
Rhee, anyhow," remarked Pandit Nehru in 1950.[39] Nor was
he, nor the many for whom he spoke, great admirers of Chiang
Kai Shek or Bao Dai, both of whom were lavishly supported by
American financial assistance.[40] And more deep-seated still was
the fact that Western policies might mean, if not a revival, at
least an unjustifiable extension of colonial rule in Asia. The
conflict in Indo-China, said Pandit Nehru,[41] despite its complexity,
was in its origin and essential character a movement of resistance
to colonialism and attempts were being made to deal with such
resistance "by the traditional methods of suppression and divide
and rule." The risk as he conceived it was that the Western
alliances might be used to maintain surviving Western colonial
outposts in Asia beyond the natural historic term of their existence.
In 1949, when asked about India's reaction to the North Atlantic
Treaty, Pandit Nehru said that India "is far removed from the
Atlantic region and the Government of India is not affected by
the Pact." They had been kept informed but not consulted
"because we are not in it at all" and he added that India's
membership of the Commonwealth did not in any way connect

[38] United States Information Services published pictures of it which had not
the effect in South Asia that was no doubt intended.
[39] *The Times*, Oct. 2, 1950.
[40] Cf. J. C. Kundra, *op. cit.*, 12, for figures of aid given to them. Indian
dislike of aid with strings accounted in part for the comparatively modest assistance
given to India.
[41] *House of the People Debates*, April 24, 1954; vol. 4, col. 5577.

India with the Pact.[42]   But in June, 1952, there appeared for the first time a new note of criticism. The North Atlantic Treaty, said Pandit Nehru, began as a defense organization but later extended its role to the defense of the colonial possessions of its members. India took "a very serious view" of this because she was unalterably opposed to colonial rule wherever it existed.[43] Subsequent Portuguese appeals to her partners in the North Atlantic Treaty about Goa and the response they elicited hardened this antipathy in India to the principal Western alliance. The apparent inclination of the Western powers towards Pakistan after 1954 further estranged India from the West. The existence of such sentiments and suspicions, whether they are thought to be well- or ill-founded, invites the question whether the military advantages of the extension of the Western system of defensive treaties to South and South East Asia outweighed the political disadvantages they incurred.

While thus opposed after 1952 to all extension whether in form or in practice of the system of Western alliances in which the United Kingdom was a principal partner the Indian Government under Pandit Nehru's leadership remained nonetheless a convinced supporter of the Commonwealth and a believer in its "healing touch." In the same speech in which the Indian Prime Minister first denounced the North Atlantic Treaty,[44] he reaffirmed in categoric terms all he had said in the past about the importance to India of her ties with the Commonwealth. "We propose to continue these bonds," he told his critics, "and I see no reason why we should break these bonds which are of advantage to us." Despite differences on major issues of foreign policy which divided India and later Ceylon from the older members of the Commonwealth, they were in accord on the broad aims of economic and financial policy. They also co-operated in the working out of the Colombo Plan and the importance of member-

[42] Constituent Assembly of India, [Legislative], *Debates*, vol. 3, pp. 2136-2137 (April 5, 1949).

[43] *Manchester Guardian*, June 13, 1952.

[44] *Ibid.*

ship remained for both. And even in respect of foreign policy India, a major power in Asia, had as a consequence of membership an opportunity of informing the Western powers of the Asian outlook; Britain and other members of the Commonwealth were thus put in a position to act at least with knowledge and usually with understanding of Asian policies. One interesting and by no means unimportant consequence of Commonwealth member- ship was the Indo-Canadian entente—for so indeed it deserves to be described. This entente was much in evidence at the United Nations in the later phases of the wars in Korea and Indo-China and during the Suez crisis of 1956, when the Commonwealth in the words of the Canadian External Affairs Minister Mr. Lester Pearson was brought to "the verge of dissolution,"[45] and it played a possibly decisive part in ensuring that Asian membership was not brought to an end in that moment of high emotion.

7. The Elaboration of Commonwealth Alliances:
A Perspective View

In September, 1939, the Dominions had no particular com- mitments binding them to go to war in Europe or in Asia. They had not subscribed to the obligations assumed by the United Kingdom in the Locarno Treaties of 1925, in the Anglo-Egyptian treaty and in the renewed guarantee of Belgian neutrality both of 1936; in the guarantees given to Poland, Roumania, and Greece in March-April, 1939, or in the Anglo-Turkish Alliance of the same year. Their policies of detachment, which was not tantamount to isolation, were expressed in the phrase "no com- mitments." They were founded not so much upon a cool assess- ment of what might best serve the cause of peace or the interests of the Commonwealth as upon an emotional revulsion against the alliances and power politics of the old world and a desire to disentangle Dominion policies from those of the United Kingdom. Consideration of status and of foreign policy at that time were

[45] See James Eayrs, "Canadian Policy and Opinion during the Suez Crisis," *International Journal*, vol. 12 (Spring, 1957), 97-108, for an analysis of Canada's role in the crisis.

thus inextricably intertwined. Once equality of status no longer needed to be asserted because its existence in fact and in form was assured, a reconsideration of Dominion policies was in any circumstances likely. The particular circumstances in which that reconsideration took place prompted a course of action in marked contrast to that generally pursued by the Dominions between 1919 and 1939 with the result that by 1956 the member nations of the Commonwealth had entered either severally or individually into a great variety of alliances, treaties, or agreements committing them to particular courses of action in particular circumstances. The freedom of action the Dominions had acquired by disentangling their policies from those of the United Kingdom was thus at their own will limited by international obligations which they had decided to assume.

The extent and variety of the alliances, treaties, and other agreements entered into by members of the Commonwealth may be placed in perspective by summarizing briefly the more important of them. In Europe the United Kingdom (alone of Commonwealth members) was a party to the Dunkirk Treaty with France 1946, and to the Brussels Treaty 1947, and was associated with the European Defense Community 1954; all of which committed her to armed assistance in the event of an attack upon one or more of the signatories to these treaties. Britain and Canada among Commonwealth members were signatories to the North Atlantic Treaty in 1949; Britain and Pakistan to the Bagdad Pact 1954; Britain, Pakistan, Australia and New Zealand to the South East Asian Treaty 1954. Canada, apart from her membership of the North Atlantic Treaty, was associated with the United States in the defense of North America under the 1940 Ogdensburg Agreement as extended for peacetime purposes in 1947 and 1949. Australia and New Zealand, pledged to mutual aid and assistance under the intra-Commonwealth ANZAC Agreement of 1944, both subscribed to the Pacific Security Agreement in 1951 with the United States and to the South East Asia Treaty in 1954. South Africa was a member of no regional pact but under an agreement signed in June, 1955, guaranteed the maintenance of the Simonstown naval base by the Union and its use by the United Kingdom and its allies in time of war whether the Union itself were neutral or not.[46] The South African Government also indicated its intention to assist in the defense of the Middle East and its Government asserted that in the event of a major war brought about by communist aggression South Africa would not be neutral. Pakistan, a member of the Bagdad Pact, was linked by bilateral treaties with Turkey, Iraq, and Iran in the Middle East and was associated with the United States not only through common membership of the South East Asia Treaty Organization but also by acceptance of U. S. military aid under an agreement reached in 1954. Ceylon was associated with the United Kingdom through the 1947 Defense Agreement until its abrogation in 1956 at the wish of the Ceylonese Government. India, like South Africa, but for altogether different reasons, was a member of no military agreements. She entered, however, into a considerable number of treaties of mutual friendship, first with neighboring countries, later with others geographically more remote. Over and above treaties, military or political in their principal purposes, members of the Commonwealth entered into a number of treaties or other arrangements for economic and social purposes. Among them may be mentioned Britain's membership of O.E.E.C. and of the Council of Europe; the participation of all members of the Commonwealth other than South Africa in the Colombo Plan; United Kingdom, Australian, and New Zealand membership of the South Seas Commission; Asian membership of E.C.A.F.E.; South African association with various organizations for economic planning and research in Africa.

The extent of Commonwealth commitments suggests the extent of the independent action taken and the responsibility assumed by individual Commonwealth members after 1945. It

[46] Cmd. 9520.

was at once the product of maturity and of experience.[47]   The
Nazi technique of picking off prospective victims one by one
disillusioned many who had believed that aggressors might be ap-
peased or their own safety assured by a policy of detachment.
Accordingly faith was widely placed, as some few distinguished
voices had advocated in the years before the Second World
War, in collective security and collective measures for defense.
But the distaste for military alliances remained.   The new agreements were rarely so described.   Canadian statesmen, once the
foremost champions of a policy of no commitments, were insistent
that their new regional security agreements were something
different from, and morally superior to, old fashioned military
pacts; and in respect of their greater awareness of the economic
and social conditions of peace perhaps the claim was warranted.
But the hard core of the regional defensive treaties was nonetheless military.   The members of the Commonwealth who
subscribed to them were brought directly, as they were not before
1939, into the area where military decisions were made.   This
brought about a significant shift in the character of their dominant
external interests to which the expansion of their diplomatic
services strikingly testifies and accounted for the fact that foreign
policy was the principal preoccupation of the members of the
Commonwealth after 1945.   That in turn posed new questions
as to the scope and purpose of their partnership, the ends it
best might serve and the means by which its members might most
usefully co-operate.   It is to be noted, however, that Commonwealth Governments evidently attached, despite their outside
commitments, much value to Commonwealth consultation; for
between 1945 and 1956 meetings of Commonwealth Prime
Ministers were far more frequent than before 1939, and Commonwealth Prime Ministers constant in their attendance at them.[48]

[47] The experience was not, of course, peculiar to them and accounts equally for
the military alliances into which the United States entered in the same period.
[48] Some parts of this paper are elaborated in a chapter in the author's forthcoming *Survey of British Commonwealth Affairs 1939-1952.*

3

The Commonwealth and the Law of Nations

ROBERT R. WILSON*

SCOTLAND'S SACRIFICE of her sovereignty in 1707 to the newly formed Kingdom of Great Britain was, a British jurist has suggested, "an unequalled example of the surrender of sovereignty for the greater good of mankind." Had the sacrifice not been made, the same speaker submitted, the history of the world would have been worse than it had been since the event.[1]

The peoples of the Commonwealth today would doubtless regard their respective countries' reversal of this process, their loosening of legal ties which once bound them together in a single empire, as equally promotive of the greater good of mankind. However true this may be, the process of moving toward independence instead of yielding up sovereignty seems to raise more questions of public international law. Particularly can this be so if the process is a gradual one, and if there is unevenness and lack of uniformity in the exercise, by the emergent new nations, of power to dissolve old legal ties.

Emergence from the old, and assumption of the new stations

* The author acknowledges with appreciation the research assistance of Mr. William Mithoefer, sometime Fellow in Political Science in the Graduate School of Arts and Sciences of Duke University, and of Dr. Robert E. Clute, Research Associate at Duke University.

[1] Presidential address of the Right Honourable Lord Normand at the Edinburgh meeting of the International Law Association in 1954, *Report of the Forty-Fourth Conference of the International Law Association* (1955), 10, 11. Lord Normand said in the course of his address that it was arguable that Scotland had made a larger sacrifice than was necessary.

may appear to be partial and incomplete from the point of view of the public law applicable between fully independent states. That law, "the sum of the rights that a state may claim for itself and its nationals from other states, and of the duties which in consequence it must observe towards them,"[2] finds application between entities which are in different stages of political advancement. If, however, new members of the family of nations while declaring their complete independence assert that certain other independent nations are not "foreign" to them (for commercial, jurisdictional, and regulatory purposes), questions arise as to what international legal rules apply between them.

The maintenance of special ties and preferences based upon sentiment and traditional political association may of course be simply matters of agreed foreign policy. Nevertheless, if the process continues for a long time, operates between a rapidly increasing group of states, and limits the legal relationships which the associated nations can or do establish with members of the family of nations that are admittedly "foreign," the effect of this practice may be considerable.

A discussion of the Commonwealth in relation to the law of nations might well proceed to an examination of the law as evidenced in the practice of each Commonwealth nation separately. It is obvious that, in a sense, the position of each will be a special one as compared with that of any other. For example, there is truth in the observation that Canada's problems in international law "are largely the problems of Canada in her relations to the United States."[3] Many questions, some of them not yet fully explored by scholars, have related to the Great Lakes, which waters the United States Supreme Court more than fifty years ago found to be "high seas" within the meaning of certain national legislation.[4] A broader approach is necessary, however,

[2] J. L. Brierly, *The Outlook for International Law* (London, 1944), 5.
[3] Norman MacKenzie and Lionel L. Laing, *Canada and the Law of Nations* (Toronto, 1938), xi. Cf. Maxwell Cohen, "Some International Law Problems of Interest to Canada and Canadian Lawyers," *Canadian Bar Review*, vol. 33 (1955), 389-423.
[4] *United States v. Rodgers*, 150 U. S. 249 (1893).

to discern the international legal significance of developments in the Commonwealth as a whole.

An authoritative writer concluded before the end of the third decade of the twentieth century that the British Dominions were "persons" of international law, but not of identically the same kind as those that are called independent sovereign states.[5] In the intervening decades it has become sufficiently clear that the Commonwealth nations are indeed "persons" for general purposes of international law. The method of the reception of the law in the jurisprudence of the respective Commonwealth countries has begun to receive deserved attention.[6]

A complete inquiry into the law of nations as it figures in the relations of Commonwealth members would necessitate examination of a wide range of questions. Of these, the capacity to conclude treaties and the possibility of remaining neutral when Great Britain has gone to war have perhaps come in for greatest popular attention. There have been, naturally, many others of practical importance, such as state succession,[7] acquisition of imperium in polar regions,[8] sovereign immunity,[9] and judicial assistance between Commonwealth nations through extradition.[10]

[5] P. J. Noel Baker, *The Present Juridical Status of the British Dominions in International Law* (London, 1929), 354, 356.

[6] See C. H. Alexander, "International Law in India," *International and Comparative Law Quarterly*, vol. 1 (1952), 289-300; D. C. Vanek, "Is International Law a Part of the Law of Canada?," *University of Toronto Law Journal*, vol. 8 (1949-50), 251-297. The last-mentioned writer concludes (p. 295) that in Canada, "legislation contrary to international law is *ultra vires* under existing Canadian constitutional law,"
   On the relation of international law and municipal law, cf. H. Lauterpacht, "Is International Law a Part of the Law of England?," *Transactions of the Grotius Society*, vol. 25 (1940), 51-88, and E. D. Dickinson, "Changing Concepts and the Doctrine of Incorporation," *American Journal of International Law*, vol. 26 (1932), 239-260.

[7] See, for example, J. Mervyn Jones, "State Succession in the Matter of Treaties," *British Year Book of International Law*, vol. 24 (1947), 354, 356.

[8] See the statement concerning the sector principle in Maxwell Cohen, *loc. cit.*, at 405-407.

[9] On this subject as relating to Pakistan and its component states, see L. C. Green, "The Status of Pakistan," *Indian Law Review*, vol. 4 (1952), 65-77.

[10] On the applicability between Commonwealth countries of the rule of international law concerning political offenses and extradition, see R. Y. Jennings, "International Law and The Commonwealth," *British Year Book of International Law*, vol. 30 (1953), 320-351, at 325-326.

The limitations of a brief study preclude consideration of more than a few selected matters—the criterion of selection being the presumed greater bearing of these, as compared with some of the more technical questions, upon international co-operation through legal means. On this basis it is proposed to consider (1) nationality questions, (2) obligatory jurisdiction for the settlement of international disputes, and (3) some features of international-organization law.

Two preliminary cautions are perhaps in order. The first is suggested in one writer's reminder that "it is not possible to discuss even the outline of the Constitution of the British Commonwealth without in the first place giving a brief consideration to the British character."[11] This doubtless touches the tradition of dealing practically with political problems without too much concern for the logical consistency of such handling with preconceived ideas or systems. The second caution would emphasize the realization today of *interdependence* rather than of complete independence or sovereignty. Of the latter two terms it has been well said that they "can only have a meaning for international law in so far as they are merely compendious designations of certain qualities of modern Statehood."[12] There now appears to be less preoccupation with the old fetish of sovereignty and more attention to the meeting of human needs through arrangements between public bodies.[13]

1. Nationality

In legalistic terms, nationality—or citizenship, used in a broad sense—connotes "membership in a political society and implies a duty of allegiance on the part of the member and a duty of protection on the part of the society."[14] It is basic in traditional

[11] Alison Russell, "The Constitution of the British Commonwealth," *Journal of Comparative Legislation and International Law*, 3rd ser., vol. 24 (1942), at 83.
[12] J. L. Brierly, "The Shortcomings of International Law," *British Year Book of International Law*, vol. 5 (1924), 12.
[13] Cf. Wilfred Jenks, "The Scope of International Law," *British Year Book of International Law*, vol. 31 (1954), 1-48, *passim*; W. G. Friedmann, ed., *The Public Corporation* (Toronto, 1954), 495-537.
[14] *Luria v. United States*, 231 U. S. 9, 22 (1913).

international law on this subject that each state shall have the right to determine who shall be its nationals. However, the right of a state to confer its nationality has never been unlimited. In fact, the International Court of Justice held in 1955 that the word of a naturalizing state was not necessarily conclusive upon other states as to the nationality of a person it had naturalized (in this instance, of an individual whose property another state has seized on the ground that the man was an enemy alien).[15]

For the purpose of diplomatic protection a state may have protégés as well as nationals. There may also be persons "assimilated" to nationals for certain jurisdictional purposes, such as the exercise of criminal jurisdiction. Such a person, for example, was the Brooklyn-born William Joyce, better known as "Lord Haw Haw" of the Second World War. Never a British subject, but a long-time resident of the British Isles, he went to Germany on a British passport ("wrapped in the Union Jack") and became prominent in the service of the Nazis. His later conviction in England for treason rested upon the proposition that one who enjoyed British protection abroad occupied the same position as he would have had he been a British subject.[16] (In this case the country of Joyce's birth, quite understandably, did not protest the proceedings.)

The idea of a natural-born British subject, one "born under the ligeance of the King," has at times rested not on legislation but on the common law.[17] There was Canadian legislation (of general application) concerning the naturalization of persons in British Dominions as early as 1881 (following passage by the Parliament at Westminster of the Naturalization Act, 1870), but naturalization in a Dominion apparently did not confer

[15] *Nottebohm* case, *I. C. J. Reports*, 1955, 4-27. For a general discussion of nationality in municipal and in international law, see Clive Parry, *Nationality and Citizenship Laws of the Commonwealth and of the Republic of Ireland* (London, 1957), 3-27.
[16] *Joyce v. Director of Public Prosecutions* [1946], A. C. 347. In cases of criminal jurisdiction the idea of allegiance seems to have received more emphasis than has place of birth.
[17] See statement in *Calvin's Case*, 77 E. R. 377, 409 (1608). Cf. Heather J. Harvey, *Consultation and Cooperation in the Commonwealth* (London, 1952), 50.

a nationality in any entity other than the naturalizing one. For example, a British court found that naturalization of a person in Australia (in accordance with Part V, Section 51 (xix) of the Australian Constitution) did not keep him from being an alien in Great Britain.[18]

The practical effect of classification for nationality purposes of course depends upon the extent to which there is discrimination against aliens. In Great Britain, in the years just before the First World War there was a tendency to put aliens on the same footing with nationals. Beginning in 1919, however, various legislative acts came to discriminate against aliens.[19] For the purpose of restricting economic rights and privileges, the classification of "British subject" became more meaningful. Its retention as and after the Dominions became fully independent states was to be one of the most striking features of Commonwealth development, but only after the Second World War was there planned, parallel action which raised new questions of public international law.

Following passage by Canada of new nationality legislation in 1946, to be effective January 1, 1947, the Government of the United Kingdom issued invitations for a conference which met in February, 1947. To it came nationality experts of the various Commonwealth countries. India did not have representation, but there were arrangements to keep the Indian Government informed of the proceedings. The United Kingdom's draft scheme, which related the idea of local citizenship in each country and the wider status of "British subject," provided a basis for discussion. The plan was for each Commonwealth member to pass its own legislation.

Of the legislation, that in the United Kingdom and Colonies,[20] while not first in chronological order, perhaps merits first mention because of the extent to which it provided a model. When the

[18] *Markwald v. Attorney General* [1920], 1, ch. 348.
[19] L. Oppenheim, *International Law* (8th ed., by Lauterpacht), I (1955), 689.
[20] The British Nationality Act, 1948, 11 & 12 Geo. 6, c. 56; *Halsbury's Statutes of England* (2nd ed., 1951), vol. 28, 137. See also Cmd. 7326.

measure was under discussion in the House of Commons the Secretary of State for the Home Department said:

The essential feature of the Bill is that each of the self-governing Commonwealth countries shall determine by its own legislation who are its citizens and shall declare these citizens to be British subjects; and shall recognize as British subjects the citizens of all the other countries of the Commonwealth. The structure of the edifice thus created would be the same for all the countries. Each would confer its citizenship, and through citizenship of a country—and through citizenship alone—will a person become a British subject. It would be contrary to the scheme . . . that a country should create British subjects without passing them through the gateway of its own citizenship.[21]

The Act distinguished what one publicist described as "nationals of His Majesty in international law" from ordinary aliens. The former might acquire British citizenship on more favorable terms (by registration) than were allowed to "aliens." As British-protected persons they were exempted from certain disabilities applicable to aliens, but still they were not nationals of the United Kingdom (if they chose to remain connected with another Commonwealth nation) in the full sense of the municipal law.[22] Special rules applied to any citizen of Eire who, having been a British subject immediately before the effective date of the legislation, desired to retain that status. A citizen of Eire who, under legislation of some other Commonwealth nation, had been enabled to remain a British subject was to be deemed to have that status also in the United Kingdom.

In Canada the legislation was perhaps even more explicit. The Canadian Citizenship Act of 1946 declared that "A Canadian citizen is a British subject." It also provided that every person who under the legislation of listed countries (other Commonwealth countries and Southern Rhodesia) had been given citizenship in the respective countries would have in Canada the status of a British subject. The expressions "British subject" and

---

[21] *Parl. Deb.*, 5th ser., Commons, vol. 453, col. 388 (July 7, 1948).
[22] Cf. Heather J. Harvey, *op. cit.*, 67.

"Commonwealth citizen" were declared to have the same meaning.[23]

The basic legislation in Ireland had come more than a decade earlier. The Irish Nationality and Citizenship Act, 1935,[24] was a move to abolish the status of British subject for Irish citizens. Section 33 set forth that specified British legislation, if and so far as it ever was in force in Saorstát Eireann, was repealed. By the same section, "The common law relating to British nationality, if and so far as it ever was . . . in force in Saorstát Eireann, shall cease to have effect." Facts or events by reason of which a person was at any time a citizen of Ireland were not of themselves to confer on such person any other citizenship or nationality. Furthermore, by Section 34, one who was a citizen of Ireland by virtue of Article 3 of the Constitution or who might become such a citizen by or under the Act was declared to be such a citizen "for all purposes, municipal *and international.*" [25] It has been seen that there was provision in British law for citizens of Eire to retain their previously acquired status of British subject. British citizens are aliens in contemplation of Irish law, since legislation of Eire has defined an "alien" as "a person who is not a citizen of Saorstát Eireann"; but apparently they are in practice "exempted from most of the disabilities imposed upon aliens."[26]

The Australian Act of 1948 followed, in general, the plan

[23] Revised Statutes of Canada (1952), vol. II, chap. 33 (pp. 1607-1626).
Amendments to the Canadian Citizenship Act since 1946 have added to the list such countries as have become members of the Commonwealth since 1946, and have extended the Act so as to apply to Newfoundland. See Clive Parry, *op. cit.* (note 15, *supra*), 472.

[24] *Saorstát Eireann, Public General Acts Passed by the Oireachtas During the Year 1935,* Act no. 13, 173-219.

[25] Italics supplied.
Cf. the definition of Irish citizen in later United Kingdom legislation, Ireland Act, 1949, Sec. 5 (1), 12-14 Geo. 6, c. 41.

[26] Cmd. 7326 (par. 17), and Irish Aliens Act, 1935, s. 2 (volume cited in note 24, *supra*, 221).

For text of 1956 legislation of Eire (supplementing earlier legislation) whereby the Government of Eire, if satisfied that under the law of another country Irish citizens enjoy there some or all the rights of citizens of that country, may by order declare that citizens of that country shall enjoy in Eire similar citizenship rights and privileges to those enjoyed by Irish citizens in that country, see Clive Parry, *op. cit.* (note 15, *supra*), 969-970.

of the legislation passed by the Parliament at Westminster in the same year, both on the status assigned to British subjects and on that assigned to citizens of Eire.[27] In the course of debate on the bill the Minister for Information and Minister for Immigration made the point that citizenship in a Commonwealth country carried with it "the common status." He pointed out that British subjects in Australia would be "free from the disabilities and restrictions that apply to aliens." He added:

They will qualify for the franchise and have the right to become members of Parliament or enter the public services. A British subject who is not Australian born will be able to become an Australian citizen by a simple act of registration, but he will not suffer in any way whatever should he fail to do this. No doubt a great many British people not born in Australia will seek citizenship, but they will not make the move as a means of obtaining any practical advantage whatever, but purely as an expression of pride in this country and its achievements. . . .[28]

The New Zealand legislation of 1948, aptly entitled the British Nationality and New Zealand Citizenship Act, provided that New Zealand citizens and citizens of listed countries (other Commonwealth members and Southern Rhodesia) should by reason of such citizenship have the status of British subjects. "Commonwealth citizen" and "British subject" were, by the Act, to have the same meaning. By Section 8, Irish citizens were included, along with citizens of Commonwealth countries, among those who might, by compliance with the prescribed procedure (which included registration) acquire New Zealand citizenship. New Zealand recognized the continuance of certain Irish citizens (who had been given the right so to continue under legislation of other Commonwealth countries) as British subjects.[29]

South African legislation of 1949 followed, in general, the

[27] Nationality and Citizenship Act, 1948 (no. 83 of 1948), *Commonwealth Acts*, vol. 46, 415-433.
[28] *Parl. Deb.*, vol. 198, 1062 (Sept. 30, 1948).
[29] *New Zealand Statutes*, 1948, vol. 1 (no. 15 of 1948), 145-169. Section 2 (4) provides that, "Any reference in this Act to India, being a reference to a state of affairs existing before the fifteenth day of August, nineteen hundred and forty-seven, shall be construed as a reference to British India as defined by section three hundred and eleven of the Government of India Act, 1935."

lines of Canadian legislation of three years earlier. It provided a method whereby citizens of another Commonwealth country or of Eire might acquire South African citizenship through a procedure which included registration. While not mentioning in very specific terms a common or Commonwealth status, it provided (s. 38) that any reference in a law of the South African Union to a British subject would be deemed to refer to a citizen of the South African Union, or a citizen of a Commonwealth country, or a citizen of the Republic of Ireland.[30]

The Ceylon Citizenship Act of 1948 created "the status of a citizen of Ceylon." Ordinary resident aliens who register for the purpose of acquiring Ceylonese citizenship are required to take an oath or affirmation of citizenship and one of allegiance, but a British subject (this term having "the same meaning as in the law of the United Kingdom") need take only the former. An alien was one who, for the purpose of this law, was not a British subject. There were no specific references to Irish citizens.[31]

In the case of India, the present Constitution does not in the articles referring to citizenship mention "British subject." There is provision whereby one who has been born in India (or either of whose parents or any of whose grandparents has been born in India) and who was on the date of the adoption of the Constitution living outside the country may register and thus be deemed an Indian citizen.[32] The Constitution leaves broad powers to the Parliament in matters relating to citizenship.

By the Pakistan Citizenship Act of 1951, the term "alien" means a person who is not a citizen of Pakistan or a Commonwealth citizen. The term "Commonwealth citizen" means a person described as such by the British Nationality Act of 1948. Every person who becomes a citizen of Pakistan under the Act

---

[30] *Statutes of the Union of South Africa*, 1949, Act no. 44 (pp. 414-453).

[31] *Laws Concerning Nationality, United Nations Legislative Series* (1954), 83-91.

[32] Articles 5 and 6. On a declaration made by the Indian President, under Articles 367(3) and 392(3) of the Constitution, that, subject to legislation which the Indian Parliament might enact, Commonwealth countries are not to be foreign states for the purposes of the Constitution, see "The Present Status Under the New Indian Constitution of Indian Citizens within the British Commonwealth," *International Law Quarterly*, vol. 3 (1950), 285-286.

has the "status of a Commonwealth citizen." One who has been naturalized as a British subject in Pakistan and who has before the effective date of the Act acquired citizenship of a foreign state and subsequently (before the date of the Act) renounced such citizenship, is deemed to be a Pakistan citizen. Legislation of 1952 substituted the words "citizen of Pakistan" for the words "British subject" in older (1926) legislation which applied to what is now Pakistan.[33]

The Ghana Citizenship Act of 1957 is generally in line with the Commonwealth Conference agreement of a decade earlier. Citizens of other Commonwealth countries and British-protected persons may, if they have been resident in Ghana for at least four years or are in the service of the government, become citizens by registration.[34]

From the foregoing it will appear that there has been, on the part of most of the Commonwealth countries, legislative effort to have a distinctive citizenship for the respective members of the Commonwealth, while preserving a status of "British subject" or "Commonwealth citizen" which differs from the status assigned to "aliens." The practical effect of the plan will depend upon other legislative policy of the individual Commonwealth states. A sampling of legislative enactments would appear to indicate that there is a substantial amount of discrimination against "aliens" which does not extend to the category of persons described as British subjects or "Commonwealth citizens."[35] Such discrimination might conceivably be overcome by most-favored-nation clauses (as on establishment matters) which a Commonwealth country might include in a commercial treaty with an outside state, provided such clauses are not read to mean most-

---

[33] Volume cited in note 31, *supra*, 361-366.

On the creation, by legislation effective in 1952, of a citizenship of Malaya, and a rule whereby that citizenship could not be held by one who was also a citizen of another Commonwealth country, see F. G. Garnell, "Malayan Citizenship Legislation," *International and Comparative Law Quarterly*, vol. 1 (1952) 504, 515.

[34] *Commonwealth Survey*, vol. 3, no. 11 (May, 1957), 479.

[35] Based upon the research of Dr. Claude S. Phillips, Jr., under a grant from the Duke University Commonwealth-Studies Center in 1956. The result of the research has not yet been published.

favored "foreign" nation so as to avoid giving to nationals of outside states what is given to nationals of Commonwealth countries.

Individuals having the "common status" may find that this entails obligations as well as benefits and privileges. Court decisions concerning compulsory military service will illustrate. The existing rule of international law on involuntary military service by aliens has been the subject of some difference of opinion (the kind of service, the type of residence which the aliens may enjoy, and the alternative of leaving the country of residence being among the considerations entering into the discussion). Although the law does not preclude the denial to an alien (who refuses to serve) of the privilege of naturalization, or even preclude his expulsion, the sound view would seem to be that it does not permit him to be drafted without his consent or that of his own state. In 1945 the High Court of Australia, in the *Polites* case, held that such drafting was a breach of international law.[36]

Are British subjects who are in the jurisdiction of a Commonwealth state of which they are not citizens in the full municipal sense, "aliens" in the international-law sense, for the purpose of the international-law rule? Certain judicial decisions suggest that they are not, or that, if they are, the states of which they are citizens in the municipal-law sense have condoned or consented to their being drafted if the law of the Commonwealth country in which they are resident so provides. For example, in *Murray v. Parkes*[37] the court held that a person who was born in Ireland in 1908 but who had resided in England since 1934 and was a natural-born British subject under the British Nationality and Status of Aliens Act, 1914, had not been deprived of that status by the legislation which made him an Irish citizen. Having continued to reside in England, he had not discharged the burden placed upon him by the National Services Act, 1941,

[36] 70 C. L. R. 60 (1945). The case involved a Greek national, not a Commonwealth citizen.

[37] [1942], 2 K.B. 123-137.

of showing that he was not a British subject.[38] Eleven years later a British court held another Irish citizen liable to compulsory military service under British legislation; by this legislation, while the territory known as the Republic of Ireland had ceased to be a part of His Majesty's dominions, it was not a foreign country.[39] In *Ullah v. Black* (1955), the Court of Queen's Bench decided that a Pakistan citizen, who had come to England uncertain about whether he would remain there, was a British subject under the British Nationality Act of 1948 and, since his residence was not merely temporary, was liable for military service under the National Service Act.[40] In all of these cases there was strong emphasis upon what the national legislative body had willed.

Another part of international law which might conceivably be affected by the nationality situation in the Commonwealth is that pertaining to international reclamations. The relevant rule is to the effect that, in general, claims of individuals or companies against foreign states may be espoused only by the state whose nationality these individuals or companies have. The question suggested is whether the "common allegiance" throughout the Commonwealth would make it possible, consistently with the stated rule, for the United Kingdom and Colonies to espouse the claim of all or any British subjects. There is, of course, considerable leeway within which states may waive the applicable rule, and there is even one reported instance of Great Britain's having interceded in behalf of Tuscan subjects who, although

---

[38] In the First World War period an Alberta court had occasion to decide whether one who had obtained a naturalization certificate in Canada and who claimed that this made him a British subject *only in Canada* was liable for military service overseas. The ruling was that he had become a British subject in *every* country—except in the one of which he had before naturalization in Canada been a national and if by that state's law he had not lost his previous nationality. *Re Solvang* [1918], 43 D. L. R. 548.

[39] *Bicknell v. Brosnan* [1953], 2 Q. B. 77-83. See discussion in Clive Parry, "International Law and the Conscription of Non-Nationals," *British Year Book of International Law*, vol. 31 (1954), 437-452.

[40] Apparently unreported. See statement in *The Times* (London), April 23, 1955, 5(7).

not its nationals, were members of the Anglican church.[41] International usage has established that states may collect in behalf of their protégés as well as their full-fledged citizens. It is reasonable to surmise, however, that under a claims convention of the usual type specifying claims by nationals of each country against the government of the other, a respondent state might successfully invoke the rule concerning nationality against the United Kingdom's presentation of claims other than those of persons who were her nationals in the full municipal-law sense.

It is, however, indicative of Commonwealth realities affecting international relations that the United Kingdom should handle certain war claims in behalf of all the Commonwealth countries. Illustrative of such handling are the agreement of 1951 with Thailand and the agreement of 1948 with Yugoslavia.[42] The latter provided for payment by Yugoslavia of a lump sum in settlement of claims of "British nationals" up to the signature date of the agreement. By the provisions, "British national" means "physical persons who are British subjects or British protected persons . . ." and also "Companies, firms and associations incorporated or constituted under the laws in force in the territory of the United Kingdom . . . or Canada, the Commonwealth of Australia, New Zealand, the Union of South Africa, India, Pakistan, Ceylon. . . ."[43]

Nationality questions arising out of Burma's election to remain out of the Commonwealth were anticipated in the Treaty Regarding the Recognition of Burmese Independence and Related Matters, signed by Burma and the United Kingdom on October 17, 1947. Article 3 provided that a person who at the effective date of the treaty was a Burmese citizen under the Burmese Constitution and a British subject by subsequent election might by declaration divest himself of Burmese citizenship.[44]

[41] I. M. Sinclair, "Nationality of Claims: British Practice," *British Year Book of International Law*, vol. 27 (1950), 125, 138-139.

[42] Cmd. 8163 (Thailand), Cmd. 7600 (Yugoslavia).

[43] Alfred Drucker, "Compensation for Nationalized Property: The British Practice," *American Journal of International Law*, vol. 49 (1955), 477-486, at 477.

[44] *United Nations Treaty Series*, no. 904. For example of an agreement between

The actual implementation of understandings between the Commonwealth countries on matters of nationality has varied to some extent from state to state. As far as national legislation is concerned, the United Kingdom has apparently been the only one of the Commonwealth countries in which all British subjects, regardless of race or origin, have been put on substantially the same footing as British subjects born in the country.[45]

2. Settlement of Disputes between Commonwealth Members

One of the steps in international relations strongly advocated by many legalists in the period since the First World War has been acceptance of a general obligatory jurisdiction.[46] By this is meant agreement, in advance of the occurrence of disputes, to their settlement by a judicial agency if they are not amicably adjusted by some other peaceful means. The outcome of effort in this direction, both during the League of Nations period and since 1945, has been the achievement of only a limited obligatory jurisdiction. The latter rests partly upon acceptances of the so-called Optional Clause in Article 36 of the World Court Statute. This applies to four broad classes of disputes,[47] but states which accept the Clause may at the time specify exceptions even within these. While such acceptances pertain to adjective rather than to substantive law, the course which the Commonwealth countries have followed in this matter has some bearing upon the application, particularly in disputes between them, of the substantive law of nations.

One reason for the slowness of states to accept obligatory jurisdiction and for their inclusion of reservations when they

the United Kingdom, India, Australia, Pakistan, and Ceylon on the one part and Burma on the other, see the loan agreement signed June 28, 1950, Cmd. 8007.

[45] Heather J. Harvey, op. cit., 57.

[46] The writer is indebted to the editor-in-chief of the American Journal of International Law for permission to reproduce in this section certain materials the substance of which appeared in condensed form in that Journal under the title, "Some Questions of Legal Relations between Commonwealth Members," vol. 51 (1957), 611-617.

[47] Questions of international law, treaty interpretation, the existence of any fact which, if established, would constitute a breach of an international obligation, and the nature and extent of reparation to be made for such a breach.

do accept it has undoubtedly been their conviction of the law's incompleteness. If authorized to settle *any type* of dispute, courts would perhaps appear to be makers of law instead of merely agencies to apply it. Distrust of a court on the bench of which a disputant state could never have more than one of its own nationals as a judge, and some feeling that there should not be too much legalism in international relations, have probably been additional factors. The result has been various types of reservations.

The specification of reciprocity, the limitation of acceptance of the Optional Clause to a term of years, and exclusion of questions that have arisen in the past or that have grown out of war, have become common. Potentially more limiting than these have been the "domestic jurisdiction" and the "national security" reservations. Of the former, perhaps the most criticized form has been the one which the United States originated in 1946—"disputes with regard to matters which are essentially within the domestic jurisdiction of the United States as determined by the United States." The latter reservation found expression in 1957 when the British Government excepted disputes "relating to any question which, in the opinion of the Government of the United Kingdom, affects the national security of the United Kingdom or of any of its dependent territories."

In the case of the Commonwealth countries, seven of which are among the more than thirty states bound by the Optional Clause, a more distinctive type of reservation has evolved. This had its origin in the period when the Dominions had not completely emerged as independent states. The considerations which inspired it found expression in the remarks of Sir Cecil Hurst at a meeting of jurists to discuss the Statute of the World Court, in 1929. On the Court's possible role in relation to inter-Dominion disputes or a dispute between Great Britain and a Dominion, Sir Cecil

replied that this matter had been discussed in London where the view was that no question arising between Great Britain and a Dominion could be brought before the Permanent Court owing to the provisions of Article 14 of the Covenant which laid down that the Court possessed jurisdiction only in international disputes. This provision excluded the submission to the Court of disputes between two of the units composing the British Empire, because the relations between them were different from the relations between two foreign States, and for this reason the relations between them *were not international*. Although the Dominions were autonomous, a dispute between two of them or between a Dominion and Great Britain was not an international matter and could not technically be brought before the Court.[48]

Three years earlier an Imperial Conference had recorded agreement that it would be premature for the parties represented to accept the Optional Clause at that time. There was an understanding that no one of the governments represented would move toward acceptance without discussion with the others. After Canada had initiated such dicussion, in 1929, there followed, later in that year and in the following one, a movement toward accepting the Optional Clause of the Permanent Court of International Justice. All of the Commonwealth members accepted it, but, with the exception of the Irish Free State, all of them reserved disputes *inter se*. By the formula used, the latter were to be settled in such manner as the parties had agreed upon or might agree upon.[49]

In the next several decades the Commonwealth members as a group moved little nearer to the acceptance of the principal world tribunal's obligatory jurisdiction for disputes of Commonwealth states *inter se*. Of the eight states which were members of the Commonwealth at the end of 1956, one, Ceylon, while a member of the United Nations, had not accepted the Optional Clause. Six other members employed formulas that followed the general line of India's declaration, which excluded

---

[48] *Minutes of the Committee of Jurists on the Statute of the Permanent Court of International Justice*, League of Nations doc. C.166. M.66. 1929, V, 71-72 (italics inserted). On the point that the law applicable in *inter se* disputes would not, at that time, have been international law, see Robert A. MacKay, "The Problem of A Commonwealth Tribunal," *Canadian Bar Review*, vol. 10 (1932), 338-348, at 344. This writer cites in support Keith, Baker, Hurst, and Wright.

[49] Cmd. 3452. The position taken with respect to obligations under the General Act for the Pacific Settlement of International Disputes was similar.

from the Court's jurisdiction "disputes with the Government of any country which on the date of this Declaration is a member of the Commonwealth of Nations, all of which disputes shall be settled in such manner as the parties have agreed or shall agree."[50]

Pakistan, while not specifically excepting intra-Commonwealth disputes, did specify reciprocity. This would presumably leave the Pakistan Government unbound as toward those Commonwealth members which did exclude disputes *inter se*. It is arguable whether a clause in India's declaration (terminated on February 8, 1957, in a communication which indicated that a fresh declaration would shortly be filed), which gave to that country the right to terminate acceptance of the Optional Clause with notice, did not provide a means of avoiding the Court's jurisdiction in *any* case involving India. However, the wording in India's declaration excluding any dispute with a country which "on the date of this Declaration" was a Commonwealth member would seem on its face to have left the Indian Government bound in relation to newcomers to the Commonwealth, if the latter had accepted obligatory jurisdiction without reserving intra-Commonwealth disputes.

It seems clear that the Commonwealth countries have now progressed to the point where international law increasingly applies to these states in their relations *inter se*. Given this fact, the continued reservation of questions between themselves would seem to suggest either (1) that ties of sentiment and tradition, as well as mutual economic interests, make desirable some special machinery to operate for disputes *inter se* (in which, for example, there would not be a majority of third state nationals as judges), or (2) that there is not sufficient confidence in the method, or

---

[50] *I. C. J. Yearbook*, 1955-56, 187. Commonwealth countries accepting in substance this formula, with the exception of India and the Union of South Africa, have the word "British" before Commonwealth.

In their "domestic jurisdiction" reservations, five Commonwealth members specify the international-law test to determine which questions are within this description. India and Pakistan use the formula on domestic-jurisdiction questions which the United States initiated, as noted above.

In Australia's acceptance of the Optional Clause, there is an exception clause for questions relating to Australia's continental shelf, natural resources of the sea-bed, and Australian waters within the meaning of Australian Pearl Fisheries Acts.

even that degree of concern about disputes *inter se,* which would make *any* continuing *judicial* machinery necessary or even desirable, or (3) that adjudication is not acceptable for really serious disputes and not needed for others. The second of these considerations seems especially to have influenced Imperial Conference action in 1929 and 1930. In 1929 there was a recommendation that there be an intra-Commonwealth tribunal, and in 1930 a more specific proposal. The arrangement was, however, to be along the lines of the old Hague Court (Permanent Court of Arbitration) in that reliance was to be upon *ad hoc* boards rather than a continuing tribunal. Each disputant party would name two persons (one to be from a Commonwealth country that was not a party to the dispute, the other from any Commonwealth country); the four thus chosen would name a fifth arbitrator who was also to be from within the Commonwealth. In the absence of "general consent" to obligatory jurisdiction, the arbitration was to be voluntary (i.e., agreed to after the occurrence of the dispute), and only "justiciable" disputes were to be referred.[51]

There has in the past been some adjudication of questions between public units of the British Empire, such as that of the Labrador boundary question between Canada and Newfoundland, which was referred to the Judicial Committee of the Privy Council.[52] In contrast, attempted arbitration of a boundary dispute between Northern Ireland and the Irish Free State did not succeed, the Government of Northern Ireland not co-operating to the extent of appointing arbitrators.[53] Certain compromissary clauses in international agreements recently concluded between Commonwealth states make provision for settlement of disputes, such as that in Article 10 of an agreement between the United Kingdom and Canada:

[51] *Imperial Conference, 1930: Summary of Proceedings,* Cmd. 3717; Robert A. MacKay, *loc. cit.,* 341-342.

[52] *In re Labrador Boundary,* 43 T. L. R. 289-299 (1926-27). At the time of this adjudication, the Privy Council could be empowered by the British Parliament to settle such a question.

[53] On co-operation between the same two entities through legislation, see A. G. Donaldson, "Co-operation between Northern Ireland and the Irish Republic," *International and Comparative Law Quarterly,* vol. 3 (1954), 319-330.

Any dispute between the contracting parties relating to the interpretation or application of this Agreement or of the Annex thereto, shall be referred for decision to the Interim Council in accordance with the provisions of Article III, section 6(8) of the Interim Agreement on International Civil Aviation done at Chicago on 7th December, 1944, unless the contracting parties agree to settle the dispute by referring to an arbitral tribunal appointed by agreement between them or to some other person or body. The contracting parties undertake to comply with the decision given.[54]

The dangerous Kashmir dispute and the sharpness of the Indian Government's accusations growing out of the treatment of persons of Indian ancestry in the South African Union prove that grave controversies can develop inside the Commonwealth. That elements of international law might apply in each of these disputes is indicated in the discussions concerning them. For example, Sir Owen Dixon of Australia, "United Nations Representative for India and Pakistan," referred to that law in his report to the Security Council.[55] Early in the history of the United Nations there was a move, which was agreeable to the Union of South Africa, to seek an advisory opinion from the International Court of Justice on the question of whether India's complaint against the Union of South Africa related to matters of "domestic jurisdiction." The effort failed. In the course of discussion the Soviet spokesman (Gromyko) observed that "To treat the Indian question as a legal matter would tend to minimize

[54] Cmd. 7857. Cf. the shorter formula in Article 8 of the United Kingdom's agreement on the same subject matter with the Union of South Africa, by which "Each Contracting Party agrees that if any matter in dispute under this Agreement . . . cannot be settled by negotiation, it shall be referred for decision to an Arbitral Tribunal. The composition of this Tribunal shall be determined by agreement between the Contracting Parties." Cmd. 7858. The compromissary clause in Article 11 of a comparable agreement with Ceylon commits the parties to use an arbitral tribunal or other agreed agency; failing agreement, either party may submit the dispute to agencies within the International Civil Aviation Organization. Cmd. 7859.

[55] Official Records, Security Council, Fifth Year (1950), Supplement, vol. 3 (Document S/1791), 24-51, at 29.

On the possible justiciability of the dispute, see comment by the present writer, loc. cit. (note 46, supra) at 614.

the political importance and weaken the prestige of the United Nations."[56]

It would appear that occasions for the application of public law in the relations of Commonwealth countries, both between themselves and with outside states, have not been lacking and are not apt to be lacking in the future. In view of the rapidly changing relationships, it is perhaps too much to expect that the long-contemplated Commonwealth tribunal for *inter se* disputes will be a reality in the near future, or that, if created, it will be a tight obligatory-jurisdiction arrangement. There remain the possibilities of mediation, conciliation, and more direct methods of amicable adjustment, some of them attainable through general international organization.

3. International-Organization Law

The possible effect of public international organization upon the further development and the application of international law requires no elaborate discussion. The Commonwealth nations' part in the process has bearing upon their general position with respect to the law. Some aspects of the subject which invite attention are (1) the assumption of membership in the principal organizations, (2) capacity to discharge obligations incident to such membership, and (3) distinctive positions on legal questions which Commonwealth states may have taken as members.

The manner in which the British Dominions became separate members of the League of Nations is well known.[57] Sir Robert Borden had an effective role in the process. His own country became not merely a member but was in due time elected to its Council, and until Mexico joined the League in 1931 Canada was the sole member from North America. The Canadians, however, apparently had no enthusiasm for a Commonwealth bloc in the League.[58]

[56] See *Official Records of the Second Part of the First Session of the Assembly,* Joint Committee of the First and Sixth Committees, Nov. 21-30, 1946, 1-50, at 29.
[57] See G. P. deT. Glazebrook, *Canada at the Paris Peace Conference* (London, 1942), 111-112.
[58] See, generally, F. H. Soward, "Canada and the League of Nations," *International Conciliation,* no. 283 (Oct., 1932).

India's membership in the League was something of an anomaly, since the country was at that time only "on the road to self-government."[59] The British Empire's panel system at Versailles enabled India to participate on an equal footing with the self-governing Dominions. President Wilson apparently hesitated about approving the admission of India but finally assented and, as an American historian of the Conference writes, "no one else seemed to care."[60] The Dominions and India were fellow-members in the League with fully sovereign states.

Membership of the Commonwealth countries in the United Nations has presented no serious legal problems. Canada, Australia, New Zealand, India, and the Union of South Africa, having been belligerents in the war against the Axis Powers and having signed the United Nations Declaration of January 1, 1942, were able to participate in the San Francisco Conference. They thus became original members of the new world organization. At the partition of India in 1947, that member's status in the United Nations continued—although a Polish representative went through the form of putting in the record a resolution to the effect that the precedent could not be used in the future to limit the Security Council's power to make recommendations concerning new members. Pakistan having been left to seek its own ties with international organizations, the General Assembly admitted that country to membership on September 30, 1947. Eire, long opposed by the Soviet Union for membership because of Irish neutrality during the Second World War, finally gained admission through the "package" deal late in 1955, as did also Ceylon.[61] Any Commonwealth nation that is a member of the United Nations is, of course, eligible to be elected to the Security Council.

[59] R. K. R. Sastry, "India and 'International Law,'" *Bombay Law Journal*, vol. 4 (1937-38), 450, 452.

[60] D. H. Miller, *The Drafting of the Covenant* (New York, 1928), vol. 1, 492.

[61] On the External Affairs Agreement between the United Kingdom and Ceylon, in which the latter agreed to observe the principle and practice observed by Commonwealth members in regard to external affairs, and the United Kingdom agreed to lend full support to any application by Ceylon for United Nations membership or membership in any of the specialized agencies described in Article 57 of the United Nations Charter, see note in the *International Law Quarterly*, vol. 2 (1948), 250-251.

As a United Nations member, apart from its membership in the Commonwealth, each Commonwealth country is in a position where the organization of its treaty-making power may affect its capacity to co-operate with other members. With the tendency to regulate a greater and greater variety of matters through multilateral conventions,[62] the question of competence to implement such arrangements becomes a very practical one (but, of course, one which is a matter of each state's internal arrangements). Without attempting here an analysis for each of the Commonwealth nations, it may be relevant to note that treaty-makers have sometimes encountered constitutional obstacles. The experience in Canada with the labor conventions is not reassuring. The "Bricker Amendment" principle in Canada's constitutional law has caused some concern; one observer has thought that limitation upon the Dominion Parliament in the matter of implementing certain types of international agreements "may well lead to an international delinquency on the part of Canada as a state. . . ."[63]

In its Constitution, India has followed the plan, employed in many of the new constitutions since the Second World War, of using wording on the relationship between international law and municipal law. By Article 51(c) the state shall endeavor to "foster respect for international law and treaty obligations. . . ." Article 253 gives the central legislature power to implement treaties, agreements, and conventions. However, a proviso specifies that "no decision affecting the disposition of the State of Jammu and Kashmir shall be made by the Government of India without the consent of the Government of that State."[64]

[62] On the nature and variety of such agreements, see John E. Read (Canadian judge of the International Court of Justice), "International Agreements," *Canadian Bar Review*, vol. 26 (1948), 520-532.

[63] R. St. J. Macdonald, "Public International Law Problems Arising in Canadian Courts," *University of Toronto Law Journal*, vol. 11 (1955-56), 224, 225. See also Maxwell Cohen, *loc. cit.* (note 3, *supra*), 389, 396.

[64] Cf. C. H. Alexander, *loc. cit.* (note 6, *supra*), at 295. The writer notes the tendency on the part of the Indian judiciary to preserve the relationship between international law and municipal law which was introduced in India under British rule. On the relatively broad scope of the treaty-making power under the Indian Constitution as compared with that in any other federation, see Robert L. Looper,

The development of constitutional law in each of the Commonwealth nations on the scope of their respective treaty-making powers will require time. The problem is one likely to be encountered in any federally organized state, not merely those of the Commonwealth. Perhaps difficulties in this connection tend to be somewhat less serious under a parliamentary form of government than in a country where there is an "independent" executive.

It remains to note, at least illustratively, distinctive positions which Commonwealth nations have taken in, and which have affected the law of, international organizations. One of these was the position which Canada took, early in the history of the League of Nations, with respect to sanctions. At the Fourth Assembly, Canada offered an interpretation of Covenant Article 10 to the effect that determination of the extent to which a member state would be bound to use its military force under the mentioned article would lie with the constitutional authorities of that state. One state (Persia) opposed, and the rule was not formally adopted, but the principle involved did have considerable effect in guiding League policy.[65] Similarity to the principle later incorporated, at the desire of United States representatives, in the NATO Treaty is apparent.

At the San Francisco Conference of 1945 Herbert Evatt became the principal spokesman for the smaller states. His effort seems to have affected decisions concerning the powers of the General Assembly. He was particularly concerned with the wording of the "domestic jurisdiction" paragraph of the Charter. In this he was not a disinterested draftsman, being concerned about what the Security Council might do under Article 39 of the Charter, and doubtless mindful of pressure which Australia had encountered in connection with its restrictive immigration

---

"The Treaty Powers in India," *British Year Book of International Law*, vol. 32 (1955-56), 300, 305.

[65] See Clyde Eagleton, "The Share of Canada in the Making of the United Nations," *University of Toronto Law Journal*, vol. 7 (1947-48), 329, 331.

policy.[66] The Australian leader helped to construct what many probably thought would be a firm dike against the new world organization's interference in the internal affairs of any state. In actual fact, it has not turned out this way, so far as the *political* (as distinct from the legal) interpretation of Article 2(7) of the Charter has been concerned. In this matter of political interpretation the Commonwealth nations have not seemed inclined to act as a bloc.[67]

As for the legal interpretation of "domestic jurisdiction," all of the Commonwealth countries which have accepted the Optional Clause of the World Court Statute have sought to reserve such questions. Two of them (India and Pakistan) have sought to retain for themselves the determination of whether a dispute involves such a question.[68]

Whether directed at legal or political arrangements, there have come, from Commonwealth sources as from other sources, varying degrees of criticism of the United Nations system. Illustrative are remarks of a United Kingdom representative at the Fourth International Commonwealth Relations Conference. He expressed skepticism about whether the United Nations could organize any real collective security system, although he admitted that the organization had dragged issues into the open and had helped to "slow down the rate at which crises developed and lowered the temperature of argument." There was a further suggestion that the "older and more experienced powers" tended to see the United Nations as impeding their policies without substituting any effective policies of its own. A Canadian speaker referred to "dewy-eyed idealism."[69]

[66] See *UNCIO*, VI, 512, and Lawrence Preuss, *Article 2, Paragraph 7 of The United Nations Charter and Matters of Domestic Jurisdiction* (Paris, 1949), 44 n.

[67] The position which the Commonwealth states have taken on the subject of domestic jurisdiction in United Nations discussions is the subject of a projected publication by Dr. John M. Howell based upon research done in 1956 under a grant from the Duke University Commonwealth-Studies Center.

[68] See note 50, *supra*.

[69] F. H. Soward, ed., *The Changing Commonwealth: Proceedings of the Fourth Unofficial Commonwealth Relations Conference* (Toronto, 1950), 89, 90, 92. With the last statement quoted may be compared Clyde Eagleton's conclusion (*loc. cit.*, at 354), based upon developments in the early years of United Nations history, that

In the dynamics of United Nations politics, the several Commonwealth nations have by no means followed a common path at all times. India's course with respect to anti-colonialism has tended to separate her from the United Kingdom, and Indian criticism of SEATO, a regional organization to which four of the other members of the Commonwealth belong, would hardly suggest anything approaching unity in foreign policy.[70] Between India and at least two of the other Commonwealth states there are powerfully divisive forces, although it is doubtless going too far to say, as did a foreign correspondent recently, that "India, Pakistan and South Africa are united chiefly by bonds of mutual detestation."[71] The positions taken by the respective Commonwealth states when the Suez crisis came in 1956 left little doubt as to the completeness of their independence.

4. Conclusions

Perhaps the Commonwealth experiment, viewed in terms of nationality, obligatory jurisdiction, and international-organization law, provides but limited guidance for the larger community of states to which international law applies. For the peculiar relationship which has continued to exist between the Commonwealth states even after they have become completely independent is not a particularist international law (such as certain Western Hemisphere jurists have distinguished as "American international law"). Held over from an era when there was a common supreme authority are, rather, habits of co-operation and consultation. Yet, as a thoughtful observer predicted as far back as 1937, the substance of rules and concepts involved is "likely . . . to approximate more and more closely to the analogy of

---

"On the whole, the record of Canadian support for the constitutional law of the United Nations is good, in spite of some impatience with pedantic legalism and occasional uncertainty as to interpretation."

[70] Even the neutralist policy of India has been thought by one observer to provide a desirable balancing force in United Nations relationships. E. B. Haas, "Regionalism, Functionalism, and Universal International Organization," *World Politics*, vol. 8 (1956), 238-263.

[71] A. M. Rosenthal, in the *New York Times*, March 5, 1956, 3.

international law."[72] This prophecy has been borne out in practice. At the same time the sense of community and the broad human base on which co-operation has proceeded in the Commonwealth may in turn have their effect upon the further development of law between elements of the still wider human community. A member of the Canadian Parliament perhaps sensed this when, in the course of debate on the Canadian Citizenship Act of 1946 he said:

A British subject . . . is not a citizen of the United Kingdom. He is a citizen, rather, of the British Commonwealth of nations. A British subject has but one king and one country—not two countries. But he has fraternal affiliations with many countries; he is close to being a world citizen . . . . He is an internationalist in a world which is still nationalist, but is groping toward internationalism. He is a member of the first united nations organization. I say . . . that the British subject is the prime hope for the future of a free world.[73]

The process by which the Commonwealth has developed has not been predominantly legalistic, but it has not been without respect for law. Speaking to the resolution by which the General Assembly of the United Nations received Ghana into membership, a representative of the United Kingdom described the process of Commonwealth development as "flexible and democratic."[74] Concerning the Federation of Malaya's emergence in the same year as a Commonwealth state, the Prime Minister of Pakistan referred to the "great and flexible association of independent sovereign states which have come together as free and equal partners."[75]

[72] R. T. E. Latham, "The Law and the Commonwealth," in W. K. Hancock, *Survey of British Commonwealth Affairs*, vol 1, *Problems in Nationality 1918-1936* (London, 1937), 510-615, at 614.
[73] Canada, *Parl. Deb.*, Commons, vol. 1, 797 (April 11, 1946).
[74] New York *Times*, March 5, 1957, 3.
[75] *Commonwealth Survey*, vol. 3, no. 19 (Sept., 1957), 812.

4

The Commonwealth: Demographic Dimensions; Implications

Joseph J. Spengler

"The most efficient cause of the prosperity of new colonies . . . is the capital, living and dead, which they acquire from old civilisations." J. S. Nicholson, *A Project of Empire*, 252-53.

"Universal states . . . are possessed by an almost demonic craving for life."—Arnold Toynbee, *A Study of History*, VII, 7.

". . . a revolution which will ever be remembered, and is still felt by the nations of the earth." Edward Gibbon, *The Decline and Fall of the Roman Empire*, chap. 1.

In his illuminating account of the origins of the British Commonwealth, Professor Underhill described it as "an experiment in co-operation among nations."[1] Co-operation presupposes considerable commonness of interests, objectives, aspirations, and mutuality of trust and understanding, together with a sufficiency of similarity in values, institutions, sentiments, and other important irrational sources of cohesion. Whether the conditions that gave rise to this experiment in co-operation will persist, let alone whether they will make for its extension, remains to be seen. Professor Underhill certainly was not overly sanguine. It is my purpose, in the present essay, to present a demographic picture of the Commonwealth, to point out some implications of this picture, and to indicate whether the demographic forces presently operative in the Commonwealth are essentially centrifugal or cen-

[1] F. H. Underhill, *The British Commonwealth* (Durham, N. C., 1956).

tripetal, it being assumed that demographic ties and associated economic interdependence reinforce various sources of subjective solidarity.

The values, together with the capacities, which give a sufficiency of cultural unity to peoples and which enable peoples to co-operate effectively, inhere in individual members of populations. Ultimately, therefore, whether or not appropriate values are present in sufficient quantity in a population depends largely upon whether the rate of natural increase is sufficiently high among those population-elements sharing these values. For educational and other value-propagating systems are quite limited in their capacities to diffuse such values among those who do not originally acquire them within familial and closely related milieus. These capacities tend to be greater, of course, when the population-elements initially possessing the values in question are looked upon as constituting *elite* groups.

The capacity of a population to carry a set of values abroad and cause them to flourish there depends largely upon the number of emigrants that it can send abroad, upon their rates of natural increase in their new environments, and upon the extent to which the populations already resident there look upon the newcomers and their descendants as constituting *elites*. When the newcomers and their descendants are possessed of relatively advanced techniques and "superior" institutions, they are more likely to be looked upon as elites than when their margin of advantage over the resident population is considered slight. Even then, however, the values of these elites will be effectively diffused among the resident populations only if the elites seek to diffuse these values and if important elements in the resident populations are disposed to acquire these values.

What has been said has great bearing upon the future composition of the Commonwealth. One or the other of two demographic conditions will be present in the countries that continue to remain active members of an effective Commonwealth. The countries in question will have been well populated by persons of British and/or West-European origin. Or their economic and political progress will be seen to depend upon the presence of a powerful elite that shares with the British the values which are prerequisite to the continuation of the Commonwealth. It is quite likely, furthermore, that such an elite must include a considerable number of persons of British and/or West-European origin. It is possible, of course, that other ties may prove effective even in the absence of demographic ties; but this does not seem likely.

For purposes of discussion I shall include in the Commonwealth not only the present members, the United Kingdom, Canada, Australia, New Zealand, South Africa, Ceylon, India, Pakistan, the Federation of Malaya (along with Singapore), and Ghana, but also several prospective members, namely, the Caribbean Federation, Nigeria, and a combination made up of Southern and Northern Rhodesia and Nyasaland. The units enumerated fall into six distinct categories: (1) the originating and still nuclear member, the United Kingdom; (2) the secondary British members, Canada, Australia, and New Zealand; (3) the Afro-British-European member, the Union of South Africa; (4) the Asiatic members, India, Pakistan, the Federation of Malaya, and Ceylon, of which at least the last is incapable of independent political survival; (5) the potential Caribbean Federation (after 1958 to be called "The West Indies"), whose prospect for political survival is conditioned by the aspirations and defense requirements of the United States; and (6) Ghana, together with the prospective African members, whose political and economic future depends appreciably upon the amount of assistance they receive from western countries, particularly from the United Kingdom and the United States.

1. The United Kingdom

The importance of the demographic dimensions of the United Kingdom derives from the fact that it remains the major source of such cohesive forces as unite present members of the Commonwealth and make membership attractive to potential members. In the past, when these diverse political units were held together by the ties of empire, the United Kingdom was almost the sole source of the linguistic, economic, institutional, demographic, and sentimental bonds which reinforced her political sway over what have since become actual or aspiring members of the Commonwealth—a sway that long rested upon a naval-military ascendancy since destroyed by two world wars and the relentless march of technological change and cultural diffusion. Between 1815 and 1930 there emigrated from the British Isles some 24 million people—nearly two-fifths of all the world's emigrants—of whom about three-eighths went to the United States, one-eighth to Canada, and the rest elsewhere, but above all to Australia, New Zealand, and South Africa. Of these, probably something like two-thirds remained abroad, American experience suggests.[2] This heavy outflow helped to spread British-type institutions and sentiments, together with the English language, which, as of 1950, was the principal tongue of about one-tenth of the world's population. It not only greatly facilitated the settlement of Canada, Australia, New Zealand, and South Africa; it also stimulated the export of British capital (which in 1870-1913 absorbed about three-sevenths of British savings) to future members of the Commonwealth, the fraction of all British foreign holdings invested within the empire approximating 42 per cent in 1914 and 50 in 1938.[3]

[2] For data on emigration and immigration, see W. S. and E. S. Woytinsky, *World Population and Production* (New York, 1953), chap. 3; Brinley Thomas, *Migration and Economic Growth* (Cambridge, 1954); J. Isaac, *Economics of Migration* (New York, 1947), and *British Post-War Migration* (Cambridge, 1954); M. R. Davie, *World Immigration* (New York, 1936); A. M. Carr-Saunders, *World Population* (Oxford, 1936); W. A. Carrothers, *Emigration from the British Isles* (London, 1929); D. Kirk, *Europe's Population in the Interwar Years* (Princeton, 1946). While Irish-born emigrants went principally to the United States, many also went to England and Scotland. See Thomas, *op. cit.*, chap. 6, and Appendix 4. See also N. H. Carrier and J. R. Jeffery, *External Migration* (London, H.M.S.O., 1953); G. F. Plant, *Oversea Settlement, Migration from the United Kingdom to the Dominions* (London, 1951).

[3] See W. S. and E. S. Woytinsky, *World Commerce and Governments* (New York, 1955), chap. 5; A. K. Cairncross, *Home and Foreign Investment, 1870-1913* (Cambridge Press, 1953), 4, 182-186; also on earlier periods, L. H. Jenks, *Migration of British Capital to 1875* (London, 1938). On the sterling-area economy, see J. M. Cassels, *The Sterling Area: An American Analysis* (Washington, G.P.O., 1951); and on the role of capital in economic progress, E. Cannan,

The United Kingdom, viewed as a source of capital and population whereby the rest of the Commonwealth, especially its less advanced members, whether actual or aspiring, might be developed, is much less important than formerly. Emigrants departing from the United Kingdom numbered only a million in 1931-50, in comparison with above 4.4 million in 1911-30, but a much larger fraction went to Commonwealth countries in the later period, and only in part because of the restriction of immigration into the United States after 1924. The capital-exporting capacity of the United Kingdom has been greatly reduced, largely through war losses, decline in saving, and failure adequately to adjust the composition of British domestic investment to export requirements. Even so, she provided seven-tenths of the £2,350 million of capital flowing into sterling-area countries in 1946-55, instead of virtually all, as before the war; but this was made possible largely by the extension of aid and credit to the United Kingdom (principally by dollar-area countries), since her favorable balance with the sterling area was approximately offset, during this period, by her unfavorable balances with other areas. Recently Britain has been investing about £250 million a year abroad, of which about four-fifths has gone into the Commonwealth and colonies—an amount somewhat in excess of her balance on current account.[4]

"Capital and the Heritage of Improvement," *Economica*, n.s., vol. 1 (1934), 381-392.

[4] See discussion of the White Paper on Commonwealth development (Cmd. 237) in *The Economist*, Aug. 3, 1957, 364. In 1954-56 gross fixed investment in the United Kingdom approximated 16 per cent of Gross National Product, with net long-term overseas capital movements approximating £ 191 million a year, or 9 per cent of gross fixed investment; but balance on current account averaged only £ 88 million. See unsigned, "Britain's Economic Positions," *British Affairs*, vol. 1 (1957), 60-65. See also A. R. Conan, "The Changing Pattern of International Investment in Selected Sterling Countries," *Essays in International Finance*, no. 27 (Princeton, 1956), 17. Net saving in the United Kingdom ranged between 5 and 8 per cent of net national product in 1948-54; net capital formation approximated 6.6 per cent in 1925-30, and 14.9 in 1904-13. See United Nations, *Economic Survey of Europe in 1955*, chap. 2, esp. 44, 50-51, 63, 69 ff.; S. Kuznets, *Toward a Theory of Economic Growth* (mimeographed) (Johns Hopkins University, Baltimore, 1956), Table 8; R. Nurkse, "The Relation between Home Investment and External Balance in the Light of British Experience, 1945-1955," *Review of Economics and Statistics*, vol. 38 (1956), 121-154. Whereas the First World War reduced the United Kingdom's foreign holdings about one-fourth and in-

The partial drying up of Britain as a source of capital, together with the failure of any other Commonwealth country to take over the capital-exporting role that Britain performed before 1914, is an important but not an insuperable obstacle to the development of the Commonwealth. Its advanced members can supply their own capital; in fact, the bulk of every advanced country's capital stock has been supplied through domestic capital formation. The less advanced members will be greatly handicapped, however, in part by dearth of capital, and in even greater measure, by shortage of that know-how which flows into countries with foreign investment and the skilled personnel who accompany it. Whether this capital can be gotten from America and Western Europe, or through plans like that inaugurated at Colombo, remains to be seen. A precondition to its being gotten, however, is political stability, together with governmental policies calculated to inspire and maintain the confidence of foreign lenders and industrialists. Even if considerable capital is gotten from abroad and through the diversion of domestic resources from ordinary "consumption," there is still likely to be a marked scarcity of capital for investment in industrial development, because, in modern societies, with the great cost of urbanization and of emphasis upon "welfare," an unduly large fraction of "gross capital formation" tends to assume shapes other than those most suited to accelerate commodity flow. Moreover, population growth will absorb a great deal of capital, since a 1-per-cent

creased her gross foreign indebtedness, the Second World War wiped out three-fourths of her net credits (which had increased in the 1920's and 1930's). In 1951 the nominal value of Britain's overseas investments was only 56 per cent of what it had been in 1938. Money return (in sterling) from these investments approximated the 1938 amount, however, but its purchasing power was much lower and it comprised only one-fourth of gross income from "invisibles" instead of one-half as in 1938. See Woytinsky, *World Commerce*, 191-215, 225; unsigned, "Britain's 'Invisible Exports,' " *Labor and Industry in Britain*, vol. 12 (1954), 82-90. Recently, T. Barna reported post-1939 British capital formation to be somewhat higher than usually estimated, but he was disturbed at the stagnation of British investment in 1951-54. See "Investment in Industry—Has Britain's Lagged?," *The Banker*, vol. 107 (April, 1957), 219-230. See also P. Redfern, "Net Investment in Fixed Assets in the United Kingdom, 1938-53," *Journal of the Royal Statistical Society*, Series A, vol. 118 (1955), 141-192.

rate of population growth absorbs the capital provided by a savings rate of 3 to 5 per cent of national income.

The capacity of the United Kingdom to supply emigrants, insofar as this capacity depends upon natural increase, may be negligible in the proximate future. Whereas the population of Great Britain increased somewhat more than 25 per cent each 20 years in 1861-1901, during which interval emigration approximated 10 per cent of natural increase, it increased only 9 per cent in 1921-41, in which period immigration somewhat exceeded emigration. While increase in the period 1941-61 will be in the neighborhood of 9 per cent, it will probably be lower thereafter, for natural increase is running slightly below 5 per 1,000, and net reproduction, close to 1.0 in England and Wales, is not much above 1.0 elsewhere in the United Kingdom. While projections differ somewhat, they agree in making the prospective rate of growth low. According to one, the United Kingdom's population will grow about 0.5 per cent per year; according to a second, the population of working age will grow 0.25 per cent per year in 1956-71; and according to a third, which supposes net emigration of 32,000 per year, the population, 51.2 millions in 1955, will grow to about 53 millions by 1975, remaining about this figure thereafter, while the number of working age increases relatively less.[5] Hence, although population growth will absorb relatively little capital and resources in the future, the rate of growth of aggregate capital resources may still remain low, and this will intensify the unfavorable influence of a low rate of emigration upon the diffusion of British culture, since capital

[5] See United Nations, *Demographic Yearbook*; also *Economic Survey of Europe in 1955*, 116 ff., C-17, and *Papers* of World Population Conference (Rome, 1954), III (New York, 1955), 322; Central Statistical Office, *Annual Abstract of Statistics* (London, 1956); *Report* of Royal Commission on Population, Cmd. 7695 (1949), 8-9, and chaps. 8-9; J. R. L. Schneider, "Local Population Projections in England and Wales," *Population Studies*, vol. 10 (1956), 95-114. It is, of course, well to keep in mind that population movements rarely conform to long-term forecasts; see John Hajnal, "The Prospects for Population Forecasts," *Journal of the American Statistical Association*, vol. 50 (1955), 309-322. Hereinafter, birth, death, and natural-increase rates, when not expressed in percentages, will signify so many per thousand inhabitants. According to a recent projection the population of the United Kingdom will grow from 53.7 millions in 1970 to 65 in 2000.

exports, particularly when in the form of direct investment, carry with them considerable skilled personnel of the lending country. However, should the United Kingdom undertake to train many technical and professional people for posts in the Commonwealth, its influence in Commonwealth countries would be greatly increased despite the smallness of British emigration, and British foreign investment might increase in consequence.

It is possible nonetheless that emigration may continue in appreciable volume from the United Kingdom, even though the British economy initially should be adversely affected if, as is to be expected, the bulk of such emigrants are of actual or incipient working age. With a population of 533 per square mile in 1950, a density exceeded only by that of Japan, Belgium, Holland, and Puerto Rico, the United Kingdom is greatly overpopulated; it could use its resource-equipment and propensity to save more effectively if its numbers were smaller, and it would then be less subject to the balance-of-payment and related problems which (as Malthus foresaw) recurrently trouble it.[6] Moreover, at the close of World War II, there was a temporary upsurge in aspiration to emigrate,[7] as at the close of earlier wars and in the wake

---

[6] Some years ago P. A. Samuelson suggested (as A. Marshall and B. Ohlin had implied and M. Longfield may have anticipated) that, so long as raw materials could be transported cheaply to the United Kingdom, it was better for Englishmen to engage in industry at home than to seek industrial or agricultural employment abroad, even in advanced Commonwealth countries. See Samuelson, "International Trade and the Equalisation of Factor Prices," *Economic Journal*, vol. 58 (1948), 163-184, and "International Factor-Price Equalisation Once Again," *ibid.*, vol. 59 (1949), 181-197. These articles have given rise to a considerable literature concerning the underlying theoretical argument, which does not concern us here. The realizability of Samuelson's suggestion turns on the magnitude and pattern of transport costs and upon the conditions under which raw materials may be had. The underlying issue of policy has been a subject of debate since the *Agrarstaat-vs.-Industriestaat* controversy of 50 to 75 years ago. See M. Gottlieb, "Optimum Population, Foreign Trade and World Economy," *Population Studies*, vol. 3 (1949), 151-169. On Britain's lack of space, see R. A. Piddington, *The Limits of Mankind* (Bristol, 1956).

[7] See J. Isaac, "European Migration Potential and Prospects," *Population Studies*, vol. 2 (1949), 379-412. In early 1948 public opinion polls indicated that of each 100 Englishmen 42 were in favor of emigrating abroad, 53 of staying, and 5 of no opinion. This favorable percentage ranged from 58 in the 21-29 age group to 37 in the 50-65 and 15 in the 66 and over age groups; it was 44 for men and 41 for women. The percentage in favor of emigration was much higher in England than in the seven other European countries polled. Of those indicating a desire to emigrate, 80 per cent preferred a British Commonwealth country; 12, the

of the recent Suez fiasco. Persisting inflation and the burdens of the welfare-state may yet, of course, permanently increase the rate of emigration. Whereas the United Kingdom experienced net immigration of about 14,000 per year in 1934-38, at which time fear of unemployment was depressing international migration, it lost 1,224,000 emigrants, most of them British nationals, in 1946-50, and about 506,000 in 1951-53. But, since 1,084,-000 persons (including at least 456,000 British nationals) immigrated into the United Kingdom in 1946-50, and 236,000 in 1951-53, net annual emigration averaged only 28,000 in 1946-50 and 90,000 in 1951-53.[8] Since 1953 net emigration to non-European countries has been exceeding 50,000 per year. Its future volume will be conditioned by Britain's policy and economic fortune and by the economic prospects confronting her population of migratory age.

British emigration policy still rests upon the Empire Settlement Act, enacted in 1922. British policy embodies four principles: freedom to emigrate, freedom from pressure to emigrate, safeguards for Britain's population and manpower needs, and no promotion of emigration except with the active co-operation of the Dominions. There being no pressure to induce a cross-section of the population to emigrate, emigration is necessarily selective, as in 1946-50 when emigrants were generally more skilled than immigrants. While one school of thought envisages the eventual emigration of 20 million persons from the United Kingdom to other parts of the Commonwealth, the Royal Commission on Population, fearing an intensification of the forces making for population decline, estimated that there could not be supplied more than a third of the 226,000 immigrants sought annually by the Dominions (bent on having their population

---

U.S.A.; 8, other countries. See *ibid.*, 390-394. According to a 1951 poll, only 33 per cent of those questioned wanted to emigrate. See Isaac, *Post-War British Migration*, 293-294. Scotch and North Irish migrants move both to England and abroad.

[8] For the 1946-50 data, see Isaac, *British Post-War Migration*, 203-209; for 1934-38, United Nations, *Sex and Age of International Migrants: Statistics for 1918-1947* (New York, 1953), 228-231; for 1951-53, *Demographic Yearbook*, 1954, 652, 662.

grow 2 per cent per year), since "a maintained net outflow of 100,000 . . . may be regarded as a maximum, short of catastrophic developments or the adoption of a deliberate policy of drastic reduction of the population."[9] Isaac argues cogently, however, that since net emigration of 100,000 a year for the next twenty years or so would reduce the population of the United Kingdom only about 1 per cent, while affecting its age composition very little, a net outward movement of 100,000 persons per year is to be regarded as desirable on balance, since it would help to maintain the British character of the Dominions despite their absorption of an increasing number of non-British immigrants.[10] A case could be made for the proposition that Britain supply double or treble this number to the Commonwealth countries during the next twenty years.

2. Canada, Australia, New Zealand

These units of the Commonwealth have a number of characteristics in common. Their occupational compositions are those of advanced economies. Their populations are racially homogeneous and of British or European origin or extraction. Their per capita incomes are among the highest in the world. They are already well-equipped with wealth and capital per head, having been spared, as was the United States, the cost of stocking the economy with people insofar as these were supplied through immigration. Their culture is European (predominantly British), but European invigorated and made flexible by the selectivity and the shock that accompany immigration into a strange land and a new environment. Their ruling sentiments make them the firmest of the oversea adherents to the Commonwealth. Their long-run economic prospects are good. But their demographic growth has disappointed the hopes of late nineteenth-century

[9] *Report*, 93, 129-130.
[10] This paragraph is based upon Isaac, *British Post-War Migration*, 214-251. In the report of the Economics Committee it is indicated that the Dominions cannot count on the United Kingdom to furnish many immigrants. See *Papers* of the Royal Commission on Population, III (London, 1950), 19-21. See also Thomas, *op. cit.*, chap. 13.

spokesmen for the British Empire who anticipated that their numbers would exceed 50 millions by now instead of approximating but half that number.[11]   At present the population per habitable square mile approximates 11.7 in Canada, 3.1 in Australia, and 24.7 in New Zealand.[12]   Canada differs from the other two of these dominions in several respects.   Australia and New Zealand are monocultural whereas Canada is bicultural, British and French-Canadian.   Australia and New Zealand have had to overcome the challenge of distance, long being separated by several months from London, whereas Canada has had to overcome the growth-retarding proximity of a powerful and expanding neighbor to the South.

a. Canada

Canada's development is less closely identified with that of the United Kingdom than is the development of Australia and New Zealand.   For, even though Canada is less affected than formerly by proximity to the United States, and its state policy is less directed now than it once was toward preserving it politico-economic autonomy from the impact of America,[13] its economic and possibly its demographic ties with the United Kingdom are much weaker than formerly.   In 1914 about 2.5 of Britain's 18.4 billion dollars of foreign investment were situated in Canada.   By 1926, of the $6 billion in Canada, the British and American portions had become 2.6 and 3.2; by 1939, 2.6 and 4.5 in a total of 7.4; and by 1953, 2.1 and 9.2 in at total of 12.3.   Canadian foreign investment had also increased to $6.6 billion, reducing its net foreign indebtedness to 5.7.   In 1956 American investment in Canada

[11] See forecasts cited in G. F. McCleary, *Peopling the British Commonwealth* (London, 1955), preface.   The *Canada Year Book* of 1868 forecast that by 1951 Canada's population would number 58.4 millions.

[12] Based on p. 128 of *Report*, cited in note 6 above.

[13] On this point see Hugh Aitken's essay, in Aitken, ed., *The State and Economic Growth*, to be published in 1958, under the auspices of the Social Science Research Council, New York.   According to G. Rosenbluth, the Canadian economy has become less sensitive to changes in the American economy in the course of the last 25 years.   See "Changes in Canadian Sensitivity to United States Business Fluctuations," *Canadian Journal of Economics and Political Science*, vol. 23 (1957), 480–503.

approximateed $12.1 billion, of which at least 7.5 was in industry, while Canadian investment in the United States slightly exceeded $4.6 billion. Canadians even were complaining that too much of Canada's industry was subject to American financial control.[14] British participation in Canadian trade, relatively low already in 1913, has steadily diminished. By 1952 the export trade of the United States with Canada was 2.65 times that of the United Kingdom with Canada; the corresponding figure for import trade was 7.65.[15] By 1951 the fraction of the Canadian population made up of British stock had fallen appreciably below the level of 1901. This change is attributable in part to the fact that net immigration contributed appreciably to Canada's population growth in 1901-30 and again after the war, and that relatively more immigrants were of non-British stock, a shift that reflects change in the selectivity principle governing the admission of immigrants.[16]

[14] Canadian savings might have financed Canada's recent industrial growth, had not so much been invested otherwise or abroad. See A. D. Knox, "United States Capital Investments in Canada," American Economic Review, vol. 47 (May, 1957), 596-609; Cassels, op. cit., 56; Canada Year Book, 1955; Woytinsky, World Commerce, 194-213; S. Pizer and F. Cutler, "Growth of Foreign Investments in the United States and Abroad," Survey of Current Business, vol. 36 (Aug., 1956), 15, 18-19, and "Record Growth of Foreign Investments," ibid. (Aug., 1957), 22 ff. On capital formation, which has been higher in Canada than in most countries, see Kuznets, Toward a Theory . . . , Table 10, and J. H. Adler, "World Economic Growth—Retrospect and Prospects," Review of Economics and Statistics, vol. 38 (1956), 273-285. For a review of Canadian criticism of the magnitude of American investment, see Bulletin of the First National City Bank of New York (Aug., 1956), 92-95; T. W. Kent, "The American Boom in Canada," Lloyds Bank Review (Jan., 1957), 17-33; also Knox, op. cit., and C. D. Blyth and E. B. Carty, "Non-Resident Ownership of Canadian Industry," Canadian Journal of Economics and Political Science, vol. 22 (1956), 449-460, and unsigned, "The Canadian Troubles of U. S. Business," Fortune (July, 1957), 139 ff.

[15] Woytinsky, World Commerce, 74-75, 96-97, 114.

[16] Emigration exceeded immigration in 1861-1901 and in 1931-45. Net immigration contributed about 40,000 persons per year to Canada's population in 1901-31 and about 65,000 per year in 1946-55. The fractions of the Canadian population of British and French origin, respectively, were 57.03 and 30.7 in 1901; 55.4 and 27.91 in 1921; and 47.9 and 30.8 in 1951; the fraction of non-British and non-French origin rose from 12.27 in 1901 to 21.3 in 1951. The relative magnitude of the French component has increased since 1921 because the French rate of natural increase is so much higher than the British. See N. B. Ryder, "Components of Canadian Population Growth," Population Index, vol. 20 (1954), 71-80; N. Keyfitz, "The Growth of Canadian Population," Population Studies, vol. 4 (1950) 47-63; W. B. Hurd, Origin, Birthplace, Nationality and Language of the Canadian People (Ottawa, 1929), 43; the Canada Year Book;

While the rapidity with which the Canadian population grows in the future will depend very largely upon natural increase, it will be conditioned by the rate of immigration. The Royal Commission on Canada's Economic Prospects estimates that, given an average annual net immigration of 75,000 persons, Canada's population will rise from 15,575,000 in 1955 to 26,650,000 in 1980, and that the labor force will grow at about the same rate, or nearly 2.25 per cent per year. Given 100,000 net immigration annually, Canada's 1980 population would number 27,535,000. In recent years crude natural increase (close to 2 per cent per year), together with immigration (recently somewhat in excess of 75,000 per year), has given a rate of population growth of about 2.5 per cent per year. Continuance of immigration at this rate, however, presupposes a marked diminution in past favoritism to immigrants of British origin and a greater recourse to continental countries whence immigrants are likely to come. For, on the premises of the British Royal Commission, Britain cannot spare enough emigrants to meet the demands of both Canada and other parts of the Commonwealth.[17] It will probably be necessary, furthermore, that Canada and other immigrant-seeking countries not insist on the immigrants's possessing much skill, since otherwise the emigrant-supplying countries will be loath to permit their departure. However, should Canada grow as forecast, its population would be about half that of the United Kingdom by 1980 and its net national product probably would be in excess of one-half that of the United Kingdom.

---

also Mabel F. Timlin, "Recent Changes in Government Attitudes towards Immigration," *Transactions* of the Royal Society of Canada, vol. 49 (1955), 95-105.

[17] See Isaac, *British Post-War Migration*, chap. 8, on composition of postwar Canadian immigration. Apparently Canadian opinion has become more favorable than formerly both to immigration and to immigration of other than British or French ethnic origin. The United Nations forecast (see *Papers*, III, 317) for Canada for 1980 is only 19.8 million. Gross immigration (which is somewhat in excess of net immigration) averaged 86,000 per year in 1946-50 and 159,000 in 1951-56 after Canadian immigration policy was liberalized in 1950. Between June, 1950, and June, 1955, 424,000 immigrant workers were added to the labor force; meanwhile natural growth added only 316,000 native workers to the labor force.

b. Australia and New Zealand

The economic and demographic ties binding Australia and New Zealand to the United Kingdom are stronger than those connecting Canada with the mother country. The principal participant in the external trade of these two dominions—which, like the Canadian, is large in comparison with gross national product—remains the United Kingdom. Trade with Asia (including Japan), still relatively small, is expected to increase. Capital inflow, formerly almost entirely of British origin, remains predominantly so. In the postwar period foreign capital, about three-fifths of it from Britain, supplied 9 per cent of the capital invested in Australia and 5 per cent of that invested in New Zealand.[18] Immigration too was overwhelmingly of British origin before the Second World War. For this reason, and because in Australia and New Zealand, as in Canada but not as in South Asia (long inhabited by anciently civilized peoples) and in Africa (occupied by relatively numerous primitive peoples), the British settlers had to compete reproductively and otherwise with relatively few primitives, only a negligible fraction of the population of Australia and New Zealand was of non-British origin, at least until very recently. This fraction is bound to increase, however, since maintenance of immigration at desired levels will make recourse to non-British sources necessary, particularly on the part of Australia, now the principal absorber of immigrants in the Commonwealth. Seeking to increase its population from about 9.6 to 20 millions in 25 years, Australia favors an annual immigration of the order of 1 per cent of the resident population, with half the newcomers preferably of British origin. New Zealand, by contrast, is presently planning on 10,000 immi-

[18] See Conan, *op. cit.*, 12, 16-17; Woytinsky, *World Commerce*, 102-103, 112. American direct investment in Australia and New Zealand totaled $599 million in 1956, and $226 million in 1950; that in Canada, $7,480 million in 1956 and $3,579 million in 1950. See Pizer and Cutler, *loc. cit.* (Aug., 1957), 24. American direct investment in 1955-56 did not exceed one-fourth of all direct foreign investment in Australia.

grants (about one-tenth the Australian quota) instead of 15,000, as earlier.[19]

Net immigration continues to contribute relatively more to population growth in these two dominions than in Canada, for natality and natural increase have been lower there than in Canada, where the overall rate has been sustained by high French-Canadian natality.[20] Since 1946 net immigration, averaging close to 90,000 per year, has furnished about two-fifths of Australia's population growth; it has provided a smaller share of New Zealand's. Of the immigrants into Australia about half have been of British origin, with the British fraction falling below one-half in recent years. Relatively more of New Zealand's immigrants are of British or other Commonwealth origin. According to one recent United Nations projection, Australia's population will increase to 11.25 millions by 1980 instead of to the desired 20; another anticipates 13 million in 1975 and 17 in 2000. New Zealand's population, as of 1980, has been estimated at between

[19] See Isaac, *British Post-War Migration*, chaps. 7, 9; also vols. I-III, 1955-57, of *Research Digest*, issued by the Intergovernmental Committee for European Migration, Geneva. Much of the immigration into Australia, New Zealand, and Canada is assisted. H. Bernardelli traces the early rise of the welfare state in Australia and New Zealand to the smallness of their populations, occasioned by the fewness of their immigrants, a condition he attributes to remoteness from Europe and to denial of admission to Asiatics. In consequence the labor force was too small, and comparatively too invariant in size, to generate enough internal employment opportunities to permit its occupational composition to adjust rapidly to great fluctuations in external demand, of the sort to which economies highly dependent upon remote export markets are subject. Hence much of the brunt of market fluctuation fell upon labor. Wage-stabilization and related welfare measures were introduced, with the eventual result that the economies of these dominions became too inflexible to adjust effectively to changing economic circumstances. See "New Zealand and Asiatic Migration," *Population Studies*, vol. 6 (1952), 39-54. On assisted migration, see L. B. Brown, "Applicants for Assisted Migration from the United Kingdom to New Zealand," *Population Studies*, vol. 11 (1957), 86-91.

[20] Since 1946 natural increase has averaged close to 1.4 per cent in Australia, just over 1.5 in New Zealand, and just below 2.0 in Canada. Family allowance systems exist in each of these Dominions and in the Union of South Africa. Expectation of life at birth is highest in New Zealand, with Australia, Canada, and South Africa following in that order; it is slightly higher in New Zealand than in the United States. In New Zealand as in the United Kingdom reproductive selection appears to be producing a downward trend in national intelligence. See Betty M. Giles-Bernardelli, "The Decline of Intelligence in New Zealand," *Population Studies*, vol. 4 (1950), 200-208. Whereas full-blood aboriginals comprise only 0.5 per cent of Australia's population, the Maori, with an annual rate of increase of 3.4 per cent, form about 6 per cent of New Zealand's population.

2.6 and 3.2 millions. Yet another projection, based on the assumption of an annual immigration of 10,000, gives that country 3.33 millions by 1980 instead of 1.94 millions as in 1951.[21]

3. Union of South Africa

In the Union we encounter a problem common to at least all of the African federations, namely, that the population is multiracial in character, with the white population ranging between a minority and a very small fraction of the total, and with much of the remainder of the population poorly educated, backward, and poverty-ridden. In the Union the white population is sufficiently large and differentiated to constitute a nucleus whence the forces of economic and cultural progress can flow in sufficient measure eventually to transform the whole of the society; but this is not yet true of other parts. When a population is of the sort described, the leadership-providing function of the elite is very difficult to perform; and there is always danger that the distribution of the fruits of economic and cultural progress, which in a relatively homogeneous society tends to be rapid and all-embracing, may, because of stratification consequent upon a population's heterogeneity, be too unevenly channeled by dikes resembling those of caste. Racial differences accentuate many of the sources of interindividual difference, great even in relatively homogeneous societies, thereby retarding economic development, augmenting the cost of substituting modern for indigenous economic and social structures, and (hence) giving rise to political instability that could affect adversely adherence to political organizations such as the Commonwealth. For then the ties of trade and investment with the outside world, though usually very powerful in underdeveloped and backward economies, may be severed in response to economically irrational political forces,

[21] See *Year Book* of the Commonwealth of Australia; United Nations, *Papers*, III, 323; G. N. Calbert, *The Future Population of New Zealand* (Wellington, 1946); and *New Zealand Official Year Book*, 27-36, 58. Given, respectively, zero, 5,000, or 10,000 (a number exceeded only in recent years) net immigrants, New Zealand's population would number 2.69, 2.81, or 2.93 millions, respectively, by 1972.

and this divisive process may be intensified as the spread of modern death-control increases the excess of births over deaths in indigenous populations.

Although Britain still supplies most of the capital flowing into the Union from abroad and remains the chief (but not the only important) trading partner of the Union, it has contributed but a minor fraction of its population and is supplying but few immigrants. Furthermore, most of the Union's capital is of domestic origin, gross capital formation usually exceeding 24 per cent of gross national expenditure. In 1951 the population of the Union, 13.7 millions in 1955, was composed as follows: white (mostly of English and Dutch extraction), 20.9 per cent; Bantu, 67.5; Asiatic (mostly of Indian extraction), 2.9; colored, 8.7. Should the population grow as recently forecast, it would number about 21.2 millions by 1980, of whom 17.8 per cent would be white, 68.8 Bantu, 9.5 colored, and 3.9 Asiatic. Should Bantu and colored mortality fall more rapidly than this projection anticipates, and such fall is not unlikely, the proportions these form of the population would be greater than indicated whilst that of the whites would be lower. Nor is it likely that net European immigration, of which recently about a third has been British, will add markedly to white increase; for while it supplied about 10,000 persons annually in 1946-50, or about one-fifth of white increase, it has not since provided quite so large an average annual number, nor did it in the prosperous late 1930's. Gross immigration, of course, appreciably exceeds 10,000 per year.[22]

[22] Concerning population growth in the Union, see the series of papers by L. T. Badenhorst in *Population Studies*, vol. 4 (1950), 3-46; vol. 5 (1951), 23-34; vol. 6 (1952), 135-162, and his report in United Nations, *Papers*, III, 159-170; Sheila T. Van der Horst, "Native Urban Employment," *South African Journal of Economics*, vol. 16 (1948), 251-259. According to the United Nations forecast (Papers, III, 317), South Africa's population will number 25 millions by 1980. On immigration and economic aspects of *apartheid*, see H. M. Robertson's paper in B. Thomas, ed., *International Migration* (Cambridge, 1958) and his *South Africa* (Durham, N. C., 1957). On investment in South Africa, see Conan, *op. cit.*; S. H. Frankel, *Capital Investment in Africa* (London, 1938) and *The Economic Impact On Under-Developed Societies* (Oxford, 1953), chap. 7. Various data are summarized in the Union's *Official Year Book*. In 1946 about 56 per cent of the African labor force was in agriculture, forestry, and fishing, and another 30

Given a multiracial population in an economy that is undergoing expansion, urbanization, and Euro-acculturation of the natives, but in which the white population grows more slowly than the native, the range of opportunities open to the natives tends to broaden and deepen greatly, in the longer run, and the services which natives can render tend to become relatively more scarce. Then social capillarity tends to develop, and the occupational composition of the native labor force, although initially one characteristic of a backward people, tends gradually to resemble a more advanced structure of the sort characteristic of the white labor force. The present bimodal distribution of income, whereunder, in given industries, average European income is four or more times as high as average native income, will probably change in a unimodal direction. Furthermore, that most powerful of all generators of democracy and equality, labor scarcity, will act as a solvent upon some of the institutional elements in the Union's sociopolitical structure which presently impair the effectiveness of its economy. These various tendencies will be strengthened by the urban character of much of the Union's population; for over two-fifths of this population is urban, and about one-fifth is situated in urban agglomerations of over 100,000.

Should the Union's economy and society evolve along these lines, because of a growing scarcity of white workers to perform economic roles presently assigned to whites, understanding of patterns of growth suited to the politico-economic development of other African members of the Commonwealth would become widespread. In this event, the Commonwealth would find inspiration, guidance, and strength in the Union's experience. It remains to be seen, however, whether economic scarcity, together with its salutary effects, becomes sufficiently ascendant.

---

per cent in mining, quarrying, and public and personal service; of the whites about 19 per cent were in the former category and 26 in the latter which, however, in the case of the whites denotes public more than personal service. On economic conditions, see the series on South Africa in *The Statist*, London, June-July, 1957, especially June 29 ff.

4. India, Pakistan, Ceylon, Federation of Malaya

Before we consider the Asiatic members of the Commonwealth, account needs to be taken of a condition they share in common with the African and Caribbean members. In nearly all of these areas gross reproduction and natality are very high, while mortality is either already relatively low, or, while still high, in a stage of decline. The populations of these areas have not, therefore, undergone that demographic evolution which has characterized the populations of advanced countries; in consequence, a multifold increase in numbers could easily take place in the populations of these areas. In the British-European populations mortality is low, fertility is under control, and net reproduction, even when high, is susceptible of rapid reduction. By contrast, unless the adoption and diffusion of effective methods of birth control[23] proceeds far more rapidly in the Asian, African, and Caribbean areas than in the West, their rates of population growth, already high, will increase still further as death control is intensified.[24] The high rates of population growth resulting will tend to produce certain effects. Immigration into these areas may be discouraged, especially if they are heavily populated already, even though there is great need for skilled immigrants in all these areas.[25] Population growth will absorb much of the capital formed, thereby retarding improvement of the average lot. This effect, together with the political instability it gives rise to, may inspire fear of confiscation of property, prevent much

---

[23] In pre-Malthusian populations of the sort encountered in parts of the Commonwealth there has developed an equilibrium between nuptiality, ability to procreate, and fertility, at least the first two of which vary greatly. Accordingly, if ability to procreate increases as economic conditions improve, fertility will increase in the absence of birth control and decrease in nuptiality. See summary of J. Bourgeois-Pichat's findings in *Population Index*, vol. 20 (1954), 161-162. On the factors principally responsible for high fertility in underdeveloped countries see K. Davis and Judith Blake, "Social Structure and Fertility: An Analytical Framework," *Economic Development and Cultural Change*, vol. 4 (1956), 211-235.

[24] See Kingsley Davis, "The Amazing Decline of Mortality in Underdeveloped Areas," *American Economic Review*, vol. 46 (1956), 305-318; G. J. Stolnitz, "A Century of International Mortality Trends," *Population Studies*, vol. 9 (1955), esp. 45-55; vol. 10 (1956), 17-42; his and other papers in F. B. Boudreau and C. V. Kiser, eds., *Trends and Differentials in Mortality* (Milbank Memorial Fund, New York, 1956).

[25] This problem is treated by T. H. Silcock in Thomas, ed., *op. cit.*

foreign investment, and discourage the immigration of skilled personnel. These various adverse political and economic consequences would tend in turn to reduce participation of the affected areas in the benefits which the Commonwealth can provide.

a. India

The population of India, the most populous member of the Commonwealth, numbered 357 millions in 1951, or 312 per square mile, of which very few were European. Of more importance than its racial, religious, and linguistic heterogeneity, is the occupational composition of India's labor force, numbering 106 millions in 1951. Within the rural category of self-supporting persons fell 71 million agriculturalists (of whom about 15 million were landless laborers) and 16.5 million nonagricultural workers, most of whom were engaged in cottage industries. Within the urban category fell 16.2 millions, or about 16 per cent of the aggregate self-supporting population; yet at least 2.1 million of these belonged in pre-industrial categories (e.g., rentiers, beggars, religious and related workers, and independent artisans and storekeepers who do not employ help). Within the truly urban class fell 14.1 millions, of whom 2.47 were factory workers, 6.28 were essentially "white collar" workers, 1.75 represented small business, and 0.68 were employers; approximately 1 million were in professions and 1.9 in civil service.[26] India thus is essentially a non-industrial country, in that employers, members of the professions, and factory workers comprise only about 4 per cent of all self-supporting persons, in that about 83 per cent of the population live in 558 thousand villages (where the traditional orientation of life is strongest), and in that per-capita income is

[26] See B. Moore, *The Western Impact upon the Structure of Authority in Indian Society*, mimeographed (Center for International Studies, M.I.T., Cambridge, 1955), chap. 5; these figures are based upon the census of 1951. For a comparative statistical picture of the working population of the world, see reports in *International Labour Review*, vol. 73 (1956), 155 ff., 501-521. On the role of the city in bringing about the modernization of society in South Asia, see R. I. Crane, "Urbanism in India," *American Journal of Sociology*, vol. 60 (1955), 463-470, and N. S. Ginsburg, "The Great City in Southeast Asia," *ibid.*, 445-462; also Davis and Golden, cited in note 35 below; also B. F. Hoselitz, "Population Pressure, Industrialization and Social Mobility," *Population Studies*, vol. 11 (1957), 123-135.

under $100 (about $56 in 1951). India's industrial and urban population, though so relatively small, still is absolutely large enough, as is its civil service, to permit widespread and accelerating industrialization and exploitation of its considerable economic potential. Moreover, Indian workers, although less effective than American workers, are more effective than workers in many parts of Asia.

Inasmuch as most of India's major problems are greatly accentuated by the excessive density and growth of its population, it is quite possible that continuation of India's adherence to the Commonwealth will depend largely upon the contribution that Commonwealth membership can make to the solution of its population problems. While high mortality—31 in and just before 1951—has kept down the natural increase to which a birth rate in the 40's—about 43 in 1951—could give rise, the rate of growth would rise appreciably above the level (just over 1 per cent) experienced in 1921-51 if, as is likely, mortality should gradually fall. With present fertility and a halving of the death rate by 1975, the population would total 775 million by 1986, averaging an increase of 2.6 per cent per year. Even if fertility declined by half between 1956 and 1981, the population would still approximate 590 millions by 1986, having grown 1 per cent per year. Whereas, because of differences in the impact of these rates of growth upon age composition, capital formation, etc., income per equivalent adult consumer (341 Rs. in 1956) would rise only 13 per cent by 1986 if fertility continued unchanged, it would increase 92 per cent, if, with conditions otherwise comparable, fertility began to fall at once as postulated.[27]

Given effective efforts to reduce Indian fertility, it is capital and technical assistance that will prove of most use. Its compara-

[27] The projections and estimates appear in A. J. Coale and E. M. Hoover, *Population Growth and Economic Development in India, 1956-1986*, Princeton Press, forthcoming in 1958. See also *India's Year Book; Kingsley Davis, The Population of India and Pakistan* (Princeton, 1951); A. Ghosh, "The Trend of the Birth Rate in India, 1911-50," *Population Studies*, vol. 10 (1956), 53-68. R. A. Gopalaswami has forecast something like 520 millions by 1981, whereas the United Nations forecasts 580 millions by 1980 (*Papers*, III, 186, 320).

tive foreign trade—carried on principally with Western Europe and the United Kingdom and with the United States and the ECAFE region, but representing only 5-6 per cent of gross national product—is smaller than that of Pakistan (8-10 per cent of GNP) and much smaller than that of Ceylon (about 33) and Malaya (50-60). Domestic capital formation remains low, having risen by 1956 to only 7-8 per cent of net national product from about 5 in 1949-51; but it is expected to rise to 10-11 by 1960. Even so, it will barely finance employment of the current normal annual increment (about 2 millions) in the labor force, together with a slight reduction in urban unemployment and rural underemployment. For this reason, and because carrying out India's development program entails expenditure of more foreign exchange than is presently supplied through export of goods and services (e.g., the Second Five Year Plan may absorb over $2 billion of foreign exchange, much of which is not yet in hand), continuation of India's economic development would be greatly aided by foreign investment and technical assistance; in fact, balance-of-payments deficits will prevent realization of the Plan unless foreign aid becomes available. Although British investment in India declined about four-fifths between 1938 and 1948, at which time it approximated about $500 million, or about 72 per cent of all foreign investment in India, it has since increased, Britain having provided about two-fifths of the £ 250 million flowing into the country in 1946-55. While the United Kingdom's capacity to supply India's requirements of sterling and technical assistance is quite limited, considerable help is likely to be forthcoming from other Dominions and the United States, at least so long as India remains within the Commonwealth. Unless, however, India is successful in reducing its rate of natural increase—an objective the success of its development program would facilitate, the amount of foreign assistance available will prove inadequate. India's economic progress, together with the degree of its participation in the Commonwealth, depends in part upon its success in clipping the wings of the stork. India's prospects will also be improved if sufficient scope and freedom are allowed to India's many competent enterprisers and to foreign firms, a number of which are alert to opportunities in India.[28]

Population pressure may operate in at least one way to increase the value India places upon Commonwealth membership. At present large numbers of Indians live abroad, many of them in Commonwealth countries. India's Commonwealth membership may give leverage, therefore, to her efforts to protect the rights of Indians living abroad and to guard them against political and economic disabilities. Pakistan may view her Commonwealth membership similarly, since many Pakistani live in foreign parts. The number of Indians and Pakistani living abroad approximates four million, 24 of the 30 millions emigrating from British India in 1834-1937 having returned. Those living abroad are situated principally in Burma, Ceylon, Malaya, Mauritius, Fiji, the Caribbean, East Africa, and South Africa.[29]

b. Pakistan

The demographic condition of Pakistan's population, which is less religiously heterogeneous than India's, resembles that of

[28] Concerning India, Pakistan, Ceylon, and Malaya much information is provided in various ECAFE studies and reports, such as the annual *Economic Survey of Asia and the Far East*, the *Economic Bulletin for Asia and and the Far East*, (of which VI, No. 1, 1955, deals with population growth), etc.; the reports of the Consultative Committee for *The Colombo Plan*; the United Nations, *A Study of Trade between Asia and Europe* (New York, 1953); and frequent reports in *The Economist*, London, and the *Eastern Economist*, New Delhi. See also Conan, *op. cit.*; U. S. Dept. of Commerce, *Investment in India* (Washington, 1953); W. Malenbaum, "India and China: Development Contrasts," *Journal of Political Economy*, vol. 64 (1956), 1-24; R. Nurkse, "Reflections on India's Development Plan," *Quarterly Journal of Economics*, vol. 71 (1957), 188-204; Supplement on the second plan, in *Eastern Economist* (March 22, 1957); W. A. Morrison, "Attitudes of Males toward Family Planning in a Western Indian Village," *Milbank Memorial Fund Quarterly*, vol. 34 (1956), 262-286; N. K. Chondhry, "A Note on the Dilemma of Planning Population in India," *Economic Development and Cultural Change*, vol. 4 (1955), 68-81; S. Swaroop, "Growth of Population and Public Health Programmes in Asia and the Far East," *Population Bulletin* of the United Nations, No. 5 (July, 1956), 13-27. American direct investment in India rose from $38 million in 1950 to only $109 million in 1956. See Pizer and Cutler, *loc. cit.*, (Aug., 1957), 24.

[29] See Kingsley Davis, *The Population of India and Pakistan*, chap. 13; unsigned paper, "International Migration in the Far East during Recent Times," *Population Bulletin* of the United Nations, No. 1 (Dec., 1951), 19-22; no. 2 (Oct., 1952), 27-58. On the conditions under which Indians have emigrated, worked, and lived abroad, see C. Kondapi, *Indians Overseas 1838-1949* (New Delhi, 1951).

the latter; but its industrial prospects are less promising, in part because 1100 miles separate the two parts of the country. Six Asian tongues are spoken, but English is the official language. While data on natality and mortality are incomplete, a number of circumstances suggest that in the future the natality (45-48 in 1951) and natural increase (23-25 in 1951) of Pakistan's 75 millions—109 per square mile in West Pakistan and 772 in East Pakistan—may exceed India's. Before partition Moslem fertility exceeded Indian fertility, and the Moslem population grew somewhat faster. Pakistan contains only four cities of over 100,000, and its population is slightly less urban than India's, only 11 per cent being urban dwellers. Pakistan's population is more agricultural than India's, 76 per cent of the labor force being in agriculture and less than 4.5 per cent in organized industry; it is slightly less literate than India's, and it includes relatively more unskilled and cottage-industry-type workers and relatively less administrative, commercial, and technical personnel. Pakistan's urbanization and industrialization are likely to proceed more slowly than India's. The United Nations forecasters anticipate, however, that Pakistan's population will increase 56 per cent to 119 millions by 1980 whereas India's population will increase 60 per cent. According to a more recent forecast, however, Pakistan's population will increase 54 per cent in 1955-75, whereas India's will increase 46 per cent.

In view of its economic state and its demographic prospect Pakistan will be highly dependent upon outside sources—especially Commonwealth members and the United States—for technical assistance and capital, and this need may strengthen other bonds which presently tie it to the Commonwealth. In 1955 net capital formation approximated 5 per cent of national income, too little to carry out its development program, and it may rise to 7 per cent; its proposed development plan calls eventually for an 8 per cent rate of saving. Pakistan's external sales are not providing enough foreign exchange to satisfy its developmental needs. In recent years foreign sources—principally

American and Commonwealth—have provided funds for public and private investment amounting to something like one-eighth of the amount the Pakistan government is investing in economic development. Foreign grants and loans are expected to supply 47.5 per cent of the public expenditures required under Pakistan's economic development plan.[30]

c. Ceylon

While Ceylon's per-capita income is above that of India and Pakistan (but much below Malaya's), its fundamental politico-economic problems are greatly accentuated by the high rate of growth (2.8 per cent per year) of its population (8.6 millions in 1955), its unfavorable land-man ratio (about 2 acres of cultivated land per agricultural worker), and its extreme populousness (about 344 per square mile). That its rate of natural increase will not rise much further, however, given its crude death rate of close to 10, affords little basis for optimism, particularly since there is no evidence that family limitation is spreading. For, the country's economic potential being so limited, it will experience great difficulty accommodating a population of 14 or more millions by 1980. Its cultivable land can be increased by little more than half, and this only at considerable reclamation cost. Its opportunities in manufacture, whether for domestic or foreign markets, are restricted by various lackings (e.g., natural resources; skilled personnel; capital per head, which a savings rate of little more than 5 per cent of national income is hardly sufficing to increase). Furthermore, the distribution and occupational patterns of its population (of which seven-tenths are Sinhalese, but very few British or European) reflect economic backwardness: 72 per cent live in rural areas, 10 on exports-producing estates, and only 18 in towns, but one of which exceeds 100,000 in size; agriculture occupies just over 51 per cent, and industry and mining little more than 10 per cent, of the labor force; and there is much unemployment and underemployment. Even if domestic

[30] See sources cited in note 28 above; United Nations, *Papers*, III, 320; K. Davis, *The Population of India and Pakistan*; U. S. Dept. of Commerce, *Investment in Pakistan* (Washington, 1954).

savings were more plentiful, Ceylon's heavy annual requirement of foreign exchange, traceable to the high ratio of its food and other imports to its national income, would not necessarily be met.

Ceylon's being a dependent economy does not presently appear to be strengthening its ties with the Commonwealth. For while Ceylon now receives capital and technical assistance from the Dominions and the United Kingdom (still its principal trading partner and formerly almost its sole source of foreign funds), private capital is moving out on the balance because of the "Ceylonization" program. This program is reducing the attractiveness of Ceylon's economy not only for Westerners, but also for comparatively skilled personnel of Indian origin and extraction, who are considered superior to the Sinhalese in a number of activities. What amounts to xenophobia is accentuating these tendencies. Under existing circumstances, therefore, Ceylon's economic ties with Commonwealth members are hardly sufficient to induce it to continue its membership. It is quite probable, nonetheless, that the smallness of Ceylon's population, together with the country's defenselessness, may prompt it to remain within the Commonwealth and seek its national security therein.[31]

d. Malaya

Malaya, which first became a Commonwealth member in 1957, differs in some respects from the three Asiatic members al-

[31] See the works cited in note 28 above; the IBRD mission report, *The Economic Development of Ceylon* (Baltimore, 1953); T. Morgan's essay in B. F. Hoselitz, *Agrarian Societies in Transition*, issued as vol. 305 of the *Annals* of the American Academy of Political and Social Science, May, 1956; Irene B. Taeuber, "Ceylon as a Demographic Laboratory: Preface to Analysis," *Population Index*, vol. 15 (1949), 293-304; N. K. Sarkar, "Population Trends and Population Policy in Ceylon," *Population Studies*, vol. 9 (1956), 195-216; Earl Huyck, "Differential Fertility in Ceylon," *Population Bulletin* of the United Nations, No. 4 (Dec., 1954), 21-29; United Nations, *Papers*, III, 320; Henry Oliver, *Economic Opinion and Policy in Ceylon* (Durham, N. C., 1957). Concerning the differential response of Ceylonese customs to westernization, see T. L. Green, "Changes in the Family in Ceylon Consequent upon Education and Social Contacts," *Famille dans le Monde*, vol. 9 (1956), 269-282. Between 1911 and 1954 expectation of life at birth for males rose from 33.43 to 60.3 years; more than a century elapsed before this improvement was achieved in the United States. On the "flight" of capital from Ceylon, see the *Financial Times*, London, September 17, 1957, 2.

ready described. Its economy, although highly dependent on rubber and tin, is fairly advanced, by Asian standards, and its per-capita income (about $280) is the highest in the Far East. While it is less densely populated than a number of Asian countries, the Federation's 6.1 millions averaging only about 120 per square mile, this average is misleading. For much of the Federation's territory, though rendered fairly accessible by a long coast line, is covered by jungle, something like three-fifths of the landed area being virtually uninhabited. Hence the number (433) of persons per square mile of alienated and cleared land is high.[32] The heterogeneity of the Federation's population is linguistically and hence politically significant: about 49 per cent are Malaysians; 38 are Chinese; 12 are Indians and Pakistani; the rest comprise about one per cent. The Federation is comparatively urban, including 22 towns of over 10,000; more than 27 per cent of its population live in urban centers of 1000 and over. Over 35 per cent of the population of the Federation and Singapore live in such centers, and over 28 per cent live in cities of 10,000 and over. This high degree of urbanization, comparable with that of France, is partly traceable to the fact that over half the Chinese have settled in urban centers, now comprising about seven-tenths of the aggregate urban population.

Malaya resembles Ceylon in having a high birth rate (over 45) and a high rate of natural increase (2.5 per cent or higher), with the Chinese outstripping both the Malaysians (whose gross reproduction is below that of the Chinese) and the Indians (whose excess of births is sometimes partly offset by emigration). Accordingly, despite its present potentialities by Asian standards, Malaya's economic and political progress will probably be checked, should the present high rate of natural increase persist, or should

[32] To the 6.1 millions must be added to 1.25 millions inhabiting the 225 square-mile Crown Colony of Singapore, which, in our discussion, we sometimes include with the Federation, it being the most advanced part of Malaya, and the Asian city with the highest per-capita income. It includes relatively more Chinese (77 per cent) and fewer Malaysians than any part of the federation; for this reason the Federation is not eager to admit Singapore to membership. It will probably be combined with the Federation at some future date, however. It is due to have local autonomy in 1959.

the country be swamped with immigrants from highly over-populated parts of Asia. Although planned parenthood now receives some support in Singapore, the behavior of urban fertility does not yet certainly foretoken a decline in natality. Further-more, the decline, when it begins in the cities and spreads from them, is likely to be gradual at best. It is expected that the Federation's population will total 10.2 millions by 1975, and Singapore's 2.2 million.

The Malayan occupational structure is underdeveloped, and effective exploitation of its resources still requires considerable foreign technical personnel and external capital (of which about $696 million, over half British, had been invested by 1938). In 1947, 61 and 7 per cent, respectively, of the labor forces of the Federation and Singapore were in agriculture; in mining, manu-facturing, etc., 10 and 20; in finance, etc., 12 and 32; and in professions, personal service, clerical, etc., 8 and 23. In the post-war period considerable capital has come in, principally from the United Kingdom and other Commonwealth members, but the net rate at which capital has been formed has been relatively low (about 6 per cent of the net national product), foreign investment income representing a considerable fraction of gross domestic savings. Trading partnerships, together with access to foreign capital, bind Malaya to the Commonwealth, just as do the requirements of defense against communism and external aggression. The ties connecting both Malaya and Singapore with the Commonwealth will be relatively strong if English is retained as the first language, or even as the lingua franca that facilitates communication between the area's three main ethnic groups.[33]

5. Caribbean Federation

Unlike other members of the Commonwealth, the Caribbean

[33] See works cited in note 28; also Woytinsky, *World Commerce*, 195, 214; IBRD mission report, *The Economic Development of Malaya* (Baltimore, 1955); T. E. Smith, *Population Growth in Malaya* (London, 1952); Eunice Cooper, "Urbanization in Malaya," *Population Studies*, vol. 5 (1951), 117-131. According to the United Nations (*Papers*, III, 320), Malaya and Singapore will number about 12 millions by 1980.

Federation, to be established in 1958, comprises not mainly one or two continuous landed areas, but a number of scattered islands embracing a territory of about 7,741 square miles. Two of these islands, however, Jamaica and Trinidad, include four-fifths of the landed area and about three-fourths of the aggregate population of the federation. The inhabitants total slightly more than 3 million, population density averaging about 380 per square mile. The islands, or groups, together with their populations, in thousands and in number per square mile, in 1954, follow: Jamaica, 1,546 and 329; Trinidad and Tobago, 716 and 361; Barbados, 227 and 1,362; Windward Islands, 307 and 370; Leeward Islands, 119 and 334. Corresponding data for several territories which, although not presently included in the Federation, may be added later, follow: British Guiana, 479 and 6; British Honduras, 78 and 9; British Virgin Islands, 8 and 113.

The population of the Federation consists almost entirely of persons of African or mixed descent from the former slave population. The whites are relatively few in number, ranging from 5.1 per cent in Barbados through 2.7 in Trinidad and Tobago to 0.3 in Dominica. Asiatics form about 3 per cent of the population of most of the islands; in Trinidad, however, this percentage is 36. Natural increase, now about 2.5 per cent per year, is greater in Trinidad, where East Indian natural increase is remarkably high, than in Jamaica. Net emigration reduces this rate slightly, but the rate of growth is still much above the average rate (1.75 per cent) experienced in the whole period 1921-56. Since the crude death rate is about 10-11 in some of the islands, the Federation's crude rate of natural increase is not likely to rise much above the current level (which is higher in Trinidad and Tobago than in Jamaica, the Leeward Islands, and elsewhere) of about 2.5 per cent per year.

The economic prospect of the Federation is not good, and it is being worsened by continuation of high natality and natural increase. Raw materials are few (principally bauxite in Jamaica and petroleum in Trinidad), sugar-cane growing being the major

source of exports and income, along with a few primary agricultural products. Furthermore, proximity to the United States is
not the remarkable source of advantage to the West Indies that
it is to Puerto Rico, where, by 1955, per-capita income had risen
to $436; for the West Indies have less access to the American
market. There is, however, Lewis believes, scope for the development of a number of labor-oriented industrial activities,
the products of which should find markets in the Americas and
the United Kingdom. Some students are less sanguine, however,
than Lewis concerning this prospect. Only through the development of tourism and nonagricultural activities is escape possible
from current unemployment, underemployment, and lowness of
income. Conducive to such development is the fact that illiteracy
is relatively low, especially among those of school age, much
lower than in the populations of South Africa and the Asian
members of the Commonwealth. Moreover, urbanization is
well advanced, running from one-fifth to over two-fifths. The
economic situation of the population of the Federation is well
illustrated by that of the people of Jamaica: there, in 1950,
income averaged $168; unemployed persons made up 15-20 per
cent of the labor force, the annual addition to which approximated
13,000; of the labor force, about 40 per cent were in agriculture
and only about 4 per cent in manufacturing. Since domestic
savings are inadequate, considerable foreign capital is required,
in addition to that now being invested in the development of
natural resources and tourism. However, should Commonwealth members supply much of this needed capital, together
with technical assistance and additional markets, it would serve to
strengthen the Federation's adherence to the Commonwealth.
This tendency might be further strengthened were more entrepreneurs to settle in the islands.[34]

[34] Efforts in the past to shift population from the Federation to British Guiana
and Honduras have not been successful, in part because a great deal of investment is
required to facilitate such shifts of population. Furthermore, concentration of this
investment in the islands may serve to bring down natality and natural increase.
On the Federation, see R. R. Kuczynski, *Demographic Survey of the British Colonial
Empire*, III (London, 1953); M. Banton, "Recent Migration from West Africa and

6. The African Members

Under this head we treat Ghana, Nigeria, and the Federation of Rhodesia and Nyasaland. Ghana, formerly the Gold Coast, became a Commonwealth member in 1957. Nigeria hopes to become a member by 1959. While the Federation already enjoys much self-government, the African population does not want Dominion status. Within each of these areas there exist, it is supposed, extensive underdeveloped resources. Within each is found a large, backward, ethnically and (sometimes) linguistically diverse, indigenous population, many of whose members still live in villages of the tribally oriented type (as distinguished from the Asian type). The institutions of the African peoples have not yet become sufficiently adjusted to the requirements of technological progress (e.g., the joint or extended family has not yet generally given place to the economically superior Western nuclear type). Moreover, the British-European population remains too small to be a source of as much institution-transforming and progress-generating power as modernization of these areas requires. Euro-acculturation is proceeding apace, however, in those parts (e.g., in the Rhodesias) where a fairly large and increasing European core is to be found. More and more indi-

the West Indies to the United Kingdom," *Population Studies*, vol. 7 (1956), 2-13; W. A. Lewis, *Industrial Development in the Caribbean* (reprinted from the *Caribbean Economic Review*, Trinidad, 1950); IBRD mission reports, *The Economic Development of Jamaica* (Baltimore, 1952) and *The Economic Development of British Guiana* (Baltimore, 1953); *The West Indies and Caribbean Year Book* (London, 1955-56). See also M. J. Proudfoot, *Population Movements in the Caribbean* (Trinidad, 1950); G. W. Roberts, "A Note on Mortality in Jamaica," *Population Studies*, vol. 4 (1950), 64-85, and "Some Observations on the Population of British Guiana," *ibid.*, vol. 2 (1948), 185-214; W. H. Knowles's paper in Hoselitz, *op. cit.*, 134 ff.; Irene B. Taeuber, "British Guiana: Some Demographic Aspects of Economic Development," *Population Index*, vol. 18 (1952), 3-19; P. H. J. Lampe, "A Study on Human Fertility in the British Caribbean Territory," *Caribbean Economic Review*, vol. 3 (1951), 93-178; G. W. Roberts, "Population Trends in the British Caribbean Colonies," *ibid.*, 179-200. Roberts anticipated an increase of only 2.1 per cent per year in 1946-61, ranging from a high of 50 per cent in Trinidad for the 15 years to a low of 30 in Jamaica. See also his later paper, "Recent Demographic Trends in Cuba, Haiti and the British Caribbean," *Population Bulletin* of the United Nations, No. 5 (July, 1956), 42-50. See also United Nations, *Papers*, III, 318 for an estimate of 4.545 million by 1980; also R. C. Cook, "The West Indies," *Population Bulletin*, vol. 14 (1958), 17-34. Per capita incomes of £100 and £71, respectively, are reported for Trinidad and Jamaica by A. R. Prest in *A Fiscal Survey of the British Caribbean*, Colonial Research Series, No. 23 (London, 1957), 11.

genes are being drawn from the subsistence economy of the bush into a money economy. Class and status relationships based largely on economic success are replacing those based on age and control of land. Older sources of social cohesion are undergoing dissolution, and geographical and social mobility is increasing. Trade, some finance, and types of industry have developed. Small-scale entrepreneurs have multiplied, and economic activity is becoming increasingly individualized. Extensive trade with the outside world, together with continuing foreign investment and the growth of an urban population, has accelerated the rate of economic and cultural change. Symbolic of the change which has taken place and perhaps prophetic of that in prospect is the metamorphosis of the Rhodesias. Seventy years ago their inhabitants were illiterate, ignorant even of the wheel and the pulley, and afflicted with malaria, sleeping sickness, and other dread diseases. Today they are somewhat literate and enjoy health and other advantages of the sort associated with the rise of a prosperous copper industry, the lure of subsoil wealth having served here, as in other parts of Africa, to introduce the society-transforming productive forces of the West. Continuation of progress in the Rhodesias, as in Ghana and Nigeria, presupposes continuation of the immigration of non-Africans with enter-preneurial and related skills.[35]

[35] See Conan, op. cit.; papers by J. L. Comhaire, Elizabeth E. Hoyt, and Pius Okigbo, in Hoselitz, ed., op. cit.; R. R. Kuczynski, op. cit., I-II (London, 1948-49), and The Cameroons and Togoland (London, 1939); L. T. Badenhorst, "Population Distribution and Growth in Africa," Population Studies, vol. 5 (1951), 23-34; C. J. Martin's papers on the East African population in ibid., vol. 3 (1949), 303 ff., vol. 6 (1953), 233 ff., and vol. 7 (1953), 181 ff.; P. T. Bauer, West African Trade (Cambridge, 1954). For criticism of immigration-control policies intended to preserve the homogeneity of the population, see P. T. Bauer and R. S. Yamey, "Economic Aspects of Immigration Policy in Nigeria and the Gold Coast," South African Journal of Economics, vol. 22 (1944), 222-232. On the revolutionary urbanization under way in Africa, see K. Davis and Hilda Hertz Golden, "Urbanization and the Development of Pre-Industrial Areas," Economic Development and Cultural Change, vol 3 (1954), 6-26; but cf. W. Bascom, "Urbanization among the Yoruba," American Journal of Sociology, vol. 60 (1955), 446-454. Figures relating to income and capital formation tend to be too low in underdeveloped countries, and particularly in countries of the sort treated in section (6). See H. T. Oshima's comments on the income-estimates of underdeveloped countries more advanced than these African lands, "National Income Statistics of Underdeveloped

a. Federation of Rhodesia and Nyasaland

In 1956 the population of Nyasaland and the two Rhodesias included about 251 thousand Europeans, 19 thousand Asians, 11 thousand colored, and about 7 million Africans, most of whom speak variants of Bantu even though they are members of diverse ethnic groups. While the average population density of the 477,000 square miles of territory is only about 15 per square mile, it approximates 70 in Nyasaland, where relatively few Europeans live and into which relatively few are immigrating. While the African population, with a birth rate in the 40's, may be growing about 3 per cent per year, the Asian and colored have been growing faster, and the European population faster still. Net immigration (most of it British or South African), sometimes four times as high as natural increase (which averages 2 per cent or better), has raised the European growth rate nearly to 10 per cent per year since the war. Accordingly, while the Federation government, aware of Britain's slow growth, stands ready to accept more immigrants from Europe, it recently (1956) limited the monthly quota to 2,100, of whom only one-seventh may be aliens. In 1956, 26,201 immigrants were admitted, of whom at least 22 thousand were from Commonwealth countries. If the present rate of population growth continues, the Federation's 1980 population will exceed the United Nations forecast of 11.2 millions.

The occupational structure is gradually assuming a more advanced form, at least in the Rhodesias. About 93 per cent of the European labor force and about seven-tenths of the gainfully employed Africans are engaged in nonagricultural activities, mining and refineries alone occupying about one-seventh of the latter. The Asians are engaged principally in merchandising, and the colored in skilled and semiskilled work. Urbanization will facilitate improvement both of the occupational structure of the Africans and of their education, to a small amount of which

Countries," *Journal of The American Statistical Association*, vol. 52 (1957), 162-174.

(usually not over three years) 33-50 per cent of the children of school age are exposed. Over three-fourths of the European population, most of the Asians and colored, and over one-tenth of the natives live in towns of over 1,000.

Per-capita income remains low—it averaged something like $109 in 1954, but was much lower among the Africans—because actual performance falls far below potential in agriculture, forestry, and power development, and possibly because too much reliance is put upon copper, to the neglect of other minerals and activities. Nonetheless, net savings have been running close to one-fifth of net domestic product, and their amount has been increased about four-fifths by foreign investment, though this has been more than offset by net income paid abroad. Much of this foreign investment is British, its nominal value approximating $321 million in 1953 as compared with $43 million American and considerable South African; moreover, it continues to flow in from these and other foreign sources. The nearby Union, besides being a source of capital and population, is also a principal trading partner of the Federation, being second only to the United Kingdom in importance. It is to be expected that the Federation will find Commonwealth membership highly advantageous, given its requirements of capital, immigrants, and technical assistance, together with the smallness of its elite, the great dependence of the Federation upon external trade (especially with the United Kingdom), and its military weakness.[36]

b. Nigeria

Nigeria's population, somewhat over 32 millions and occupying 373,000 square miles of territory, averages over 86 persons per square mile. This average is misleading, since in some

[36] See Colonial Office reports, *Northern Rhodesia* (London, 1956); U. S. Dept. of Commerce, *Investment in Federation of Rhodesia and Nyasaland* (Washington, 1956); J. R. H. Shaul and C. A. L. Myburgh, "Vital Statistics of the African Population of Southern Rhodesia in 1948," *Population Studies*, vol. 4 (1951), 432-438; Frankel, *Capital Investment*, chap. 5. Illustrative of complaints of the smallness of the amount of annual investment made by the United Kingdom in the Commonwealth are the remarks in *East Africa and Rhodesia*, vol. 33 (1957), 735, 1239, 1279, 1527, 1659.

areas density exceeds 400 per square mile, and since only about
9 per cent of the land is in farm crops. The non-African population, mostly of British or Commonwealth origin, is very small,
having been estimated at 15,000. The African population em-
braces at least 13 major language groups. While its rate of growth
has been put at 1.5 per cent per year, it is certain only that fertility
is very high, that mortality is quite high, and that the rate of
growth will increase if mortality declines. The United Nations,
supposing an increase of only 1.25 per cent per year, forecasts
a population of 41.7 millions by 1980. According to a more
recent forecast, however, the population is expected to number
at least 42 millions by 1975.

While economic conditions in Nigeria have been improving,
they have not been improving so rapidly as they would if more
European or other entrepreneurs and skilled people resided there
and the attitudes of Nigeria's native leaders were more economically rational. All this has a bearing upon the country's prospective adherence to the Commonwealth. The comparatively urban
character of the population (of those living in the North, the
East, and the West, respectively, 9, 14, and 47 per cent are urban;
and at least 4 per cent live in "urban" agglomerations of over
100,000) is not reflected in its occupational or its educational
structure. About four-fifths of the labor force is engaged in
extractive activities; about 7 per cent, in crafts and industry;
and about 6 per cent, in trade and commerce. Less than one
person in ten of school age is literate, and only about one-
fourth of the children of primary school age are on the school
rolls. Per-capita income in 1952-53 was $59, while domestic
investment approximated only 7 per cent of gross national product.
Foreign investment, which has been financing 12-25 per cent
of private fixed investment, in 1950-52 amounted to only about
2 per cent of gross national product. Moreover, although foreign
investment is essential to Nigeria's development, present Nigerian
attitudes tend to discourage it; and exports, principally to the

United Kingdom, are too small (about one-sixth of gross national product) to countervail these attitudes.[37]

c. Gold Coast

The Gold Coast in 1957 became Ghana, the second full-fledged member of the Commonwealth situated in Africa. The total population of the areas usually included in the Gold Coast was estimated at 4,478,000 in 1953. Non-Africans numbered only about 11,000, of whom 7,100 were British, and the balance, of many nationalities, above all, Lebanese or Syrian. At least 10 of the African tribes exceeded 100,000 in size. Geographically the population was distributed as follows, in thousands: 2,456 in the Colony; 912 and 1,110, respectively, in Ashanti and the Northern Territories; and 416 in Togoland, under United Nations Trusteeship. Some published estimates of changes in the size of the African population suggest that it is increasing about 1.5 per cent per year. A recent United Nations estimate supposes, however, that Ghana's population will increase little more than one per cent per year, from 4.92 millions in 1955 to 6.1 millions in 1975. Between 1948 and 1953 the very small non-African population increased about three-fifths, principally through immigration. Most of the non-African population live in large towns and mining areas. About one-eleventh of the African population lived in urban agglomerations of 10,000 and over in 1948.

The economy remains backward. Average income in 1950 seems to have been close to $100 (though several recent estimates put it as high as $140), with about two-fifths originating in agriculture, fishing, and forestry, and a similar amount in wholesale and retail trade. Subsistence agriculture and cocoa farming

---

[37] See IBRD mission report, *The Economic Development of Nigeria* (Baltimore, 1955); Colonial Office, *Report on Nigeria for the Year 1953* (London, 1955); Bauer, *op. cit.*; United Nations, *Papers*, III, 316; O.E.E.C. *Investments in Overseas Territories in Africa, South of The Sahara* (Paris, 1951); R. M. Prothero, "The Population Census of Northern Nigeria 1952: Problems and Results," *Population Studies*, vol. 10 (1956), 166-183. In his *Economic Analysis and Policy in Underdeveloped Countries* (Durham, N. C., 1957), Peter Bauer estimates conventional national income per head in Nigeria at about £ 25; in the Gold Coast, at about £ 50; and in Malaya at about £ 100.

occupied most of the adult males, nearly half of the males of working age being engaged in the former and about 15 per cent in the latter. Only about 4 per cent were engaged in mining and quarrying, and about 6 per cent in manufacture. Most of the rest were occupied in commerce, services, and transport and communication. In recent years (but not in 1956 when export prices were lower) exports have been exceeding imports in value, with the United Kingdom doing about half the trade. Moreover, exports have furnished much of the national income (over half in recent years). The rate of investment in recent years apparently has been somewhat in excess of one-tenth of gross national product. There is danger, in the Gold Coast as in Nigeria, that long-run economic development will be retarded through diversion of too large a fraction of the community's disposable resources to less productive forms of "capital formation" and through the pursuit of politico-economic policies that check the inflow of foreign capital and skilled personnel.[38]

Conclusion

While the stork is not always the arbiter of the future, he tends to become such when the technological spread between peoples becomes small and the bond of common sentiment is not very strong; and he always plays a role in determining historical outcomes. It is virtually inevitable, therefore, that the comparative lack of population growth in the United Kingdom, together with the great diminution in the movement of its people to outlying members of the Commonwealth, will reduce the capacity of that organization to hold fast in the face of external or centrifugal forces making for its partial dissolution, unless the United Kingdom is willing to send out emigrants in excess of its natural increase. Nor is it likely that Canada, Australia, and New Zealand will in time provide enough emigrants to other parts

[38] Colonial Reports, *Gold Coast 1953* (London, 1954). Income data are given in United Nations, *Statistics of National Income and Expenditure*, Series H; W. A. Lewis, *Report On Industrialisation and the Gold Coast* (Accra, 1953). A United Nations projection relating to most of the population of the Gold Coast as described above suggests an annual rate of increase of 1.75 per cent per year in 1950-80 (*Papers*, III, 316).

of the Commonwealth to strengthen the British element in South Africa, and make it an effective nucleus in Malaya and in the African (with the possible execption of Rhodesia) areas. There is no likelihood, of course, that a British nucleus will ever be established in any of the remaining Asian members, or in the West Indies.

The adherence of members not bound to the Commonwealth by ties of essentially common ethnic origin and by the resulting possession of similar values and sentiments must rest on other grounds. Among these grounds is the capacity of the Commonwealth, and above all, the United Kingdom, to supply capital, technical assistance, and opportunities for profitable trade. Insofar as the United Kingdom is concerned, however, this capacity is not likely to be great enough or to grow rapidly enough; for its population is increasing very slowly, and there no longer exists a strong disposition to accumulate surpluses and invest them productively and abroad as in the late nineteenth century. Moreover, such capacity has not yet developed in any other member. It is quite possible, therefore, that the participation of India and Pakistan in the Commonwealth will diminish, as will that of Ceylon, unless guarding national security becomes a paramount motive. Malaya is more likely, on economic and politico-military grounds, to continue its adherence. For South Africa there is no practical alternative to adherence, and much the same may be said of the Federation of Rhodesia and Nyasaland. A similar, but less overpowering, argument might be made for the continued adherence of Ghana and Nigeria; but it is not yet evident that the inhabitants of these territories will perceive the nonexistence of a suitable alternative and the great advantage of belonging to the Commonwealth. For the Caribbean Federation there is little choice; because of its proximity to the United States it must either participate in the Commonwealth or pass under American protection.[39]

[39] Research underlying this paper has been facilitated by grants from the Ford and the Rockefeller Foundations.

Appendix

For the reader's convenience there are reported, in Table I below, the estimated populations of the countries dealt with, as of 1955, 1975, and 2000. These are the so-called medium figures, the United Nations Secretariat, whence these figures were gotten, having prepared high, low, and intermediate or medium estimates for 1975 and 2000. In the last two columns of the table the rates of growth, in per cent, for the periods 1955-1975 and 1975-2000 are given. Inasmuch as these projections have been made in the absence of knowledge respecting prospective economic growth and removal of existing obstacles to continuing population growth, they are to be viewed as extensions into the future of current populations on the basis of postulates which may or may not prove tenable.

Table I

Country	Population (in millions)			Population Growth (in per cent)	
	1955	1975	2000	1955-1975	1975-2000
United Kingdom	51.0	55.5	65.0	9	17
Canada	15.9	22.3	29.0	40	30
Australia	9.3	13.0	16.9	40	30
New Zealand	2.2	3.0	3.9	36	30
Union of South Africa	13.7	21.9	42.0	53	92
Ghana	4.6	6.1	9.7	33	59
Nigeria	31.3	42.3	67.5	35	60
Rhodesia, Nyasaland	7.1	10.2	16.2	41	59
India	386.0	563.0	1000.0	46	78
Pakistan	83.2	128.0	228.0	54	78
Ceylon	8.7	14.1	25.1	62	78
Malaya, Singapore	7.3	12.4	22.0	70	77
West Indies	3.0	4.7	8.3	57	77

5

The Emergence of Ghana

JAMES L. GODFREY

IN ACCRA AT midnight on March 5-6, 1956, as the Speaker
of the Legislative Assembly read the message of prorogation
from the Governor, colonial rule for the Gold Coast came to an
end and Ghana emerged as the first all-black member of the
Commonwealth. On the morning of the sixth, the former Governor was sworn in as Governor-General and, following British
ceremonial closely, the Duchess of Kent, representing the Queen,
read the speech from the throne to the new Parliament. The
constitutional documents establishing the independent and sovereign state were presented to the Prime Minister, Dr. Kwame
Nkrumah, who, upon the withdrawal of the Duchess and Governor-General, moved an address to be sent in reply to the speech
from the throne. All of the Commonwealth countries were
represented, with Great Britain marking the significance of the
occasion by sending Mr. R. A. Butler. Admission of the new
country to the Commonwealth circle had been "without difficulty," to quote Nkrumah, though some slight unease may have
been created for the future when the Prime Minister seized an
early and conspicuous occasion to condemn South African policy
by the statement that "if he had his way he would smash the
South African system of *Apartheid*." This was too little, however, to mar a gala occasion.[1]

In a very real sense the emergence of Ghana as an indepen-

[1]*The Times*, March 6-8, 1957, gives a good coverage of the ceremonies.

dent nation was as much a tribute to the efficacy of the British policy of matching political power to advancing maturity in colonial areas as it was a recognition of a remarkable and rapid growth of political leadership and sophistication within the Gold Coast itself. Indeed the rapidity of the change is of great significance since it is hardly necessary to go beyond 1946 in tracing the admission of the African to the central area of governmental power. But even if one goes farther back, Britain's experience as a colonial power in most of the Gold Coast area is relatively recent and hardly seems part of the traditional story of backwardness and retardation in colonial development.

The first appearance of the British on the Gold Coast in 1631, at Fort Koromantin, to take part in that trade which was both "sordid" and "lucrative" need not detain us. Briefly we must relate, however, that as late as 1828 the British Government had decided to leave the Gold Coast and remained only at the insistence of merchants and some of the native chiefs. Not until 1843[2] was a legal basis given to the exercise of British authority within the "Settlements," and only in 1874 was a colony established by letters patent and an order in council which was so vague in defining the area of its operation that the boundaries of the present colony did not become fixed until a second order issued in 1901.[3] Thus, on a formal basis, the British colonial experience has been restricted in the "old colony" to four generations and in the inland areas to less than two. This is not a long time for the journey from African tribal conditions to those of a partially modern state resting upon the most complex and delicate of political institutions and practices.

During most of this period African political experience was limited to that which could be had in the local councils operating under the system of "indirect rule."[4] The chiefs, assisted by councils of elders, exercised authority over local matters and

[2] By the British Settlements Act of that year.
[3] This account is drawn largely from Lord Hailey, *Native Administration in the British African Territories* (London, 1951), III, 194-199.
[4] David E. Apter, *The Gold Coast in Transition* (Princeton, 1955), chaps. 6 and 7.

jurisdiction over both civil and criminal cases subject to intercession by, or appeal to, higher and English authority. In the "old colony" provincial councils of head chiefs made a direct link with central government. The central authority was vested in the traditional colony forms of governor, executive council, and legislative council. It was only in the last of these that the native had any chance of participation. The legislative council of the Gold Coast was established in 1850, but not until 1889 was the first African appointed as one of the unofficial members.[5] This council, maintaining through various numerical changes a majority of one official over unofficial members, did not receive its first elected member until the constitutional revision of 1925. This change provided for a legislative council of thirty members: the Governor, fifteen official and fourteen unofficial members. Of the unofficial members only nine were to be African. Of these six were to be elected by the provincial councils and three by municipal electorates composed of voters, male and female, able to meet a high property qualification.[6] It is rather remarkable to recall that only within the past thirty years has the Gold Coast known the electoral process even in a restricted form, and that at the beginning of the period less than one-third of the legislative body was of African origin. It was not until almost twenty years later—1943—that the first Africans, a barrister and a paramount chief, were appointed to the executive council.[7] By this time the Gold Coast, despite its meager preparation, stood on the edge of the phenomenal constitutional advance that would bring it within fifteen years from almost complete tutelage to independence.

It was during the war on October 5, 1944, that Mr. Oliver Stanley, Colonial Secretary, announced that plans submitted to him by the Governor of the Gold Coast, following consultation with representatives of African political opinion, had the approval

[5] *Ibid.*, 136.
[6] Martin Wight, *The Gold Coast Legislative Council*, vol. II of *Studies in Colonial Legislature*, ed. Margery Perham (London, 1947), 41-45.
[7] William E. F. Ward, *A History of the Gold Coast* (London, 1948), 318.

of the British Government and would be placed in operation at a suitable time.[8] This plan became effective, through an order in council, on March 29, 1946. The new arrangements undoubtedly recognized that the war years had been a forcing period for the political growth of the Gold Coast which had served as an Anglo-American base during much of the conflict. Political changes also had the undergirding of prosperity brought on by the boom in the cocoa and raw-materials market, and the increasing competency of the native African as marked, in his part of the world, by a relatively high rate of literacy and a relatively efficient system of education.[9]

Undoubtedly from the standpoint of the constitutional development of the colony the most important change occurred in the composition of the legislative council. Although the membership remained at thirty the elected Africans had a majority of eighteen to twelve. This might go even higher for six of the twelve were to be nominated—the other six were official members—and the choice would likely include some natives. The eighteen were to be elected by joint provincial councils, the Ashanti Confederacy council, and by municipal elections.[10] This assured that the members thus returned would be largely chiefs and intellectuals but they would be African and they would be in a majority. The territorial authority of the legislative council was also expanded. Until now the "old colony" only had been included while the Ashanti lands and the Northern Territory of the hills and savannahs had been governor's territories under direct central authority. Five of the representatives in the new council were from Ashanti and marked the political union of this area with the original colony; it was intended that the Northern Territories come in at some later period.[11] Despite the system

[8] *Parl. Deb.*, 5th ser., Commons, vol. 403, cols. 1161-1162 (Oct. 5, 1944). Some publicity was given the changes by a debate in the House of Lords on Dec. 20, 1944. See *Parl. Deb.*, 5th ser., Lords, vol. 134, cols. 461-477 (Dec. 20, 1944).

[9] "Self-Government in the Gold Coast," in the *Round Table*, vol. 42 (Sept., 1952), 326.

[10] Wight, *op. cit.*, 203-204.

[11] *Parl. Deb.*, 5th ser., Commons, vol. 403, cols. 1759-1760 (Oct. 11, 1944).

of election—indirect or heavily restrictive—the council had now become representative and was bound to excite hopes that it would soon become democratic. Since the only precedents for the establishment of a non-European majority in a colonial legislature were in Ceylon and Jamaica, the Gold Coasters might well feel themselves to be pioneers.[12]

The shift in majorities from official to unofficial inside the legislative council was accompanied by the grant of reserve powers to the Governor, who might legislate in defiance of the council to secure the public order and the maintenance of the faith and credit of the government. The British Government further kept the executive authority clearly defined by refusing the suggestion that two unofficial members of the legislative body be appointed to the executive council and thus become advisory to the Governor while being representative of the people, and that a standing committee of the legislature be made consultative to the Governor.[13] The garment thus given was designed to change the looks of the colony without giving too bold an appearance; it was obviously intended for more than a season's wear.

This intention probably would have prevailed had the garment been a better fit. The new constitution did not put political power sufficiently into the hands of groups standing below the chiefs and professional men. The times had created able but frustrated groups within the country who wished to participate and who felt the surge of political passion. External inflation sharpened demands and created difficulties for the government. Racial feelings of inferiority spurred on the demand for greater recognition. The material for political action was at hand if only the leader could be found. In this case the need was soon met.[14]

On December 16, 1947, Kwame Nkrumah returned to the Gold Coast, after an absence of twelve years. During this period he had studied, seriously in the United States and superficially in England. In this country he took degrees from Lincoln University and the University of Pennsylvania; in London he

[12] Wight, *op. cit.*, 206-207.   [13] *Ibid.*, 204-205.
[14] One of the best discussions of this interval is in Apter, *op. cit.*, 159-170.

remained briefly and degreeless at University College and at Gray's Inn. While London did not qualify him in the law, which he intended to study, it gave him the opportunity to come briefly under Professor Laski and thus fortified him, as so many others, in the mission of colonial reform. In both countries he engaged in movements associated with African causes and became familiar with radical thought.

He was now called back to the Gold Coast by Dr. Danquah, a rather conservative leader, to serve a new political movement known as the United Gold Coast Convention. As its general secretary he supplied drive, oratorical ability, personal and national ambitions, and a good working knowledge of the organization and group dynamics of the Communist party. Unquestionably Nkrumah's natural ability as an agitator and his close attention to party organization furnished the pivot upon which party fortunes were to turn. Within eighteen months he emerged as the leader of a more radical and vital movement—the Convention People's party—formed from schism in the UGCC. Under his control this party became the instrument that was to transform the political position of his native land.[15] Here was the "god" to exorcise the "devils" of colonialism and imperialism.[16]

The narration of political events, however, demands a return to chronology. On February 28, 1948, an affray occurred in Accra in which a procession of ex-servicemen was opposed by police and troops with the tragic results that some twenty persons were killed and over two hundred wounded. Riots followed and it was widely believed that the disturbances had grown out of an attempt to establish a "Union of Africa Socialist Republics." Precautionary arrests were made and the suspected persons, including Nkrumah, were sent to the Northern Terri-

[15] Nkrumah's career can best be followed in his autobiography, *Ghana: The Autobiography of Kwame Nkrumah* (London, 1957). Some use has also been made of the biography by Bankole Timothy, *Kwame Nkrumah: His Rise to Power* (London, 1955).
[16] See Apter, *op. cit.*, 166.

tories.[17]   Mr. Creech Jones, Colonial Secretary of the Attlee Government, announced the appointment of a commission under Mr. Aiken Watson, K. C. to investigate and to make recommendations.[18]   By August 4, 1948, the report was ready. While exonerating the central authorities for the use of emergency measures, the commission pointed out that political frustration and discontent had been fundamental in creating the tense situation out of which the disturbances had come. The government thus bore its share of the basic guilt. Economic problems of high prices on imported goods, tribal lands, the cocoa marketing board, competition for jobs, and housing with the varying standards between those for European and Africans had contributed to the feeling of governmental inadequacy and indifference. The constitutional reforms of 1946 were outmoded before they were introduced, and the commission now recommended the administration of a stronger mixture to set the patient on his feet: a legislative assembly with a board of ministers acting as an executive council, and a reorganization of local government on a local-council basis.[19]

These recommendations received immediate attention. They were discussed in both London and Accra, and general agreement was secured that a fully representative committee be appointed to examine the new constitutional proposals. The Gold Coast Governor, Sir Gerald Creasy, took the first step in selecting a distinguished African jurist, Mr. Justice James Coussey, as chairman of the new committee and on January 1, 1949, the Colonial Office released the names of his associates.[20]   The committee was at least large if not representative.[21]   Its thirty-eight additional

[17] Timothy, op. cit., 59-60. The Times gave little space to the disturbances. See, however, the editorial of March 5, 1948. The Governor's use of emergency powers was defended by Mr. Creech Jones on March 24, 1948. Parl. Deb., 5th ser., Commons, vol. 448, cols. 3001-3004.
[18] Ibid., p. 471. The terms of reference were: "To inquire into and report on the recent disturbances in the Gold Coast and their underlying causes; and to make recommendations on any matter arising from their inquiry."
[19] Report of the Commission of Enquiry into Disturbances in the Gold Coast 1948 (London, 1948).
[20] Apter, op. cit., 170, 173, 178.
[21] Ibid., 173 n. 32.

members had been secured in a rather cumbersome way: four were paramount chiefs appointed by the joint provincial council of the Colony; four, including two chiefs, were appointed by the Ashanti Confederacy council; four, including two chiefs, were nominated by the Northern Territories territorial council; the remaining twenty-six, including some of the municipal members of the legislative council, were chosen for their familiarity with local affairs and their ability to represent various sections of the community.[22] The committee began its work knowing that the British Government agreed with portions of the Watson Committee report advocating a reorganization of local government, an increase in the size of the legislative council, and the introduction of a majority of African members in the executive council. There seemed no serious obstacle in the way of another constitutional advance.

By August, 1949, the report was ready and was put in the hands of a new Governor—Sir Charles Arden-Clarke had replaced Sir Gerald Creasy—but the political scene had also shifted. Nkrumah's break with the UGCC had occurred and the Convention People's party had been launched. Most of the members of the Coussey Commission were affiliated with the UGCC and were too conservative in outlook to have a natural sympathy with the "positive action" policy of the new group.[23] The proposals of 1949 were, therefore threatened with the same fate as the reforms of 1946—too little and too late. By the time the new proposals were ready for implementation, Nkrumah was in jail under a twelve month sentence for "inciting others to take part in an illegal strike,"[24] but Nkrumahism and positive action were making vigorous advances.

There had been ample time for agitation. Prepared in August, 1949, the report had been published in October and the assent of the Colonial Secretary for its principal provisions secured,

[22] *Commonwealth Survey*, no. 15 (Jan. 22, 1949), 25-26. *The Times*, Jan. 3, 1949, gives the committee as one of forty members.
[23] Apter, *op. cit.*, 170-171.
[24] As quoted in Timothy, *op. cit.*, 108.

but it was not until late 1950 that the details were worked out, and letters patent putting them in operation became effective on December 22.[25] At the center of government the changes were considerable. The legislative council was enlarged to eighty-four members. Of these, however, only five would be elected in a direct manner. These five would come from the four municipalities. Of the rest thirty-three would be elected by electoral colleges themselves elected by primary elections in rural constituencies; thirty-seven would be elected by traditional bodies (ninteen, for instance, would be chosen by the Northern Territories council); six would represent chambers of commerce and of mines; and three would be official members.[26] The arrangement reflected clearly the difficulty of moving into a more democratic system and the reluctance of the commission to abandon the influence of traditional bodies.

Of somewhat greater significance were the changes in the executive council. This body was now to have a majority of African members—three ex officio members were to be European—drawn from the legislative council on terms suggesting those prevailing in the traditional cabinet system.[27] The Governor was to prepare the list of ministers, for such they were, but their acceptance and authority would rest upon a resolution of the legislature. The ministers in turn would elect one to serve as Prime Minister (known initially as "Leader of Government Business") though the Governor himself was to preside over meetings of the executive council. British precedent from the first was followed in fixing responsibility in the majority party and consulting it about the list. Nkrumah was in fact to be released from Jamestown prison by an act of clemency so he might undertake the post of "Leader" in recognition of the sweeping electoral victory of his party, the C.P.P. The effect of British practice would be to make the council a cabinet, though

[25] The letters patent were issued on Dec. 19, 1950.
[26] The best summary of this is found in *Commonwealth Survey*, no. 60 (Nov. 24, 1950), 23.
[27] The term cabinet was given to this in 1952. Apter, *op. cit.*, 189.

134 COMMONWEALTH PERSPECTIVES

something a bit less than this had probably been intended. As an emergency device the Governor was still left with reserve powers of the veto and the authority to certify measures considered vital to the well-being of the colony. The exercise of the second power, however, was subject to the prior consent of the council or, failing this, to the consent of the Secretary of State for Colonial Affairs.

While it is impossible to follow the changes in local government, they were considerable. The old native authorities system was largely abolished, despite the Coussey Commission's intent to preserve the authority and prestige of the chiefs, and new councils, two-thirds elective and one-third appointive in membership, were established. In local matters of taxation and administration the newer democratic forces replaced the older autocratic tendencies of the chiefs. The territorial councils, which were strongholds of resistance against the unitary preferences of the C.P.P., were reduced in status though their limits of action were left vague. Municipal councils were democratized and given powers modeled upon their British counterparts.[28]

The election, early in 1951, gave an overwhelming victory to the C.P.P. which almost swept the board on seats open to any kind of electoral appeal. This party won all five of the municipal seats and twenty-nine of the thirty-three seats chosen by electoral colleges which in turn had been selected by primary voters. In opening the new legislative council on February 20, 1951, the Governor placed six C.P.P. members on his list of eight African ministers and called upon Nkrumah, who from prison had demonstrated great strength in taking an Accra seat, to become "Leader of Government Business." The victory was a tribute to organization and the more radical program of the new party that demanded national unity, freedom and independence *now*. The arrangements of late 1950 and the results of the election pointed clearly the road for the future: the extension of direct elections

[28] It is difficult to piece together exactly what happened in local government. The entirely inadequate account given here is taken from *ibid.*, 193-198. See also *Report by the Select Committee on Local Government (Colony) 1950* (Accra, 1951).

and the elimination of the three official members of the executive council. Once these two changes were accomplished it would be hard to make the distinction between the Gold Coast and a Commonwealth member.[29]

Accompanying the constitutional question step by step were several other associated problems. Unquestionably the political progress of the Gold Coast had rested upon its economic progress. The area, considered next to Malaya in its economic potential, has enjoyed a long period of prosperity coming from boom times in the export of cocoa, minerals, and timber. High external prices had not brought equivalent internal inflation, and the resultant prosperity had created the proper economic circumstances for political advances.[30] The Gold Coast was fortunate in having its economic wealth rather widely distributed and in escaping the prying attentions of a large foreign corporation. To economic prosperity was added a relatively high level—for Africa—of educational attainment.[31] This helped the government in its determination to retain in its civil service the existing British standard of performance but at the same time to replace white with black in the governmental hierarchy. The Africanization of the service went on with reasonable speed. Certainly one of the great blessings was the absence of the color question in any really serious form. The population of somewhat less than 5,000,000 had a white element of only a few thousand. Divided though the blacks were by religion and cultural orientation, they did not have to contend with the color question on any basis other than rather isolated and personal prejudice. With 1951 the weather seemed to have set fair though, as we shall see, a few squalls did develop.

The *now* part of the demands of the C.P.P. was not idly

[29] Basil Davidson, "The New West Africa III. Problems of the Gold Coast," *New Statesman and Nation*, vol. 43 (May 24, 1952), 606.

[30] Barbara Ward Jackson discusses the favorable economic situation of the Gold Coast in "The Gold Coast: An Experiment in Partnership," in *Foreign Affairs*, vol. 32 (1954), 609-610. For a brief description of the plans for economic development, see *Commonwealth Survey*, no. 84 (Nov. 9, 1951), 44-47.

[31] *Ibid.*, no. 83 (Oct. 26, 1951), 53-54.

meant. By the summer of 1952 Mr. Lyttleton, the Colonial Secretary in the Conservative Government, visited the Gold Coast. While there he was approached on the subject of self-government and independence within the Commonwealth. The Gold Coasters were assured that when proper consultations were made the British Government stood ready to examine and discuss with the Gold Coast proposals leading to the desired ends.[32] Though no commitments were given, the way was clearly open and passable.

Seeing that his Government was to take the initiative, Nkrumah proposed consultations with the chiefs and people to formulate the proposals that should be made. The problems included those of relationships with Great Britain and the alteration of the internal pattern of institutions and the distribution of powers. In the first instance the Gold Coast would have to consider the replacing of the *ex officio* ministers with Africans, though here the ticklish problem of defense would have to be kept in mind should a representative minister replace the Minister of Defense and External Affairs. Internally suggestions should be forthcoming concerning the method of appointing the Prime Minister and the ministers, electoral reform, the desirability of a second house, the powers of the chiefs, and the protection of the integrity and ability of the civil service. Upon the completion of the consultations, the Prime Minister would present the recommendations for debate and prepare the suggestions to be made in London.

These were embodied in a White Paper, and the long negotiations with the Colonial Office ended in a substantial success for the Gold Coast Government. An order in council, signed on April 29, 1954,[33] accepted in the large all of the proposals save

[32] See the statement made by Lord Munster, Parliamentary Under-Secretary of State for the Colonies, in the House of Lords on July 24, 1952. *Parl. Deb.*, 5th ser., Lords, vol. 178, col. 285.
[33] See an editorial in *The Times*, April 17, 1954. Also see *A Monthly Survey of Commonwealth and Colonial Affairs*, no. 17 (May, 1954), 9. The White Paper bore the title *The Government's Proposals for Constitutional Reform* (Accra, 1953).

one: the Secretary of State for Colonial Affairs could not agree that at this stage the affairs of the Gold Coast should be transferred to the Commonwealth Relations Office. Otherwise there was to be an enlarged, single-chamber legislature directly elected, a fully responsible cabinet with the Governor, however, continuing in the enjoyment of reserve powers and his responsibility for external affairs. Also guarantees were to be established for the independence of the judiciary and the public services. These changes would bring in an interim arrangement which would give way in due course to independence and Commonwealth status. June was designated as the month for the election to bring the new constitution into operation. The British Government was thus left with the minimum powers necessary to her so long as she retained any responsibility for the Gold Coast. Mr. Hopkinson, who had replaced Mr. Lyttleton, in announcing the changes to the House of Commons stated that these "must therefore be regarded as the last stage before the Gold Coast assumes full responsibility for its own affairs."[34] Full membership in the Commonwealth, he went on to say, was a different matter and would involve consultation among the existing members.

The arrangement undoubtedly redounded to the credit of Nkrumah and the C.P.P. and was reflected in the winning, by that party, of seventy-one of the one hundred four seats in the new legislature.[35] On June 17, Nkrumah was asked to form the first all-African cabinet and to serve as Prime Minister. The difficult problem of defense and external affairs was temporarily solved by removing it from the cabinet and lodging it in the hands of a deputy to the Governor. The remaining seats in the cabinet went to several small parties, but an ominous sign appeared in the growing demand for a federal structure of government for the future. This movement was strongest in the Northern Territories, where there was a feeling of neglect and the actuality of poverty and retardation, and amongst the Ashantis, who were bitter over the activities of the Cocoa Marketing Board and

[34] *Parl. Deb.*, 5th ser., Commons, vol. 526, col. 1625 (April 28, 1954).
[35] Apter, *op. cit.*, 231.

more than suspected that a disproportionate share of the public funds was coming from their region but was being spent in the old colony. This rising quarrel marred the triumph of Nkrumah and constituted the greatest obstacle in the way of the final step which the Government hoped quickly to take. In the consultations leading to the new Government there had been strong sentiment for a second house, which the C.P.P., with its predilection for a unitary state, ignored as a symbol of federalism and as a possible haven for the waning powers of the chiefs.

The question of federalism became the issue on which a rather weak opposition could bedevil the Government party. An opposition of about thirty members was formed of the representatives of the Northern People's party and a number of independents who accepted the leadership of Dr. Samuel Dombo. At first Nkrumah refused to recognize the group as a true opposition party since it did not possess the capacity to form an alternative grovernment. The ruling of the Speaker, no doubt much influenced by the necessity of securing an opposition from some source, went against this contention and the Dombo group formed itself into a National Liberation Movement designed very largely to exploit the issue of the federal vs. the unitary state.[36] Several defections occurred from the ranks of the C.P.P.—perhaps the most interesting was that of Mr. Appiah, who as a representative of Nkrumah in London had married the daughter of Sir Stafford Cripps—and on October 21, 1954, the Ashanti council adopted a resolution endorsing a federal constitution and requesting the Queen to establish a commission of inquiry. This was a serious check to the fortunes of the C.P.P., which in June had won eighteen of the twenty-one Ashanti seats.[37] Recognizing the seriousness of the issue, Nkrumah suggested round-table conferences and the establishment of representative regional councils. Both were rejected. Early in 1955 rioting took place in Kumasi, and the Northern Territories joined in pushing the demand for federation. The

[36] Keesing's *Contemporary Archives*, July 29, 1954. See also *A Monthly Survey of Commonwealth and Colonial Affairs*, no. 23 (Dec., 1954).
[37] *The Times*, Oct. 22, 1954.

appeal for a commission of inquiry was turned down by the Colonial Secretary, who refused to be drawn into an internal quarrel. The seriousness of the situation was recognized, however, in the warning that a failure to reach a solution of such differences would undoubtedly delay the granting of independence.

On April 5 Nkrumah appointed a select committee of the Gold Coast legislature to consider both the question of a federal system of government and a second house. This procedure was boycotted by the opposition. The committee pointed out that the Gold Coast could hardly afford the expense or provide the talent that would be required by federal government and that nothing in the history, geography, religion, or language of the region made a federal government necessary. In debating this report in the Legislative Assembly, Nkrumah suggested a degree of devolution to the regions and indicated that the Government was willing to discuss this proposition. He also invited the British Government to send an expert to advise on this problem. The question of a second chamber was to be postponed until after the granting of independence.[38] The opposition, still holding aloof, prepared a constitution of its own providing for four regions with bicameral legislatures all round.

The expert, Sir Frederick Bourne, formerly Governor of the Central Provinces in India, found the National Liberation Movement unwilling to co-operate officially though some of the leaders did hold private conversations with him. The publication of his report in December, 1955, supported the position of the C.P.P. but did suggest that the objections of the N.L.M. could be cared for by less extreme measures than federalization. He found the answer to the problem of decentralization in the creation of regional assemblies which would link the regions with the central government, formulate and express regional opinion, and use local knowledge and experience in implementing action within the regions. This would be of positive aid to the central govern-

---

[38] *A Monthly Survey of Commonwealth and Colonial Affairs*, no. 30 (Aug. and Sept., 1955).

ment in removing from Accra a great deal of local business that could better be handled in the regions.[39]   The N.L.M. was dissatisfied that the proposals fell short of the local autonomy which it wished and refused to participate in the Achimota Conference held in February and March, 1956, to consider the Bourne Report.[40]

The answer to the Bourne Report was embodied in the White Paper of April 19, 1956, in which the Gold Coast Government formally advanced its proposal for independence and for admission as a member of the Commonwealth.   The White Paper stipulated that the name of the country be changed to Ghana, that a Governor-General be retained, that the legislature—elected for a life of five years—have supreme powers, that appeals to the Judical Committee of the Privy Council continue, and went on to concede a devolution of powers to six regions with some protection for the position and privileges of the chiefs.[41]   This was far from enough for the N.L.M., which contended that while there was no quarrel over independence, the question of the constitution must be settled before and not after the attainment of independence.

In commenting upon the White Paper in the House of Commons, Mr. Lennox-Boyd, the Colonial Secretary, emphasized the desire of Her Majesty's Government that the Gold Coast receive its independence within the Commonwealth at the earliest moment.   The constitutional dispute, however, was referred to the Gold Coasters themselves.   Mr. Lennox-Boyd here said:

I have made my view clear to him (Nkrumah) that because of the failure to resolve the constitutional dispute we can only achieve our common aim of the early independence of that country within the Commonwealth in one way and in one way alone; that is, to demonstrate to the world that the peoples of the Gold Coast have had a full and free opportunity to consider their Constitution and to express their views on it in a general election.

[39] *The Times*, December 24 and 28, 1955.
[40] *Ibid.*, Jan. 23, 1956 and March 8, 1956. The controversy over the Achimota Conference can best be followed in the *Daily Graphic* (Accra), Jan. 2-March 21, 1956.
[41] *A Monthly Survey of Commonwealth and Colonial Affairs*, no. 37 (May, 1956); the *Daily Graphic*, April 20, 1956.

I have told Dr. Nkrumah that if a General Election is held, Her Majesty's Government will be ready to accept a motion calling for independence within the Commonwealth passed by a reasonable majority in a newly-elected Legislature and then to declare a firm date for this purpose.[42]

About the same time that the Colonial Secretary was making this commitment at Westminister a plebiscite in British Togoland, a trust territory, declared for integration with the Gold Coast by a vote of 92,775 to 66,529.[43] This preference, however, remained to be approved by the United Nations. Independence and an enlarged country were now clearly in view.

The election for a new legislature was held in the Gold Coast on July 12 and 17. Bitterly contested and observed by six members of the British Parliament, it happily passed off without a major clash. The C.P.P. advanced candidates in all of the one hundred four constituencies and was successful in seventy-one. With an over-all majority of thirty-eight, it seemed certain that the "reasonable majority" required by Mr. Lennox-Boyd was in hand. Though victorious the C.P.P. was, nonetheless, sobered by the fact that its strength was down from seventy-nine in the previous legislature and by its inability to do better than twelve out of twenty-one seats in Ashanti. In the popular vote the C.P.P. received 398,000 to 299,000 cast for all of the opposition candidates. Resentment and resistance against a highly unitary constitution were evident.[44]

On August 3 the newly convened Legislative Assembly by a vote of seventy-two to nil—the opposition members refusing to vote on the ground that the constitution should be settled prior to independence—passed a resolution calling for independence and the honoring of the pledges given by the British Government.[45] Nine days later a delegation of the opposition left Accra for London to press for the appointment of a Royal Com-

[42] *Parl. Deb.*, 5th ser., Commons, vol. 552, cols. 1557-58 (May 11, 1956). See editorial in *The Times*, May 12, 1956.

[43] *The Times*, May 12, 1956.

[44] *Ibid.*, July 21, 1956. The *Daily Graphic* gives the final results of the election in its issue of July 20, 1956.

[45] *The Times*, Aug. 4, 1956.

mission and to lay its fears before the Colonial Office. On September 18 the announcement was made, subject to parliamentary approval, that the Gold Coast would be granted self-government on March 6, 1957,[46] the anniversary of the day in 1844 the bond between the British Government and certain chiefs was signed and from which was derived the early jurisdiction and authority of the British Government. The bill to extend this independence was placed before the House of Commons on December 11, 1956. On this occasion the Colonial Secretary expressed his great pleasure and announced his intention of approaching the Commonwealth members in the very near future to secure for Ghana inclusion in that group. Mixed in with the optimistic voices, however, were those that feared the unresolved constitutional issues would result in bloodshed in the country. No one could have doubted, and several remarked upon, the speed with which the African nation had progressed from representative to responsible government.

We have now come full turn. The future of Ghana will be watched with the closest interest. In a very real sense the African is on trial and his success or failure will be of consequence to the political prospects of black Africa. Success is in a degree jeopardized by several factors in the political circumstances of the new Commonwealth member. These must be briefly noted.

In the first place the speed with which the country passed through the phases of its political experience, from 1946 to independence, leaves misgivings with many of its friends. The Gold Coast was pushed along the path to nationhood and may have arrived at self-government without the balance and maturity required for the operation of a democratic political system. Indeed, some see in this inexperience and the strong personality of Nkrumah the danger of dictatorship and have wondered aloud if critical days ahead may not edge Ghana towards the exercise of personal and dictatorial powers by its leader. The constitutional problem has not been solved, and regionalism presses hard against the centralizing tendencies of the government, creating fracture lines along the edges of diverse native cultures.

Questions also have been raised concerning the efficiency of an Africanized civil service. Many of the English have remained in their former posts, but more and more the positions of responsibility will be filled by Africans. Will they be up to maintaining the British level of public service which the country professes to want and which it certainly needs? While educational services are good by African comparisons and one college at least is educating to London standards, there must long be a shortage of trained ability that may become increasingly acute if and as industrial and professional demands compete more keenly with the government. But it is not solely a question of ability. Will the African, accustomed to responsibility for family welfare on a wide basis, be able to resist the use of public funds for private responsibilities? Charges and examples of corruption have not been lacking. Undoubtedly one reason for the decision to request Commonwealth membership is that Ghana will not soon be able to do without the services of the white man and the help that can come from Commonwealth sources.

It is also quite true that the rapid political advance would not have been possible without the underpinning of prosperity. Could the country surmount an economic crisis? Will it be able to push beyond the economic level of a supplier of raw materials? Since the war the Gold Coast has flourished under world demand for cocoa, manganese, gold, and timber. The Government has enjoyed a tremendous financial boon in its ability, through the Cocoa Marketing Board, to keep the internal price paid to the farmer for cocoa much below the world price. The difference has gone into internal improvements and the creation of a surplus of about £100,000,000. Despite this shield any depression in world prices in raw materials would be strongly and adversely felt. At the same time the country is trying to get a second string to its bow by the development, with British and Canadian participation, of the water power of the Volta River and the use of electricity for the smelting of tremendously rich and convenient sources of bauxite and as the power for small industries. The success of this venture would significantly change the economic profile of the country and provide an element of economic welfare and political stability of importance in the effort to secure a viable and successful government. In Accra the African has taken his place on the balance: meanwhile a continent, indeed a world, watches with friendly interest.

6

The Development of Health and Welfare Programs in Australia: A Case Study

B. U. Ratchford

During the past twenty years most nations of the world have greatly increased their expenditures for health and welfare. The effects of this movement extend far beyond the narrow confines of governmental budgets; they have important implications for the constitutional, political, sociological, and economic development of the countries involved. It is the purpose of this paper to trace briefly the development of governmental health and welfare programs in Australia since 1900.

This paper is based on a study of public expenditures which is concerned, among other things, with the effect of the federal form of government on the development of expenditures and the effect of those expenditures upon the balance of fiscal powers and activities between the federal government and the states.

Most of the programs considered here fall into one of two large groups. The first is composed of programs designed to maintain incomes; it includes such measures as old age, invalid and widows' pensions, unemployment benefits, and family allowances (or child endowments). The second group includes measures to provide medical, hospital, pharmaceutical, and other similar benefits. Specialized programs, such as workmen's compensation, veterans' benefits, and farm relief measures are not included. Further, the limitations of this paper make it necessary to omit most details of the different measures.

1. Constitutional Powers

In the beginning, the specific constitutional powers under which the Commonwealth government could enact social security legislation were quite limited indeed. The original Constitution of 1900 only empowered the federal government to pay old age and invalid pensions. In 1912 the Commonwealth went beyond this specific grant of power by establishing a system of maternity benefits and, beginning in 1940, it started several other welfare programs. These expenditures could be justified, if at all, only under the broad and indefinite powers of the Commonwealth to raise money and spend it "for the purposes of the Commonwealth." In 1945 the legislation establishing pharmaceutical benefits was challenged and the High Court held it to be invalid. This action of the Court cast grave doubt upon the validity of all other health and welfare legislation except that pertaining to age and invalid pensions. As a result an amendment to the Constitution was proposed and adopted in 1946 which gave the Commonwealth a broad grant of powers to legislate for health and welfare purposes.[1]

In the Australian federation the legislative powers of the states are residual and state Parliaments can exercise any powers which are not given exclusively to the Commonwealth. Except where it is specifically forbidden (which is not the case with health and welfare matters) the states can legislate concurrently with the Commonwealth on subjects which are within the domain of the federal government so long as the state legislation does not conflict with federal laws. Each state has a constitution, but state Parliaments ". . . have the right to decide the manner of alteration of their constitutions, which are short documents concerned with the form that the parliaments themselves take, and not with the sort of legislation which the parliaments shall pass."[2] In the British tradition, this means that in most cases an act of the Parliament would take precedence over any

---

[1] Par. xxiiiA of Sec. 51 of the Constitution. For further details see below, pp. 158-159.

[2] Miller, J. D. B., *Australian Government and Politics* (London, 1952), 81.

conflicting provision of the Constitution. Further, with minor exceptions, the Australian Federal Constitution contains nothing corresponding to the Bill of Rights in the American Constitution, so there is little chance that any state legislation would be held invalid on procedural grounds. In summary, these provisions taken together seem to mean that the states have full power to legislate on health and welfare questions so long as that legislation does not conflict with federal legislation.

2. *The First Period: 1900-1912*

Before federation in 1900 the Australian colonies had been active in social legislation and had earned for Australia the title of "social laboratory of the world." They had enacted shop and factory acts, minimum wage laws, antisweating legislation, had set up wage boards, and adopted compulsory arbitration.[3] Then in 1900 and 1901 New South Wales and Victoria adopted old age pensions. This was the setting and the explanation for the old age and invalid pension provision in the Federal Constitution. The Commonwealth, after the lapse of a few years, used this grant of power and legislated for old age pensions in 1908 and for invalid pensions in 1909. In 1912 it went further and, without specific constitutional power, established a system of maternity benefits. The Commonwealth was able to do these things, however, only after it had freed itself of a provision requiring it to pay to the states three-fourths of all receipts from customs and excises as well as all surpluses. In the meantime, the Commonwealth Statistician, while on a trip to Europe, had studied the various social insurance schemes there and, in 1910, suggested the creation of a compulsory state social insurance plan in Australia. In the 1910 election—and again in the 1913 election—the Liberal party proposed a comprehensive plan of social insurance to be financed on a contributory basis and to cover sickness, accidents, unemployment, widowhood, and maternity but no action resulted.

[3] Mendelsohn, Ronald, *Social Security in the British Commonwealth* (London, 1954), 113.

What accounted for the widespread interest and energetic action in the welfare field at this early date? Undoubtedly one reason was the existence of a strong and aggressive Labor party. After the disastrous strike of the early 1890's, labor turned to political means to achieve its ends and organized the Labor party. In most of the years since that time, that party has been a major force in Australian politics. Birch thinks that a more fundamental reason was the absence of "an expanding frontier." True, there was much land to the west, "but it was nearly all desert" and did not afford "individual opportunities" to migrate, as in Canada and the United States, and so led to the development of different social and political attitudes.[4]

3. The Barren Period: 1912-1941

Up until 1914 Australia could reasonably be looked upon as a social pioneer. Thereafter social disturbances, and a widespread complacency caused an extraordinary barren period for nearly thirty years.

The best feature of the long pause in social development was the progress made in such matters as child welfare, provision of infant and maternal services, and the beginning of the school medical and school meals services. Here Australia probably kept abreast of other countries, but made little distinctive contribution.[5]

While there was some activity among the states, at the federal level there was, during this period, not a single positive achievement of major importance. There was much study, debate, and negotiating—at times even violent disagreements—but no action.

Among the states, Queensland established a system of unemployment insurance in 1923. New South Wales started paying widows' pensions in 1926 and family allowances in 1927. During the depression of the 1930's all states assisted to some extent with relief activities and finance. These and the programs noted above were the major state activities.

a. Proposals for Social Insurance

At the federal level a royal commission recommended a

[4] Birch, A. H., *Federalism, Finance and Social Legislation* (London, 1955), 205.
[5] Mendelsohn, *op. cit.*, 132.

system of family allowances in 1919 to supplement low incomes and alleviate the pressure for higher wages, but no action resulted. In 1924 a royal commission was appointed to study the whole field of social security. Over the next five years it submitted several reports dealing with different aspects of the problem. In general its recommendations were for a system of *insurance* to be financed on a contributory basis and with benefits limited to insured members and their dependents. During these years the Commonwealth and the states negotiated at length over the problem of how to divide the responsibility for financing and administering any scheme that might be adopted. The states contended that they were not able to assume the main burden of financing, but they wanted to have a substantial role in the administration. To a considerable extent this latter was logical, if not necessary, because of the states' extensive powers in the fields of arbitration, labor exchange, and control of basic wages. On the other hand, the Commonwealth was reluctant to acknowledge its primary responsibility in this field and to assume the basic financial burden but at the same time pointed to the obvious need for a high degree of uniformity throughout the country in regulations, administrative practices, and benefits. On the political front, the Labor party was strongly opposed to any contributory plan, while other political groups favored that principle.

Generally the 1920's was a period of prosperity; and, while there was a demand for more social security benefits, it was not sufficiently urgent to force action in the face of the constitutional and political obstacles. Also, the Labor party was weakened by the deep split which developed over conscription during the First World War; this split undoubtedly was partly responsible for keeping the party out of power until late in 1929. The reports of the royal commission were debated in Parliament in 1928 and a bill to set up a contributory system advanced as far as the second reading, but stopped there.

The Labor party returned to power in October, 1929, and

no doubt would have pressed strongly for action on social security matters had not all of its energies been required to cope with the financial storms of the depression. It remained in power a little more than two years and was on the defensive the whole time. On all of its major programs it was almost completely frustrated.

Circumstances forced it to take drastic measures which helped to stabilize the situation, but it did not remain in power long enough to reap the rewards and the credit went to the opposition ministry which supplanted it in January, 1932. This period of frustration accentuated differences within the Labor party and further divided and weakened the party when certain of the leaders went over to the Opposition.

b. The Depression

The depression caught Australia with no system of poor relief, no unemployment insurance, and no plan for dealing with the gigantic economic and financial problems presented by the depression. The depression hit Australia early and hard. The primary burden of caring for unemployment fell upon the states. Commonwealth aid was erratic and unplanned and was mainly in the form of loans to the states. The Commonwealth acknowledged no responsibility until the latter part of 1934 and then only indirectly.[6] The states depended heavily upon food relief and work relief to care for the unemployed. No accurate statistics on the cost of unemployment relief in Australia during this period are available. One estimate is that from 1930 through 1937-38 the total was over £111,000,000.[7]

c. More Proposals for Social Insurance

When the worst of the depression was over attention again turned toward the establishment of a comprehensive system of social security. The demand for action was now strengthened by the experience during the depression and by the great feeling of insecurity which had spread around the world. But there were

[6] McLaurin, W. R., Economic Planning in Australia, 1929-1936 (London, 1937), 181.
[7] Unpublished manuscript by A. G. Colley.

still the same differences and disagreements over constitutional and political problems as before 1930—and the Labor party was again in the opposition. In 1937 there were two comprehensive reports by British experts—one on unemployment insurance and one on health and pensions insurance. On the basis of the latter report Parliament, in 1938, enacted the National Health and Pensions Insurance Act.[8]

This was a *compulsory, contributory* plan to cover most *employed* persons earning up to £7 per week. Neither the self-employed nor most government employees were to be covered. The plan offered limited medical and pharmaceutical benefits, sickness and disability payments, and pensions for widows, orphans, and the aged; it did not include unemployment insurance or family allowances. Benefits were to be related to contributions, with no means test. The plan was to be financed on a strict actuarial basis. Employees and employers were to make equal payments up to 1s. 6d. per week and the remainder was to be provided by annual Commonwealth grants estimated to reach £10,000,000 eventually.

It was estimated that the number of contributors would be 1,850,000 and that benefits would be provided to about 3,500,000, or over half of the population of the country at that time. Benefits were limited to contributors except for widows' and orphans' pensions and limited payments on account of dependent children. The Commonwealth Government, however, announced its intention of providing financial assistance toward medical benefits for dependents of insured persons and toward a supplementary scheme for the self-employed.[9]

A commission was appointed to administer the Act, a considerable part of the administrative machinery was set up, and preliminary instructions and regulations were issued. Difficulties developed, however, which made it necessary, first to postpone

[8] Act no. 25 of 1938.
[9] National Insurance Commission, *National Insurance: A Summary of the Principles of the Australian National Health and Pensions Insurance Act 1938* (Canberra, 1938), 1.

the effective date of the Act, and ultimately to abandon it entirely. The medical profession strongly opposed the arrangements for medical benefits. Labor opposed the plan because it was contributory and was too limited in scope. The farmers were indifferent to it because it did not include them. Then, in the spring of 1939, the Prime Minister died and was succeeded by the former Attorney-General, Mr. Menzies, who had opposed the plan all along, saying that it violated commitments he had made to his constituents. About this time, too, Mr. R. G. Casey, Commonwealth Treasurer, who had introduced the bill and led the fight for it, was appointed Minister to the United States and left the country. And, finally, the Second World War broke upon the world, and it was not considered possible to proceed with the plan. Thus it happened that Australia entered upon a second great war with little more social security than it had when it embarked upon the first great conflict twenty-five years earlier. The way in which the National Insurance Act was managed was symptomatic of the troubles within the United Australia-Country party coalition which had been in power since early 1932. The loss of the Prime Minister weakened the coalition, there was dissension among the members, and there was popular dissatisfaction with the way in which the war was being managed. It was inevitable that this should redound to the advantage of the Labor party—the official Opposition and the only other major party. Mr. Menzies reshuffled his cabinet several times and invited the Labor party to enter the coalition and form a National Government, but the invitation was declined. After that the days of the coalition government were numbered.

In the fiscal year 1939 the Commonwealth spent £16.5 million for health and welfare, of which £16.0 million was for age and invalid pensions and £0.4 million was for maternity benefits. The states spent £14.6 million, mostly for hospitals and, in New South Wales, for widows' pensions and family allowances. Local governments spent only £1.2 million. The total for all governments was £32.2 million, which was 15.3 per cent of all public expenditures and about 3.5 per cent of the gross national product. Ten years earlier, in 1929, the total had been £21.5 million, which was 11.6 per cent of all public expenditures and 2.4 per cent of gross national product.

A great many factors, combined in different proportions at different times, were responsible for this long period of inaction on social security in Australia. They include: (1) the constitutional division of powers between the Commonwealth and the states; (2) a strong and lasting difference of opinions between the Commonwealth and the states concerning their respective duties and responsibilities for financing and administering social security measures under that division of powers; (3) the insistence of the U. A.—Country party group on the contributory principle and the opposition of the Labor party to that principle; (4) the deep split in the Labor party arising out of the First World War; and (5) the depression of the 1930's.

4. Building the Welfare State, 1941-1955

a. Family Allowances

In 1940-41 the Menzies Government lost strength and failed to draw Labor into a coalition. Early in 1941, in an effort to bolster his political strength and to woo Labor support, Menzies introduced a bill to provide a system of family allowances (child endowment). Political expediency was undoubtedly the principal reason for the introduction of the measure at that particular time, but there was a widespread demand for a program of this kind, and it would have been adopted sooner or later in any case. Other reasons which have been given for its introduction during the war are: (1) the need to alleviate the pressure for wage increases and (2) the importance of the plan as an element in the postwar reconstruction program.

The plan was universal with no means test, was noncontributory, and was financed from general revenues. It provided an allowance of 5s. per week for each child in a family after the first one.[10]   The bill was quickly passed, apparently with no debate on its constitutionality, and became effective on July 1, 1941. In its first year payments were made for the account of over 900,000 children in nearly 500,000 families at a cost of £11.3 million.

Another significant development at this time was the appointment of the parliamentary joint committee on social security. This committee was continued by the Labor party and had great influence on later developments.

Menzies' struggle to retain power was unsuccessful, and in October, 1941, a Labor Government took over. Remembering its long period in the opposition and the frustrations of 1929-32, the party now determined that it would not let the opportunity slip through its fingers this time. Taking advantage of its wide war powers and the accumulated demand for more security, it started at once to build a comprehensive system of social security. In May, 1942, it instituted a scheme of widows' pensions; it was noncontributory but included a means test. It has never been a major program, it has never covered more than 45,000 persons, and its cost rose from £2.6 million at the beginning to over £8 million now.

b. Constitutional Reform Proposals

The Labor party's most ambitious undertaking was a proposal to effect a sweeping change in the Australian Constitution. This was first announced in 1942 as the basis for a program of postwar reconstruction and would have given the Commonwealth broad and indefinite powers to legislate in fourteen major areas covering the financial, industrial, agricultural, and social segments of the economy. The areas covered were: postwar rehabilitation, em-

---

[10] Originally the basic wage was supposed to cover "about three" children in addition to man and wife. In a vague and uncertain way this was reduced to two, then to one, and now, apparently to a half, since family allowances have been extended to cover the first child although at only half rate. The 1941 Act abolished income-tax allowances for the second and later children, ". . . so that persons earning high income were worse off after the Act than before—a very substantial concession to have been made by a right-wing party." Birch, *op. cit.*, 225. Later, however, income-tax allowances for children were restored.

ployment and unemployment, marketing, company law, trusts and monopolies, price control, the production and distribution of goods, foreign exchange and investment, air transport, uniformity of railroad gauges, public works, health, family allowances, and aborigines. The powers to be granted here were to have precedence over other parts of the Constitution with which they might conflict and were to be exempt from court review. A constitutional convention was called to consider these proposals but it was composed of Commonwealth and state officials and legislators rather than delegates elected by the people for the purpose of considering proposals for constitutional reform.

The initial proposals aroused widespread opposition and fears because they came at a time of great national crisis and because the party in power was apparently asking for a blank check. When the convention met, the proposals were toned down; the powers were to be limited to five years after the war and the provision exempting them from court review was eliminated. Nevertheless, the convention refused to approve them as constitutional amendments but instead voted to have the states "refer" these powers to the Commonwealth by individual actions. Several of the states refused to take such action and the plan failed.

The Commonwealth Government then determined to proceed with a vote on the amendments. The timing and the tactics of the campaign were poorly planned. The decision came in the midst of a great war, the Government had not explained what it planned to do with the powers it was requesting, no convention of elected representatives had considered the proposals, and the original proposal for exemption from court review had aroused many suspicions. Further, by 1944, when the vote came, some of the sense of urgency had passed and many people were beginning to chafe under wartime restrictions and controls. Finally, the fourteen amendments had to be voted upon as a unit. In August, 1944, the proposals were defeated by a vote of 2,305,418 to

1,963,400; only two states—South Australia and Western Australia—returned a majority in favor of them.[11]

c. Other Benefits

In the meantime the Labor Government was not waiting upon additional constitutional powers. In 1943 it established a system of funeral benefits for pensioners. The benefit, with no means test, was £10 for each deceased pensioner and has not been changed since the beginning. The present annual cost is about £300,000.

In March, 1944, two acts were passed establishing unemployment, sickness, and pharmaceutical benefits. The unemployment act, Australia's first, was a noncontributory plan financed out of general revenues and carried a means test only as to income. It provided payments for unlimited periods to unemployed and sick persons. Rates varied with age and marital status, reaching 25s. per week for an unmarried adult and, for a married person, 35s. plus 5s. per child not covered by family allowances. The rates remained unchanged until 1953, when they were doubled. This act also contained a provision for "special benefits," at equal rates, to any person who was not eligible for unemployment, sickness or other benefits and who was unable "by reason of age, physical or mental disability or domestic circumstances, or for any other reason," to earn a sufficient livelihood for himself and his dependents. The Pharmaceutical Benefits Act was designed to cover the cost of all drugs bought on doctor's prescriptions. It was universal in application, with no means test and was financed from general funds. It was to operate by reimbursing chemists for the prescriptions they compounded. In order to assure orderly administration and prevent abuse, it was necessary to prescribe forms and procedures and to establish penalties for fraud and improper practices. The Act aroused the violent opposition of the medical profession and an overwhelming majority of the doctors refused to co-operate in administering it.

[11] For an excellent account of this matter, see Gordon Greenwood, *The Future of Australian Federalism* (Melbourne, 1946), 253 ff.

In 1945 two more major welfare programs were established; the Hospital Benefits Act and the Tuberculosis Act. The Hospital Benefits Act established Commonwealth grants which were to be paid to public hospitals (operated by the states) on condition that they would abolish all charges for treatment in public wards and admit all persons to such wards without a means test. Commonwealth payments of 6s. per day (later raised to 8s.)were made on account of patients in private hospitals or the private wards of public hospitals. Arrangements were also provided for covering hospital deficits in case these payments were not sufficient. This program was to undergo extensive changes in later years, as noted below.

The purpose of the Tuberculosis Act was to wage an intensive campaign against this one disease. After extensive changes in 1948, the program emerged with two main purposes: (1) to provide free treatment for all TB patients and (2) to provide liberal allowances in addition to normal sickness benefits so that the patients would give up work, remain isolated from their families when necessary, and undergo treatment for the full time required. Adequate facilities for treatment were assured when the Commonwealth agreed to reimburse the states for all approved capital expenditures for this purpose after June 30, 1948, and also to assume all approved maintenance expenditures for this same purpose in excess of those of the base year, which was 1947-48. The allowance has purposely been made liberal as a public health measure and not for welfare reasons. It has been raised several times and stood at £9 2s. 6d. per week in 1955; it carries a means test as to income.

d. Status at the End of the War.

During the seven years of the war period 1938-39 to 1945-46 —Australia had gone a long way toward building a comprehensive social security system. She had installed five major programs— family allowances, unemployment and sickness benefits, TB benefits, hospital benefits, and pharmaceutical benefits—and two minor programs—widows' pensions and funeral benefits for pensioners.

Commonwealth expenditures had more than tripled, rising from £16.5 millioñ to £53.8 million, while state expenditures had dropped slightly from £14.5 million to £12.3 million. The total had risen from £32.2 million to £67.4 million, which was 12.0 per cent of total public expenditures and about 4.5 per cent of GNP, contrasted with 15.3 per cent and 3.5 per cent, respectively, before the war.

e. Pharmaceutical Benefits and a Constitutional Amendment

The Pharmaceutical Benefits Act aroused strong opposition, and in 1945 the Attorney-General of Victoria brought suit to test its constitutionality. The High Court heard the case and handed down a momentous decision which held the Act unconstitutional.[12] With respect to the spending or appropriating power alone, the Chief Justice held that the constitutional power given to Parliament to appropriate "for the purposes of the Commonwealth" is

a general and not a limited power of appropriation of public moneys. It is general in the sense that it is for the Parliament to determine whether or not a particular purpose shall be adopted as a purpose of the Commonwealth.

. . . [Further], it is the Commonwealth Parliament, and not any court, which is entrusted with the power, duty and responsibility of determining what purposes shall be Commonwealth purposes.[13]

But that was power over expenditures *alone*.

It does not follow that the Commonwealth Parliament, because it can, as it were, subscribe towards the support of what it considers to be worthy objects, can take legislative control of matters relating to any such objects in respect of which there is no other grant of legislative power. A company may have the power to subscribe to a hospital or a football club without having power to conduct a hospital or to organize and control a football club.

. . . [The Act under consideration] is far more than an appropriation act; it is just the kind of statute which might well be passed by a parliament which had full power to make such laws as it thought proper with

---

[12] *Attorney-General for Victoria v. The Commonwealth*, 71 C. L. R. 237 (1945).
[13] *Ibid.*, at 254, 265.

respect to public health, doctors, chemists, hospitals, drugs, medicines and medicinal and surgical appliances.[14]

This language cast serious doubt on the constitutional power of the Commonwealth to operate all the other welfare programs except age and invalid pensions. The Labor Government immediately proposed an amendment to the Constitution which would give the Commonwealth Parliament power to make laws for

The provision of maternity allowances, widows' pensions, child endowment, unemployment, pharmaceutical, sickness and hospital benefits, medical and dental services (but not so as to authorize any form of civil conscription), benefits to students and family allowances.

The amendment was approved in the general election of 1946, receiving a majority in all states and a majority of 54.4 per cent of all votes cast. At the same time two other amendments, giving Parliament power over marketing and industrial employment, were rejected. Parliament soon afterward enacted another Pharmaceutical Benefits Act requiring that all prescriptions should be on prescribed forms. An overwhelming majority of the doctors refused to co-operate and brought suit, claiming that the new act constituted a form of civil conscription. The High Court, one justice disagreeing, held that the requirement was a form of conscription and ruled the Act invalid.[15] Before there could be more legislation there was a change of governments.

f. Labor's Postwar Program

In the postwar period Labor's main efforts were directed to-

---

[14] *Ibid.*, at 256-257, 263. There is an interesting contrast between the position of the High Court with respect to expenditures "for the purpose of the Commonwealth" and the position of the Supreme Court of the United States and expenditures for the "general Welfare of the United States." In 1936 the Supreme Court construed the general welfare clause in such a way as to invalidate the Agricultural Adjustment Act, which embodied one of the major New Deal programs. But in 1937 it altered its position somewhat and construed the clause in such a way as to sustain the Social Security law which established our unemployment insurance and old age insurance programs. See my article, "Some Constitutional Aspects of Federal Expenditures," *Journal of Finance*, X (1955), 466-470.

[15] *British Medical Association v. The Commonwealth*, 79 C. L. R. 201 (1949).

ward providing for Australia a comprehensive system of pharmaceutical, hospital, medical, and dental benefits much like those
being provided in England. These plans were embodied in the
National Health Service Act of 1948,[16] which authorized the
Commonwealth to do the following:

(1) Make grants to medical schools to finance education and
research;

(2) Make grants to the states to finance hospital construction,
equipment and maintenance;

(3) With the consent of state governments, to take over
hospitals and other state medical facilities and services;

(4) Provide or arrange for the provision of medical and
dental services and establish and maintain hospitals,
laboratories, health centers, and clinics;

(5) Arrange for or undertake the provision of medical and
dental supplies, appliances and equipment;

(6) Establish a scheme of medical benefits.

These plans were almost entirely frustrated by the difficulties
with pharmaceutical benefits noted above, by an acute shortage
of hospital facilities, and by the determined opposition of the
medical profession to Labor's plans for medical benefits. Before
any major parts of the 1948 Act could be implemented, Labor
was defeated in the 1949 election. The Liberal-Country party
coalition which took over in 1949 has attempted to provide benefits in most of the areas noted above, but at a slower pace and by
considerably different methods.

g. The Liberal Program since 1949

Under the Liberal party since 1949 the various social service
(income-protecting) programs such as pensions, allowances, unemployment and sickness benefits, have been continued and enlarged without any significant change. In fact, in partisan
political debate, the Liberal party claims that it has been far more
liberal in these matters than was the Labor party. To a very
considerable extent this was made necessary by the sharp inflation

---

[16] Act no. 81, 1948.

which started in 1948. Whatever the reasons, however, there can be no doubt that the Liberal party has been active in increasing pensions and in liberalizing the conditions of eligibility. As one high official put it, "The politicians make capital of these benefits and the Liberal party has not been far behind the Labor party in using them as vote catchers."

In the area of pharmaceutical, medical, and hospital benefits, the Liberal party has initiated several programs which the Labor party was unable to get started, but its approach has been quite different. Generally these features have characterized the Liberal programs: (1) The pace has been slower and more gradual; the programs have been limited rather than universal in application, adapted to the limited funds and facilities available. (2) The contributory principle and the co-insurance principle have been employed wherever feasible. With medical and hospital benefits, this has been done by encouraging or requiring membership in voluntary insurance organizations as a condition of eligibility for benefits. The requirement prohibiting charges for treatment at the public ward level was eliminated. (3) Strong efforts were made to gain the confidence and co-operation of the medical profession. Attempts to set a compulsory scale of fees were abandoned. Sir Earle Page, a prominent political leader who is himself a physician, was appointed Minister of Health and worked diligently to enlist support for his programs within his profession.

Four major programs in this area have been revised or initiated since 1949. In 1950 the Pharmaceutical Benefits Act was extensively revised. I n 1951 the Hospital Benefits Act was radically changed. Also in 1951 a new program was initiated to provide medical and pharmaceutical benefits for pensioners and their dependents. Finally, in 1953, the Medical Benefits Act was implemented after extensive changes. Brief descriptions of these acts are given in a later section. All of these acts were consolidated into the National Health Act of 1953.[17]

[17] Act no. 95, 1953.

In addition to these four major programs in the health field, the Liberal Government has enlarged and broadened the social services significantly. In 1950 the family allowance scheme was revised to make the first child in a family eligible for benefits at 5s. per week—one half the normal rate. In the same year a plan was initiated to provide free milk for school children—one-third of a pint per child per day. In 1952 unemployment and sickness benefits were doubled, raising the amount for a married adult to £4 10s. per week. In addition, there were increases every year except 1954 in the rate of pensions for the aged, invalid, blind, and widows. For the first three the rate was raised from £2 10s. in 1950 to £4 in 1955. The conditions of eligibility for pensions were steadily relaxed, at least in part because of rising prices. At the same time the "perquisites" of the pensioners were increased; these took the form of increased allowances for dependents, free medical and pharmaceutical services, and hospital benefits. Despite sharply rising prices, there were no changes in the rates for funeral benefits, maternity benefits, and family allowances; this meant that in real terms these benefits lost about two-fifths of their value during this period.

5. State Programs

The above discussion has been concerned almost exclusively with Commonwealth activities. Before the Second World War the states (together with their semi-autonomous authorities) were spending almost as much for health and welfare as was the Commonwealth (expenditures by local authorities were insignificant). In the past twenty years Commonwealth expenditures have forged far ahead. Nevertheless, and despite the fact that in several cases Commonwealth programs took over activities which some of the states had started and developed, the states have maintained and increased their expenditures in this field. From a level of about £15 million in 1939, state expenditures dropped below £10 million during the war. Thereafter they increased steadily and rapidly and reached a level of nearly £70 million in 1955.[18]

The construction and operation of hospitals make up by far the largest item in the states' expenditures. In recent years outlays for hospital construction alone have been running at about £15 million per year. Other state services which are important include: child and maternal services, relief for the unemployables, and medical and dental services in the schools.

6. Financial Aspects

Table A shows, in summary form, how the costs of these activities have developed and indicates the relative financial importance of the different programs. It shows also the rapid growth of the health and medical services in the postwar period, particularly since 1949. The last two lines of the table show the increasing importance of the costs of these programs in relation to the total of public expenditures and to GNP.

In terms of cost, age and invalid pensions and family allowances dominate the field. They account for over two-thirds of all Commonwealth expenditures in this field and for more than half of total expenditures for health and welfare. However, the four major health programs are growing steadily and rapidly and will undoubtedly account for a larger share of the costs in the future.

Despite the strong preference of the Liberal party for the contributory principle, the Australian system is essentially non-contributory. In 1943 the National Welfare Fund was set up and special taxes were levied to finance the various welfare programs, but the taxes were essentially income taxes, the only distinguishing feature being that they dipped a little further into the low incomes. In 1950 the Liberal Government consolidated these taxes into the regular income taxes. The Fund is still maintained in form but it has no real significance. For the individual, no file is opened and no record kept until he applies for a benefit. This

---

[18] These figures on expenditures are from a special compilation made by the Commonwealth Bureau of Census and Statistics.

avoids the great expense and trouble of keeping records for individuals; but, except for maternity benefits and family allowances which are universal, it requires the application of a complicated means test. It means also that the amount of the benefits depends upon the status of the individual rather than upon previous income or contributions.

In the hospital and medical programs a limited application of the contributory and co-insurance principles has been obtained in two ways. First, contributions have been encouraged or required by limiting part or all of the benefits to those who carry insurance. Second, an effort is made to see that insurance payments and government benefits do not cover all the costs but leave some part to be paid by the individual. In the pharmaceutical program a crude form of co-insurance is obtained by limiting the benefits to the costs of the more expensive drugs.

7. Some Results

Age and invalid pensions constitute by far the largest program in this field. The number of pensioners rose from 315,782 in 1944-45 to 510,186 in 1954-55—an increase of 58 per cent. In the same period the cost quadrupled, rising from £21.7 million to £88.0 million. The proportion of pensioners to total population rose from 2 per cent in 1925 to 5.6 per cent in 1955. The proportion of age pensioners (excluding invalid) to those of pensionable age rose from 32.5 per cent in 1938 to 41.1 per cent in 1953, partly because of the transfer of some invalid pensioners to this category but mainly because of the liberalization of the means test. In 1953 the Director-General of Social Services noted that

many people who had not applied for a small reduced pension have decided to do so because of the supplementary services now offered to pensioners; e.g., the free medical and pharmaceutical services provided for pensioners by the Commonwealth and the concessions, such as transport concessions, provided by some state governments.[19]

[19] *Twelfth Report of the Director-General of Social Services,* (1955), 9.

Family allowances, or child endowment, comprise the second largest program in this field. From 1944-45 to 1954-55 the number of endowed children rose by 200 per cent—from 920,427, or 12.5 per cent of total population, to 2,764,167, or 30.4 per cent of the population. The great increase was caused by the admission of the first child in 1950, by the increase in the birth rate, and by heavy immigration. In 1953 it was estimated that payments were being made for the account of 99 per cent of all children in Australia.

TABLE A

THE DEVELOPMENT OF HEALTH AND WELFARE COSTS IN AUSTRALIA
(£ MILLIONS)

	1938-39	1945-46	1949-50	1954-55
Social Security Programs				
1. Age and Invalid Pensions	16.0	27.0	44.6	88.0
2. Family Allowances	....	18.0	30.3	52.5
3. Maternity Allowances	0.4	2.5	3.0	3.4
4. Widows' Pensions	....	3.2	4.4	6.9
5. Funeral Benefits for Pensioners	....	0.2	0.2	0.3
6. Unemployment and Sickness Benefits	....	1.1	2.5	2.6
7. Community Rehabilitation	....	....	0.2	0.5
Total Social Security	16.4	52.0	85.3	154.2
Health and Medical Services				
1. Hospital Benefits	....	1.1	6.3	9.3
2. TB Benefits	....	....	0.5	5.7
3. Pharmaceutical Benefits	....	....	0.3	9.4
4. Medical Benefits	....	....	....	4.2
5. Medical and Pharmaceutical Benefits for Pensioners	....	....	....	3.8
6. Milk for School Children	....	....	....	2.2
7. Benefits for Mental Institutions	....	....	0.3	0.2
8. Miscellaneous	....	....	0.1	0.3
Total Health and Medical	....	1.1	7.5	35.2
Other Commonwealth Expenditures	0.1	0.7	2.6	5.0
Total Commonwealth Expenditures	16.5	53.8	95.4	194.4
State and Local Expenditures	15.7	13.6	32.3	73.2
Total—All Governments	32.2	67.4	127.7	267.6
Total in £s 1954-55	82.6	139.0	201.7	267.6
Per Cent of All Public Expenditures	15.3	12.0	19.1	21.1
Per Cent of GNP	3.5	4.5	4.7	5.5

Other pensions and social service programs are of minor importance, both as to costs and as to numbers affected. Almost unbroken full employment has kept unemployment benefits down to insignificant proportions except in one or two years. From 11,904 beneficiaries in 1951, the number rose to 175,375 (and a cost of £4.5 million) in 1953 but fell to 24,300 (and a cost of £0.7 million) in 1955.

The number of people to whom, or on account of whom, pensions and allowances were paid in 1955 were as follows:

Age and invalid pensions	510,186
Wives of invalid pensioners	19,947
Funeral benefits	33,368
Widows' pensions	41,561
Maternity benefits	208,179
Family allowances	2,764,167
Unemployment and sickness benefits	85,614
Total	3,663,022

The number of recipients was approximately 40 per cent of the total population. If to this are added those receiving war and military pensions (over 600,000) and other miscellaneous benefits, it would appear that the total number of people receiving cash benefits from the Commonwealth (excluding recipients of health and medical services and benefits) approached one half of the population. There is some duplication between several of the categories but it would not seem to be large enough to affect the general conclusion.

The health and medical programs are in earlier stages of development and are beset by more complex and difficult problems of administration. The Hospital Benefits program, in particular, followed a very troublesome course. The policy of the Labor Government, in essence, was to make hospital care, at the public ward level, free to all with no means test. The charges were abolished at a time when there was an acute shortage of hospital facilities. The drastic change in the plan of financing and rapidly rising inflation created chaos in hospital finances. The Liberal

Government turned toward a plan of prepaid hospital insurance and, in 1952, allowed the states to restore charges for hospital services. Voluntary hospital insurance was encouraged by an extra Commonwealth benefit of 4s. per day for insured patients in addition to the basic payment of 8s. for all patients. From 1952 to 1955 the number of people covered by insurance doubled, rising to 5,121,277, or 56 per cent of the total population. While hospitals receive a very large majority of their revenues from governmental sources, the amount of nongovernmental revenues doubled between 1950 and 1955. There are 129 approved insurance organizations which offer policies with varying benefits. In 1954-55 the Commonwealth paid £9.3 million in hospital benefits while insurance funds were paying £4.1 million—a total of £13.4 million. State governments, however, still carry the main burden of hospital costs and in 1955 probably spent more than three times the above amount for hospital operations.

Medical benefits are administered entirely through approved insurance organizations, of which there were eighteen in 1955. An individual must carry insurance in order to participate in the Commonwealth benefits. The insurance may provide benefits on a fee-for-service or on a group-contract basis. The Commonwealth pays a prescribed amount for each medical service received by an insured patient provided the insurance organization pays at least a similar amount. In 1945-55 total costs of medical services to insured patients were paid roughly one third by the Commonwealth, one third by the insurance funds, and one third by individual patients. The present scheme was started in 1953 and expanded rapidly; by 1955, 4,154,103 people were covered, or about 45 per cent of the total population, and they received a total of 9,226,396 medical services.

Since it was instituted on the present basis in 1950, the Pharmaceutical Benefits program has grown steadily and rapidly. It covers the cost of a prescribed list (about 250 in 1955) of lifesaving and disease-preventing drugs. These drugs are available without cost or a means test to all who require them. From

1951-52, the first full year of operation, to 1954-55, the number of prescriptions rose from 6,518,283 to 9,268,369 and the cost from £6.7 million to £9.4 million. That means that on the average there was about one prescription during the year for every person in the country at a cost of about one pound each.

Two major problems have arisen in the administration of this program. The first is a tendency on the part of doctors to overuse these so-called miracle drugs; the second is collusion between certain doctors and chemists to defraud the government. Attempts have been made to curb overuse by regulations which: (1) limit the use of certain drugs to the treatment of certain diseases; (2) limit the frequency of prescriptions for an individual item; and (3) set a maximum quantity for each prescription. Heavy reliance for the control of collusion has been placed on the professional organizations of the doctors and chemists, but there have been several public prosecutions which have attracted widespread publicity.

The Tuberculosis Benefits program has been a most successful one. It has been aided by extensive publicity, mass x-ray clinics, and a compulsory notification requirement. Four states have laws requiring compulsory chest examinations for everybody, but the authorities have been reluctant to invoke this power. The number of cases of TB reported rose from 3,884 in 1949 to 4,948 in 1954. The proportion of cases arrested among those receiving allowances rose from 12 per cent in 1951 to 36 per cent in 1954. The death rate from TB fell from 24.3 per 100,000 of population in 1949 to 10.9 in 1953. The administrators of the program are hopeful that they can reduce the incidence of TB in Australia to insignificant proportions.

The medical and pharmaceutical program for pensioners, together with related hospital benefits, affords comprehensive medical and hospital benefits for a fairly large group of people. It provides general medical practitioner services and all prescribed drugs for all who receive age, invalid, widows' or service pensions or a TB allowance and for all their dependent wives and children. Pensioners and their dependents must enroll to be eligible. Doctors who wish to participate enroll and receive a set fee for each service. The Commonwealth pays the entire cost of the program. About 97 per cent of pensioners and dependents and over 80 per cent of the doctors have enrolled. A few summary figures will indicate how the program has developed:

	1951-52	1952-53	1953-54	1954-55
Number of Pensioners and Dependents Enrolled (000)..................	468.0	535.2	575.8	620.1
Total No. Services (000)..............	2,334	3,332	4,168	4,721
Average No. Services per Person Enrolled	5.0	6.2	7.2	7.6
No. Prescriptions Written (000)........	1,579	2,662	3,477	4,419
Average No. Prescriptions Per Service...	.67	0.80	0.81	0.93
Cost: Med. Benefits (£000)............	1,035	1,740	2,115	2,516
Phar. Benefits (£000)...........	345	707	1,011	1,295
Total Cost....................	1,380	2,447	3,126	3,811

The number enrolled increased by a third, services per person increased by a half, and total costs almost tripled. In 1955 the number of prescriptions averaged almost one for each service. On the average, each participating doctor rendered about 1,000 services per year, for which he received £552. In this short period there is evidence of a strong upward trend in the use both of medical services and drugs.

In this program, too, there is the problem of the overuse of drugs and an attempt has been made to curb it by regulation. The regulations provide that: (1) not more than two benefits may be included in one prescription; (2) not more than one prescription may be written by a doctor for the same patient on the same day; (3) the quantity of drugs permitted in one prescription and the number of times the prescription may be repeated are limited.

8. Conclusions, Problems, and Issues

In the first decade after the Second World War Australia made great strides in expanding its health and welfare services. From 1945-46 to 1954-55, total costs quadrupled, rising from

£67.4 million to £267.5. They rose from 12.0 per cent of all public expenditures to 21.1 per cent, and from 4.5 per cent of GNP to 5.5 per cent. All of this occurred in a period of high employment and unprecedented prosperity when both monetary and real incomes were far higher than ever before and unemployment was insignificant.

What were the reasons for the great growth of expenditures in these fields? In part this movement was a process of catching up—of adopting measures which had been held up by the political deadlock before the war. In part, also, it was a reflection of the worldwide quest for greater security. Finally, partisan political considerations played an important part in the movement. In the first four years after the war the Labor Government was driving hard to complete its comprehensive system of security. But when the Liberal-Country party coalition took over in 1949 there was no noticeable change in the trend of expenditures despite some changes in principles and methods. In fact, the present Government has tried hard to convince the voters that it has been more active than the Labor Government in expanding benefits, services, and expenditures in these fields.[20]

Now that Australia has the major programs needed for a comprehensive social welfare system, what are the principal issues and problems remaining? The limits of this paper will not permit a discussion of this question but a few of the problems and issues are listed below.

[20] A conservative Government is in a better strategic position than a Labor Government to use pensions and allowances for political advantage. When it proposes, largely for political purposes, a substantial increase in benefits, Labor cannot oppose the increase on its merits since it has a basic commitment in favor of larger benefits. Labor can only claim that the increase comes too late and for political ends, but it dare not vote against it.

Flagrant examples of these tactics were afforded by the Menzies Government in the 1955 election in a series of *National Health Service Information Bulletins* and a brochure entitled "The Achievements of the Menzies Government, 1949-1955." A chart in the latter (p. 11) purported to show that from 1949 to 1954 the amount of age and invalid pensions had been closely adjusted to keep their value constant in terms of retail prices. But then, in 1955, these pensions were increased by 10s. per week to give them an increase in real value of more than 10 per cent. A high governmental official admitted that only a small part of this increase could be justified on welfare grounds and that it had been made mainly for political purposes.

A few years ago Mendelsohn listed the following as the major issues in these fields: (1) the extent of the responsibility of the community to provide income security and the level of benefits the country can afford; (2) how the services are to be financed; (3) the division of administration between states and the Commonwealth; (4) the means test versus universal benefits; (5) the need for and means of achieving a national health service; and (6) humane administration.[21]

The means test, although not as harsh as in England, is increasingly unpopular. All parties help in relaxing it and the principal disagreement is as to how and when it will be removed. But the inevitable result of abolishing the means test would be to make benefits universal. To make old age pensions universal would at least double their cost. Australian benefits are high in relation to income and are closely tied to the movement of prices. To make such benefits universal would entail a great increase in costs and a tremendous commitment for the future. In particular, it would mean a heavy investment in the aged at the expense of the youth of the country. For a young and growing country such as Australia that would have far-reaching implications.

The absence of extremes in wealth and income has often been noted as a feature of the Australian economy. Such a feature imposes strict limits on what can be accomplished in the redistribution of incomes through social security measures. Mendelsohn notes that

demands for extra pensions are regarded by their proponents as attempts to redistribute the national income in favor of the poor; but . . . a considerable proportion of social service expenditures is derived from taxation of lower income groups, and there are severe limits to the process of "soaking the rich."[22]

One major problem posed by the large amount of welfare expenditures is their effect upon savings. Australia has an acute need for investment funds to finance its development programs. It has often been pointed out that the means test for old age

[21] Mendelsohn, *op. cit.*, 155.   [22] *Ibid.*, 159.

pensions operates as a penalty on thrift, and there can be little doubt that a comprehensive system of welfare payments and health services has the net effect of encouraging and subsidizing consumption. Further extension of health and welfare benefits would almost certainly operate to discourage the increase in savings which Australia greatly needs.

Health and welfare expenditures have made an important contribution toward accentuating the problem of federalism in Australia. Before the Second World War, Commonwealth expenditures were less than 40 per cent of all public expenditures in the country. At that time the federal government was making a little over half of all expenditures for health and welfare purposes. Since that time the Commonwealth has multiplied its expenditures for health and welfare about twelvefold—more than for any other single function, even including defense. Its proportion of health and welfare expenditures has risen to almost three fourths and its proportion of total public expenditures stands at nearly 65 per cent. The pressing need for money to finance the health and welfare programs is one of the principal factors which makes it difficult to release any major source of revenue to the states and therefore works toward a continuance of Uniform Taxation. Since there is very little chance of any decline in health and welfare expenditures, either absolutely or relatively, this amounts to a permanent shift in the "center of gravity" of public expenditures from the states to the Commonwealth.

Large expenditures for health and welfare purposes also have an important bearing on the fiscal policy which the national government is able to pursue. The usual goal of fiscal policy is to manage the government's finances so that they will act as a counterweight to offset to some extent the fluctuations in the private economy. This requires, among other things, that the government expenditures be increased in depressions and reduced in periods of boom or inflation. To some extent health and welfare expenditures may act as "built-in stabilizers," especially in periods of depression. Unemployment insurance payments and relief expenditures automatically increase in depressions. Other cash benefits remain fixed in nominal amounts and, if prices fall, increase in real terms. So it would seem that in periods of depression extensive health and welfare programs, in their very nature, encourage adherence to sound fiscal policy. In periods of inflation the probable results are not so clear. It is true that unemployment and relief payments will decline, but the total may not decline for two reasons. First, the larger revenues which the government will be enjoying will produce strong demands for liberalization of benefits—easing of the means test (which will be almost necessary if prices rise substantially), and widening the conditions of eligibility.

Second, it is the unwritten law that when prices rise the rate of pension payments must rise in proportion. Since the numbers involved here are so large, any significant rise will more than offset automatic declines in other payments. Further, these payments bring about a redistribution of income and the payments go to those who have a high propensity to consume and a low propensity to save, which means that the forces of inflation will be strengthened. This argument is frequently used, and properly so, as an argument to show that programs of this kind produce a desirable effect in a period of depression. The same force is at work to produce an undesirable effect in an inflationary period. In summary, large expenditure programs for health and welfare aid a government in fighting a depression but hamper it in fighting an inflation and may even force it to follow policies which aggravate the inflation.

Finally, large expenditures for health and welfare introduce an element of inflexibility into a country's budget which reduces its ability to channel resources into new lines which may appear desirable in the future. Australia is a young and rapidly developing country, and its economy needs all the flexibility possible so that it can take advantage of changing circumstances. That may require, as it has in the past, substantial aid from the government. But when a country undertakes extensive welfare programs, it makes broad commitments and gives hostages to the future. Large expenditures for debt service may eventually be reduced by paying a part of the debt or by the country's "outgrowing" the debt. Heavy defense expenditures may be alleviated by a fortunate development in the international field. Similar developments may reduce the burden of most other expenditures which are heavy at any given time. But welfare expenditures are peculiarly inflexible on the "down" side. There is almost no chance that they can be reduced, and they are quite likely to grow over a considerable time.

For a free-enterprise economy there must be a limit or "ceiling" to the proportion of its national income which governments can take as taxes and spend for their various programs. That limit must be substantially below 100 per cent, and there are some who contend that it lies in the area of 25 to 30 per cent for the type of economies we have in the Western World today. Australia, along with Canada, the United States, and several other countries, is already in or near that supposedly critical area. In any event, there can be little doubt that if a situation arose in which large additional public expenditures were required, governments would be handicapped if they were already heavily burdened with large outlays for health and welfare programs. In an era when much thought and effort is being devoted to economic development, usually with substantial government aid, it should be recognized that expenditures for welfare are to a considerable extent competitive with expenditures for economic development when the levels of taxing and public spending are as high as they are today.

The Evolution of the Sterling Area and Its Prospects

BRINLEY THOMAS

1. The Era of Sterling Supremacy

THE INTERNATIONAL GOLD standard which operated in the nineteenth century could be described as a sterling exchange standard; its characteristics were determined by the economic nexus between Great Britain and the countries within her orbit. London was the financial center of the world; bills drawn on London were acceptable everywhere; and many countries maintained not only commercial bank reserves but also central bank reserves in the form of sterling balances which had the advantage of yielding interest and of being readily convertible into gold at a fixed rate.[1]

The core of this system consisted of the United Kingdom and the colonies; the currencies of the latter were backed by sterling reserves held in London. It was in 1825 that Great Britain began to supply her own currency to the colonies; up to that date they had been left to use any type of medium of exchange which happened to circulate, mainly of Spanish, Portuguese, French, Dutch, Sicilian, Indian, and Eastern origin. The Treasury Minute of February 11, 1825, proved an important turning point; the shilling now became legal tender in the colonies, and it eventually drove out of circulation the miscel-

---

[1] For an analysis of the "rules of the gold standard," see R. G. Hawtrey, *A Century of Bank Rate* (London, 1938) and *The Gold Standard in Theory and Practice* (5th ed.; London, 1947); W. A. Brown, *The International Gold Standard Reinterpreted* (2 vols.; New York, 1940); R. S. Sayers, *Central Banking after Bagehot* (Oxford, 1957).

laneous coins which were there already. Here was the foundation of a sterling exchange standard. A historian of its growth has summarized the outcome in the following words:

The Colonial Sterling Exchange Standard has been adopted throughout the colonial territories, except in Aden, which uses the rupee, in Basutoland, Bechuanaland, and Swaziland, which use South African currency, in British Solomon Islands, the Gilbert and Ellice Islands, Tonga, and, with French complications, the condominium of New Hebrides, which use Australian currency or are linked with it, and, finally, in St. Helena, which from 1949 is directly sterling (including Bank of England notes). Under that Standard, their currencies are convertible into sterling and sterling into them at par either for a small commission or within narrowly limited rates of exchange. Coin is now relatively unimportant, except in West Africa, where paper money would suffer from termites; private bank notes are also now relatively unimportant except in the Eastern territories, such as Hong Kong. The predominating paper money is the local government currency note, backed 110 per cent in sterling (cash in London and sterling securities).[2]

Around the core which we have just described there was an inner ring of countries such as Australia, New Zealand, and South Africa, which were gradually building up independent financial institutions. British emigrants, especially Scotsmen, carried with them the banking traditions and methods of the mother country; and the bonds of trade and capital supply made it natural for the new nations overseas to keep their monetary reserves in London and to maintain their currencies in line with sterling. In the outer ring were countries, not necessarily in the British Empire, which made extensive use of the facilities of the city of London and would be prepared to hold sterling almost without limit.

What were the outstanding characteristics of this international economy of the nineteenth century with London as its apex? Great Britain was a highly specialized industrial unit relying heavily on imports of raw materials and foodstuffs; almost every country was involved to a considerable extent in the network of international trade centered on London. Imports for Great

[2] H. A. Shannon, "Evolution of the Colonial Sterling Exchange Standard," International Monetary Fund, *Staff Papers*, vol. 1 (April, 1951), 349-350.

Britain were not just marginal supplements to domestic output: on the contrary the bulk of them were a major and indispensable element in the growth of production. In the period 1869-1913 merchandise imports comprised on the average 30 per cent of the net national product in the United Kingdom; the corresponding proportion for the United States was 6 per cent. Oversea suppliers of primary produce found it convenient to use sterling for most of their transactions and to hold working balances in London; sterling assets were always convertible into gold. The City possessed a unique expertise in the financing and insuring of international transactions, and this in itself acted as a magnet.

Great Britain was also the chief source of loanable funds for the development of new countries. By 1913 her foreign investments had reached an aggregate value of £3763 million, distributed geographically as follows: 47 per cent in the British Empire, 20 per cent in the United States, 20 per cent in Latin America, and 6 per cent in Europe. The service of these loans was another reason why the oversea borrowers always kept sterling reserves in London. One of the striking features of the nineteenth century pattern of growth was the parallel fluctuations in Britain's foreign lending and oversea emigration from Europe; the economic significance of this mechanism deserves to be emphasized.[3] There were four big outflows of population from Europe—1844-54, 1863-73, 1878-88, and 1898-1907; and each of these was accompanied by a boom in capital exports from Great Britain. In the upward phase of this lending-migration cycle, Great Britain was investing heavily in the capital equipment of the younger nations and thereby supplying sterling liberally to the outside world. In the downward phase of the cycle British loanable funds went mainly into domestic capital formation; but since this entailed a relatively large increase in her demand for imported raw materials and foodstuffs, sterling was again being supplied to the outside world. Thus, as a result of these alternat-

---

[3] For a detailed anaysis, see Brinley Thomas, *Migration and Economic Growth: A Study of Great Britain and the Atlantic Economy* (Cambridge, 1954), chaps. 7, 10, 11, and 14.

ing spurts in home and foreign investment, sterling was never a scarce currency; the international economy did not run into periodic crises caused by a fundamental disequilibrium.

It may also be significant that during the era of sterling supremacy the rate of economic growth in most of the borrowing countries was higher than in the chief creditor country. For the half-century ending in the First World War the average increase in real product per capita each decade in certain countries is shown in the following table:

TABLE I
RATES OF ECONOMIC GROWTH

Country	Period	Percentage Change in Real Product per Capita per Decade
United Kingdom	1860-69 to 1905-14	12.5
Germany	1860-69 to 1905-14	21.6
Sweden	1861-68 to 1904-13	26.2
United States	1869-78 to 1904-13	27.5
Canada	1870-79 to 1905-14	24.7
Japan	1878-87 to 1903-12	33.7

Source: S. Kuznets, "Quantitative Aspects of the Economic Growth of Nations, 1. Levels and Variability of Rates of Growth," in *Economic Development and Cultural Change*, vol. 5, no. 1 (Oct., 1956), 13.

Nations in Europe and overseas which experienced their industrial revolution later than Great Britain were advancing more rapidly than Great Britain in the half-century ending in 1913. The rate of growth of income per capita in the United States and Canada was twice as high as in the United Kingdom. This led to a diffusion of economic power and economic welfare; and it was not difficult for the less mature economies to adjust themselves to changes in the center country. The secular shift in the balance of economic power is shown in Table II.

The United Kingdom was at the height of her power in 1870 when she produced nearly one-third of the world's manufacturing output. By the early eighties the United States had overtaken her; and by 1906-10 Germany had done the same. In such conditions the currency of the center country was a successful international medium of exchange.

TABLE II

PERCENTAGE DISTRIBUTION OF THE WORLD'S MANUFACTURING
PRODUCTION BY COUNTRY, 1870-1938

Period	World	U. S. A.	U. K.	Germany	France	Russia	Canada	Other Countries
1870......	100	23.3	31.8	13.2	10.3	3.7	1.0	16.7
1881-85...	100	28.6	26.6	13.9	8.6	3.4	1.3	17.6
1896–1900.	100	30.1	19.5	16.6	7.1	5.0	1.4	20.3
1906-10...	100	35.3	14.7	15.9	6.4	5.0	2.0	20.7
1913......	100	35.8	14.0	15.7	6.4	5.5	2.3	20.3
1926-29...	100	42.2	9.4	11.6	6.6	4.3*	2.4	23.5
1936–38...	100	32.2	9.2	10.7	4.5	18.5*	2.0	22.9

* U. S. S. R.
Source: League of Nations, *Industrialization and Foreign Trade* (1945), 13.

2. *The Inter-War Sterling Bloc*

The First World War undermined the supremacy of sterling, but its place was not taken by the dollar. The United States, which in 1913 owed other countries a net sum of over 3 billion dollars, was by 1919 a net creditor to the extent of 4 billion dollars. World payments were now to be based on a two-centered system—London and New York; but New York still lacked the necessary technical apparatus. Mistaken notions of prestige led the British Government to return to the gold standard in 1925 at the prewar parity of 4.86 dollars.[4] The Cunliffe Committee, which had recommended it in 1917, had thought of postwar reconstruction as a return to where Great Britain had left off in 1914; its whole outlook was heavily influenced by the high moral traditions of private banking and the absolute need to maintain confidence. The committee wrongly concluded that the only way of convincing the world that sterling remained a strong currency was to restore the prewar standard at the old parity. They overlooked the change in the economic environment.

The consequent overvaluation of the pound sterling had a serious effect on the competitive power of Britain's exports; not long after the onset of the world depression the strain proved too

[4] The Chancellor of the Exchequer at the time was Mr. Winston Churchill. Mr. Keynes dealt faithfully with the episode in his pamphlet, *The Economic Consequences of Mr. Churchill* (London, 1925).

great, with the result that the gold standard had to be suspended in September, 1931. Countries had then to decide whether they were going to maintain their currencies stable in terms of gold or in terms of sterling; those which took the latter step formed the Sterling Bloc. It was composed of the British Commonwealth and Empire (except Canada which steered a course midway between the pound and the U. S. dollar), Portugal, the Scandinavian countries (in 1933), and Iran and Latvia (in 1936). Although a great gold producer, the Union of South Africa came into line with sterling in 1933, thus demonstrating that she was in fact on a sterling exchange standard and her gold exports were means of keeping up her sterling reserves.

Thus during the thirties the world saw a successful and stable exchange standard which was not anchored to gold. According to a League of Nations study, ". . . the prestige of the pound sterling must have been an important factor, implying confidence in the policy of the British monetary authorities. Without this psychological element it would not be easy to explain the fact that a currency severing its century-old link with gold in time of peace nevertheless retained the allegiance of a considerable number of more or less independent currencies."[5]

The three tests of membership in the Sterling Bloc were (a) maintaining a fixed currency relationship with the pound sterling, (b) keeping considerable reserves in London in the form of sterling balances or other assets, and (c) using sterling as an international means of payment. A variety of motives would lead countries to do these things, but among the strongest was the determination not to lose their share of the British market. The great, all-embracing network of international trade, centered on London, which had evolved in the pre-1913 era, was still powerful enough to keep the participating nations on a sterling standard. The reality of these commercial ties is brought out in Table III.

[5] League of Nations, *International Currency Experience: Lessons of the Interwar Period* (1944), 48.

TABLE III
PERCENTAGE SHARE OF THE UNITED KINGDOM IN
THE FOREIGN TRADE OF CERTAIN COUNTRIES

	Exports 1933	Imports 1933		Exports 1933	Imports 1933
	%	%		%	%
Australia.........	54	42	Latvia...........	43	22
Denmark.........	64	28	Norway..........	20	23
Egypt...........	41	23	New Zealand.....	86	51
Eire............	94	70	Portugal.........	22	28
Estonia..........	37	18	Sweden..........	26	18
Finland..........	46	21	South Africa......	78	50
India...........	30	41			

Source; League of Nations, *International Currency Experience* (1944), 48.

Another reason for the decision of so many countries to maintain the sterling connection was the comparative stability of the British economy during the world depression.   Between 1929 and 1933 the index of industrial production in the United States fell from 100 to 63, but in the United Kingdom the decline was more moderate, namely, from 100 to 88.   Furthermore, whereas the volume of imports into the United States between 1929 and 1933 fell by 33 per cent, the volume of imports into the United Kingdom went down by only 10 per cent.   The successful operation of an international exchange standard requires that the center country should display a fair degree of economic stability.

In spite of these favorable features the position of sterling in the thirties was far from strong.   In a two-centered system of world payments, the weaker one was liable to crises of confidence. The effect of the American recession of 1937-38 was coped with successfully; but in the months before the outbreak of war foreigners were withdrawing long-term as well as short-term sterling assets at a time when the rearmament program was causing the volume of imports to rise fast.   An acute analysis by an American expert in 1939 found ". . . the pound sterling in a highly vulnerable but not a hopeless position.   The possibility of a further flight of capital from London is the most pressing near-term problem.   The persistent tendency of the excess of outpayments on merchandise and service transactions to be greater than the annual production and dishoarding of gold within the Area is the principal element of weakness from the long-term point of view."[6]   There is no doubt that a sterling payments crisis would have developed out of the situation in 1938-39; the shadow of war drove most of the non-Commonwealth countries out of the Sterling Bloc, and the outbreak of hostilities changed the entire nature of the problem.

3. The Origin of the Present Sterling Area

The Sterling Area as we know it today owes its origin to the Second World War, although some of its roots go back for well over a century.   The outbreak of war made it essential for the United Kingdom to secure concerted action to safeguard the reserves of gold and hard currencies, and the necessary powers were bestowed upon the Treasury by a series of regulations promulgated between August 24 and September 3, 1939.   The Treasury was given a monopoly in dealings in gold and foreign exchange, and no payments could be made to residents outside the United Kingdom without its permission. All holdings of gold and specified foreign currencies were to be handed for sale to the Treasury; and control over all securities marketable abroad was vested in the Treasury.   The decision which brought the Sterling Area formally into existence was taken on September 3, 1939,[7] when the ban on payments to residents outside the United Kingdom was not applied to those countries which kept their currency reserves in sterling in London and which put into force a system of exchange control similar to that of the United Kingdom. The first of the statutory rules and orders to define the membership of the Sterling Area was issued on July 17, 1940.

What did membership of this group of countries involve? The essential bond was a common housekeeping in regard to

[6] Imre de Vegh, *The Pound Sterling: A Study of the Balance of Payments of the Sterling Area* (New York, 1939), 107-108.

[7] S. R. & O. 1168 of 1939, issued at the same time as the Defense (Finance) Regulations of Sept. 3, 1939.

supplies of hard currency, freedom from controls in their dealings with one another, and a joint policy in their transactions with countries outside the group. The Exchange Equalization Account in London was to keep the pool of gold and hard currencies for the whole area, and each member was to have access to it according to its needs. The paramount common interest of these countries was to win the war, and the Sterling Area was an indispensable part of their armament. In 1940 members were the United Kingdom and the Isle of Man, the Dominions (except Canada and Newfoundland), the colonies, dependencies, and mandated territories, Egypt and the Anglo-Egyptian Sudan, and Iraq. The absence of Canada was explained by her very close commercial and financial ties with the United States. It is interesting to note that the British Treasury excluded Hong Kong because of its special economic relationship with the Asian hinterland. Although Canada was not a member of the Sterling Area, she made a special payments agreement with the United Kingdom which guaranteed that Canadian industry and agriculture would not be hampered by financial obstacles in making their fullest contribution to the war effort of the British Commonwealth. In 1941 the membership of the Area widened to include Iceland, the Faroe Islands, Syria, Lebanon, the Belgian Congo and "Free French" colonies; most of these returned to their former status with the coming of liberation in 1944.

The Sterling Area which came into existence at the beginning of the Second World War differed in important respects from the Sterling Bloc of the interwar period and still more from the system which had prevailed up to 1913.

4. The Situation Immediately After the War

a. The Sterling Balances

The postwar history of sterling has been dominated by the existence of very large debts incurred by the United Kingdom as a direct result of the war; these are usually referred to as sterling balances. In order to strengthen the dollar pool of the

Sterling Area the dollar proceeds from the sale of primary produce and other output were exchanged for sterling. The goods and services needed by Great Britain when she fought the campaigns in Asia and the Middle East were supplied on credit; no less than £1732 million were entered up in London as sterling debts due to military expenditure in India, Burma, Egypt, and the Middle East. These sums were unduly large partly because of the inflationary prices which ruled at the time. The change in Britain's capital position is set out in Table IV and the distribution of sterling balances in 1945 and 1957 in Table V.

TABLE IV
BRITAIN'S INTERNATIONAL CAPITAL POSITION

	Dec. 1938 £ million	Dec. 1945 £ million
U. K. Liabilities		
In sterling to countries....................	598	3694
Govt. debt in external currencies (chiefly U. S. and Canadian)...............	....	369
U. K. Assets		
Gold and dollars held for Sterling Area.......	615	610
Oversea Investments (nominal value) March 31, 1946......................	3545	2417

TABLE V
DISTRIBUTION OF STERLING BALANCES AT DEC., 1945

	1945 £ million	1957 £ million
Countries outside the Sterling Area:		
Dollar Area...........................	34	35
OEEC................................	351	258
Otʀer................................	785	275
	1170	568
Countries within Sterling Area:		
Colonies.............................	411	1269
Other...............................	1986	1430
	2397	2699
All Countries........................	3564	3267
Non-territorial organizations..................	—	645
Total.......................................	3567	3912

Source; *Economic Trends*, H. M. Stationery Office, London, no. 55, May 1958, p. ix.

We must also note the repatriation of long-term debt which India and South Africa carried out during the war; for example, it has been estimated that it took India only six years to wipe out what she had borrowed in the previous sixty years, and she ended up as a creditor nation.[8]

Two world wars had transformed Great Britain from the world's greatest creditor country into the world's greatest debtor country.   Moreover, as a deliberate act of Allied policy British exports had been drastically curtailed so as to release resources for the war effort; in 1945 British exports by volume were down to 40 per cent of the 1938 level.   The merchant shipping fleet of the United Kingdom and the colonies was 30 per cent smaller in mid-1945 than it was when the war began.[9]   It was clear that Great Britain required a breathing space in order to rebuild her economic resources.

b. A Chasm between Informed Opinion in the United Kingdom and the United States

Article VII of the Mutual Aid Agreement signed in February, 1942, stated that the final settlement of lend-lease should "include provision for agreed action by the United States of America and the United Kingdom, open to participation by all other countries of like mind, directed to . . . the elimination of all forms of discriminatory treatment in international commerce, and to the reduction of tariffs and other trade barriers."[10]   Here was a commitment on the part of the United Kingdom to move toward a nondiscriminatory system in the postwar world.   When it came to winding up lend-lease, the United States, in an act of great generosity, wiped the slate clean.   In September, 1945, the balance in favor of the United States in the U. S.-U. K. books amounted to 21 billion dollars, and Britain had to pay only

---

[8] H. A. Shannon, "The Sterling Balances of the Sterling Area, 1939-1949," *Economic Journal*, vol. 60 (Sept., 1950), 540.

[9] On the costs of the war, see *Statistical Material Presented during the Washington Negotiations*, Dec., 1945, Cmd. 6707, and W. K. Hancock and M. M. Gowing, *British War Economy* (London, 1949), 546-555.

[10] *Agreement on the Principles Applying to Mutual Aid*, Cmd. 6341 (Feb., 1942).

650 million dollars.[11]   It was only natural that, when the terms of the Loan Agreement were being negotiated, the American representatives should have regarded the sterling balances as a contribution by the holders to the common war effort; there was a strong case for winding them up in a generous settlement.

Much that has happened to the Sterling Area since 1946 was predetermined by the unfortunate atmosphere in which Anglo-American negotiations took place as soon as the war was over. It can best be described in the words of a recent authoritative American study.

> It is axiomatic that without a flexibility of mind, a sympathy for the other fellow's difficulties, no institutions, however perfect, can be made to work.   Yet Anglo-American economic collaboration in the period we have described was constantly impeded by doctrinaire attitudes on both sides of the Atlantic.   The United States pressed for non-discrimination both in and out of season and adopted an unbecoming evangelism in its assault on the sterling area and Imperial Preference.   British opinion, in turn, yielded to an overweening insistence on the sanctity of these institutions and of ambitious programmes of domestic expansion.   The resulting controversies inflamed public opinion and impeded essential adjustments in national policy.   They led eventually to immoderate and inflexible positions not founded in the genuine interests of the two countries.[12]

In the loan negotiations in the autumn of 1945 Keynes began by appealing to "equality of sacrifice," but the American negotiators preferred to stress the need for nondiscrimination and multilateralism in the future. Articulate American opinion was emphatic. The National Association of Manufacturers demanded as a condition of assistance that ". . . the commitments the British make toward relaxing and eliminating discriminatory trade practices are definite, tangible, and practical from the standpoint of American industry."[13] A spokesman of the banking world, Mr. Winthrop Aldrich, declared: "The British Commonwealth should agree to do away with exchange controls on current account and give up the so-called sterling area . . . relinquish the system

[11] Hancock and Gowing, *op. cit.*, 547.
[12] Richard N. Gardner, *Sterling-Dollar Diplomacy* (Oxford, 1956), 384.
[13] *Ibid.*, 197.

of imperial preference . . . and eliminate quantitative trade controls."[14] Meanwhile, the British people had elected a Labor Government on issues which were largely domestic in character. "Yet here was Keynes making multilateralism the keystone of his appeal for American aid. Did he do this with the support of his countrymen? If not, the negotiations now beginning were founded on sand; they could only bring new difficulties to the Anglo-American alliance."[15] And, to crown everything, there was a clash of temperament and personality between the heads of the two delegations, Vinson and Keynes; ". . . between the grave, cautious border-state politician and the urbane product of Cambridge University there was no *rapport* at all."[16]

The American negotiators wished to see the sterling balances scaled down drastically; but the British Government opposed any American participation in their settlement.[17] The two basic conditions laid down for the Loan of 3750 million dollars were: (*a*) that sterling earned in current transactions should become convertible one year after the date when the Agreement would come into force, and (*b*) that the principle of non-discrimination was to govern international trade and payments.

c. Failure of Convertibility in 1947

The first step towards convertibility was taken when the British authorities decided that after February, 1947, sterling currently earned by countries in the "transferable Account" category could be freely transferred to any other country in this category or could be used for dealings with countries in the "American Account" category.

[14] *Idem.*

[15] *Ibid.*, 191-192.

[16] *Ibid.*, 199.

[17] Several drafts of an article dealing with sterling balances went back and forth across the Atlantic. At last Keynes lost his patience and cabled London: "We are negotiating in Washington repeat Washington. Fig leaves that pass muster with old ladies in Threadneedle Street wither in a harsher climate." The source of this is Paul Bareau, "Future Prospects," in Institute of Bankers, *The Sterling Area* (London, 1949); quoted in Gardner, *op. cit.*, 205.

The members of these two categories were as follows:

American Account		Transferable Account (July 15, 1947)	
Bolivia	Honduras	Belgium	Uruguay
Colombia	Mexico	Netherlands	Brazil
Costa Rica	Nicaragua	Portuguese and	Finland
Cuba	Panama	Spanish monetary	Italy
Dominican Republic	Philippines	areas	Egypt & Sudan
Ecuador	El Salvador	Sweden	Canada
Guatemala	U.S.A. &	Norway	Newfoundland
Haiti	Dependencies	Czecho-slovakia	Ethiopia
	Venezuela	Argentina	Iran

On the appointed day the experiment of full convertibility began; it lasted exactly five weeks and was suspended on August 21, 1947, the outflow from the reserves during the last seven days having been at the rate of 35 million dollars a day. At the rate at which the reserve was falling, the whole of the dollar loan would have been exhausted early in September.

After the failure of convertibility countries in the transferable Account category were not prepared to accept sterling for all current payments; Canada now moved into the Dollar Account category. The United Kingdom had to restore the machinery of exchange control, and the practice developed under the wartime regulations was codified in the Exchange Control Act which came into effect on October 1, 1947.

The fiasco of July-August, 1947, might have been a fatal blow to confidence. It was inconceivable that sterling could be viable at a time when the British economy was still bruised and distorted as a result of the war while the outer Sterling Area countries were equipped with ample liquid resources—the sterling balances. In retrospect one can look upon the 1947 convertibility episode as a blessing in disguise, because it drew attention in a dramatic way to the underlying economic realities.

5. The Post-1947 Sterling Area

a. Structure and Administration

Before we proceed with the analysis of the difficulties faced by the Sterling Area since 1947, it is necessary to glance at its structure.   One would not be far wrong in saying that it comprises the British Commonwealth and Empire excluding Canada and including Eire.   The members fall into three groups: the core, namely, countries whose currencies are rigidly tied to the amount of sterling held as reserve in London, e.g., Eire and the colonies; countries with independent currencies linked only indirectly with sterling reserves, e.g., Australia, New Zealand, India, the Union of South Africa; and countries in process of evolving from a colonial to an independent currency status, e.g., Ceylon, Burma, Pakistan, and Iraq.

One of the ironies of the system is that Eire combines the highest degree of political independence with a monetary standard which is indistinguishable from a colonial currency board.   Indeed it is not too much to say that, thanks to the extreme conservatism of Irish banks, the supply of money in Eire varies with sterling reserves even more automatically than it does in certain colonies.[18] It is natural and fashionable for a colony when it attains independence to wish to have a central bank of its own; but Irish experience demonstrates that the presence of a central bank does not necessarily add much to a country's economic autonomy.   No less than 90 per cent of Eire's exports are taken by the United Kingdom.   The degree of dependence of colonial territories in Africa on the British market is shown in Table VI.

The effectiveness of a central bank in minimizing short-period fluctuations and promoting economic development will vary from one territory to another; but until adequate security and capital markets are brought into existence, the scope for monetary policy as an instrument of planning will be very limited.[19]

[18] "Irish legal tender issued by the central bank is, like colonial currencies, 100 per cent backed by sterling, and the issuance is completely automatic. . . .
". . . The Irish Sterling Exchange Standard as it has operated during the post-war period is thus identical to the exchange standard of the British colonies, the only difference being that, as an independent country, Ireland is presumably freer to alter the exchange rate or the legally required backing for its currency than is a British territory."   Philip W. Bell, *The Sterling Area in the Postwar World* (Oxford, 1956), 8.
[19] See W. T. Newlyn and D. C. Rowan, *Money and Banking in British Colonial Africa* (Oxford, 1954), 267-292; A. F. W. Plumptre, *Central Banking in the British Dominions* (Toronto, 1947), 159-172; and R. S. Sayers, ed., *Banking in the Commonwealth* (Oxford, 1952), 401-460.

TABLE VI
Foreign Trade of Colonial Territories in Africa

Territory	Per Cent of Exports taken by U. K.	Per Cent of Imports coming from U. K.
Nigeria	77	56
Gold Coast	43	56
Kenya	30	57
Tanganyika	40	56
Uganda	30	53
S. Rhodesia	32	47
N. Rhodesia	59	40
Nyasaland	66	58

Source; W. T. Newlyn and D. C. Rowan, *Money and Banking in British Colonial Africa* (Oxford, 1954), 6-7.

The Sterling Area does not have a written constitution; and there is no provision for regular meetings of members for the formulation of policy. The wisdom of continuing this tradition of informality was called into question when India, Pakistan, and Ceylon joined the system as independent members. Matters came to a head when Great Britain devalued sterling in 1949 without consulting other members in advance. The Finance Minister of India, Dr. John Matthai, complained about this; and he revealed that, when the Finance Ministers of the Commonwealth met in London in July, 1949, two months before the pound was devalued, that vital question was not in the brief which was being considered for the Washington talks.

In his speech to the Indian Constituent Assembly on October 5, 1949, the Minister said that, in his opinion, the British Chancellor of the Exchequer at the Washington talks had exceeded the brief which the Commonwealth Ministers' Conference had given him. He then added these words:

I cannot help thinking that in a matter which so vitally affects the whole economy of every country in the sterling area, steps should have been taken to arrange for a secret meeting of the Finance Ministers of the Commonwealth countries before this decision was sprung upon them, regarding three matters: the need for devaluation, the extent of devaluation and the time of devaluation . . . . Let me say again that I make this statement because I feel we have been placed in a position which led not merely to inconvenience to ourselves but also inconvenience to our neighbors, Ceylon and Pakistan, and I think every effort should have been made to avoid the inconvenience that was caused in that way.[20]

Mr. Ghulam Mohammad, Finance minister of Pakistan, in a speech on October 15, 1949, in which he explained why Pakistan did not devalue her rupee, showed every consideration for the British Chancellor of the Exchequer. These were his words:

Considering the delicacy of the question involved, there was in my opinion considerable justification for the procedure adopted by the Chancellor of the Exchequer in this matter. In our desire to be consulted about a matter which so deeply and intimately affects the economic life of the Commonwealth countries, we should not overlook the injury which would have been caused by all-round premature disclosures.[21]

There has, however, been some progress in equipping the sterling system with administrative and policy-transmitting organs. In 1947 the British Treasury set up the Sterling Area Statistical Committee, which co-ordinates information. It is composed of officials representing Great Britain, Australia, New Zealand, South Africa, Southern Rhodesia, India, Pakistan, Ceylon and Eire, with a representative of Canada as observer. The other body is the Commonwealth Liaison Committee brought into existence by the Cabinet Office. Its function is to keep members fully informed about policy and to secure co-ordination. Canada is a full member of this committee, but Eire is not. The Bank of England has Commonwealth representatives among its advisors. It is doubtful whether there would be any advantage in having more elaborate machinery. It would mean, to quote *The Economist*,

. . . a rigidity and formalism wholly out of keeping with the political traditions of the Commonwealth. Any such evolution would, moreover, call for the withdrawal of Canada from its present constructive collaboration in the financial affairs of the sterling Commonwealth . . . . More frequent meetings between the finance ministers of the Commonwealth and improved permanent liaison through the SASC and CLC, are the

[20] Nicholas Mansergh, *Documents and Speeches on British Commonwealth Affairs* (London, 1953), II, 1034.
[21] *Ibid.*, 1038.

best answers to the problem of maintaining the essential community of economic interest and cohesion of policy between the various members of the sterling area.[22]

One must not, however, underestimate the difficulties of securing a continuous common policy for the Sterling Area as a whole; even when a meeting of the Finance Ministers can be quickly organized, there is a lag between taking decisions and reaping results. In the 1951 crisis it was not even possible to convene a meeting. Mr. Hugh Gaitskell, after he had left office as Chancellor of the Exchequer, described the position in the autumn of 1951 in these words: "I do not think anyone concerned would deny that it is a pity that we could not get, for instance, an agreed sterling area policy at once. It was not possible. I asked the Finance Ministers to meet me last September but for various reasons they could not do so. There was no way of getting any decisions taken in the absence of such a conference, and six months will, therefore, have gone by before agreement or action is possible."[23]

Some American commentators seem to think that the Sterling Area is the modern economic equivalent of the old imperial system —an organization in which the center of power lies in London and whose main purpose is to maintain imperial preference. This is a serious misconception. Indeed, the structure is so loose and decentralized that much would be gained if the members would evolve more permanent machinery for determining and giving effect to a common policy without too much delay.

b. Conflicts of Interest

In the thirties the deficit of $300-350 million which the United Kingdom had with the countries which now form the Dollar Area was offset by her surplus with the Outer Sterling countries and by the sales of newly mined gold which realized no less than $500 million. This triangular system was shattered

[22] *The Economist,* vol. 158 (Jan. 14, 1950), 92.
[23] Hugh Gaitskell, "The Sterling Area," *International Affairs,* vol. 28 (April, 1952), 176.

by the war. In its place we have a union of countries which have to discriminate against the Dollar Area. The reason is that, at given levels of income, prices and exchange rates, there has been a chronic tendency for the supply of dollars in current transactions to fall short of the demand for dollars. If this "gap" were temporary, it could be met out of the gold and dollar reserves of the nondollar countries; but there is an obvious limit to this process where the "gap" is persistent. There are two permanent ways of coping with the problem: the nondollar countries must restrict their dollar expenditure to the level of their dollar earnings, or the Dollar Area must finance the "gap" through grants or loans. What we have had since the war is a mixture of the two.

The advantages of discrimination are not distributed evenly through the Sterling Area. A conflict of interest exists between the United Kingdom and the colonies. The dollar pool of the Sterling Area gains substantially from the sale of such colonial produce as rubber, cocoa, sisal, tin, and newly mined gold; the surplus of dollars earned by the colonies in recent years has been well over £100 million a year. By handing over these dollars to the United Kingdom in exchange for sterling assets, the colonies are in effect indulging in short-term lending, while sharing in the regime of austerity in consuming dollar imports. Between December, 1951, and December, 1955, the sterling balances of the colonies rose from £928 million to £1281 million; in the same period the United Kingdom's sterling liabilities to nonsterling countries fell from £1018 million to £770 million. It is only fair to add that Great Britain has done a great deal of long-term investment in the colonies since the war; the estimated total for the period 1946-55 comes to about £450 million.[24] As the colonies become independent they will themselves decide the use of their dollar surpluses; they are also likely to depart from the pound-for-pound rule which operates in the colonial currency systems, thereby enabling their own securities to be held as assets

[24] A. R. Conan, *The Changing Pattern of International Investment in Selected Sterling Area Countries,* Essays in International Finance, no. 27 (Princeton, Dec., 1956), 17.

against their currency issues. No abrupt changes are likely. The Finance Minister of the Gold Coast, speaking in the Legislative Assembly on April 5, 1955, made the following statement. "The unit of the new currency will be exchanged and maintained as now at a value equivalent to that of the pound sterling, and will be fully backed by sterling, for the Government is firmly convinced that for many years to come the interests of this country will best be served by a close link with sterling." Britain's administration of the colonies endowed them with two valuable assets—a sound currency and a sound system of financing economic development out of export earnings. These are not to be lightly cast aside at a time when underdeveloped countries are threatened by inflation in their efforts to promote rapid expansion without an adequate supply of capital.

There has also been a conflict of interest between members of the Outer Sterling Area and the United Kingdom. Expression was given to it by Sir Douglas Copland in 1950 when he argued that the resources of the Sterling Area were insufficient to provide Australia's imports on the required scale and that it would be better for Australia to seek dollar loans in the United States.[25] Copland's thesis would have been more convincing if Australia's record had been different from what it had been since 1945. The answer to him was given by Sir Sydney Caine, writing from Malaya: "It is a very odd 'direction of investment' which has strictly limited 'inessential' investment in the U. K., but lent every facility to the remittance of funds for investment in luxury flats in South Africa and milk bars in Australia; to a large extent, purely profit-seeking investment in the outer sterling area has cashed in on the artificial cheapening of money in London."[26] Between the end of 1945 and the end of 1949 the Outer Sterling Area took $905 million more gold and dollars out of the central pool than it put into it.

[25] Sir Douglas Copland, "The Australian Economy, 1950," *Lloyds Bank Review*, no. 18 (Oct., 1950), 14-15, and "The Dollar Gap and the Commonwealth," *Foreign Affairs*, vol. 28 (July, 1950), 671-675.
[26] Sir Sydney Caine, "Some Doubts about Sterling Area Policy," *Lloyds Bank Review*, no. 32 (April, 1954), 16-17.

If there is a genuine conflict of interest it is between the primary producing and the industrial countries. Absence of discrimination would benefit the members of the Outer Sterling Area, for they would develop profitable trade with the Dollar Area and they would enjoy freedom of choice as consumers; the United Kingdom would probably lose, at least in the short run. But this is only one facet of the problem. Even on the purely economic plane the advantage of a higher real income may be offset by its increasing instability.

c. Strains and Stresses

Space does not allow more than a brief reference to the crises experienced by the Sterling Area in 1949, 1951-52, 1956, and 1957. Up to 1951-52 the system was running into serious difficulties every other year. The United Kingdom was making a gigantic effort to recover from the effects of the war. She was bent on raising the volume of her exports from the 1945 level, which was 60 per cent below that of 1938, to a level which would be 75 per cent above that of 1938; and at the same time she had to raise the volume of home investment. The effort was of course inconceivable without a careful control of imports. There was an alternation of declining foreign exchange reserves and declining inventories. In one year increased home investment would entail a sharp rise in imports and in inventories, and the import surplus would deplete the foreign exchange reserves; then in the following year imports would be cut back, inventories would fall and the exchange reserves would rise again. In 1949 the crisis was brought on by the recession in the United States and by a wave of speculation against sterling based on the view that the pound was overvalued. The trouble in 1951-52 was caused mainly by over-importing by the Outer Sterling Area. The Korean war and stock-piling by the United States gave the primary-producing countries a hectic boom accompanied by inflated export earnings in the second half of 1950 and early 1951. After a lag of a little over six months the increased incomes of these countries led to a sharp rise in their imports, and the Area's exchange reserves were depleted.

The gold and foreign exchange reserve of the Area may fluctuate considerably owing to the so-called "leads and lags."[27] For example, a phase of overimporting in the United Kingdom may induce short-term speculation; Dollar Area importers will postpone making payment as long as they can on the chance that the pound may be devalued, whereas the same expectation will prompt sterling area importers to make payment as soon as possible. The swing of this pendulum of "leads and lags" can make a serious breach in the dollar reserve of the Sterling Area.

After an interlude in 1953-55 when it looked as if the dollar gap had at last been closed, another crisis developed in 1956. The seizure of the Suez Canal Company in July of that year and the consequent British and French action in Egypt led to a strong wave of speculation against sterling; the reserve fell by no less than $279 million in the month of November. This serious threat was repelled by the mobilization of reserves, namely Britain's quota of $1,300 million from the International Monetary Fund and British-owned American securities worth between $700 and $1000 million in the custody of the Exchange Equalization Fund. The mobilization of these substantial second-line reserves defeated the speculators and gave an opportunity for the "leads and lags" to swing in favor of the pound.

The favorable experience of 1951-55, when the gold and short-term dollar holdings of the Free World other than the United States increased from 18.9 billion to 25.9 billion dollars, led some commentators to think that the dollar problem had been merely a sign of temporary postwar dislocation. This conclusion seemed all the more impressive considering that the level of activity in the outside world continued to increase during the American recession of 1953-54; the supply of dollars through capital movements (including economic and military aid) more than offset the effect of the fall in U. S. merchandise imports, so

[27] See Samuel I. Katz, "Leads and Lags in Sterling Payments," *Review of Economics and Statistics*, vol. 35 (Feb., 1953), 75-80.

that the gold and dollar reserves of the outside world went on rising. The relevant figures together with the ratio of reserves to merchandise imports are set out in Table VII.

TABLE VII

FREE WORLD OTHER THAN THE UNITED STATES:
RESERVES AND INTERNATIONAL TRADE, 1947-56

Year	Gold and Short-term Dollar Holdings* (1) $ Billion	Imports (c.i.f.) (2) $ Billion	Ratio: Column 1 to Column 2 Per Cent
1947................	14.6	45.3	32
1948................	14.5	52.1	28
1949................	15.0	52.4	29
1950................	18.3	49.6	37
1951................	18.9	69.5	27
1952................	20.0	68.5	29
1953................	22.6	64.7	35
1954................	24.7	68.4	36
1955................	25.9	76.3	34
1956................	27.9	83.7†	33

*End of year. Excluding holdings of international institutions.   †Estimate.
Sources: Gold and dollar holdings: Federal Reserve. Imports: *International Financial Statistics* for Feb., 1957, except for 1947 and 1949, which are from issues for Dec., 1950, and 1953, respectively. See *Federal Reserve Bulletin*, March 1957, 254.

It would be a mistake to attach much importance to the coincidence in 1953-54 of expansion in Europe and contraction in the United States; it was due to special factors which cannot be relied upon for the future. Nor should we be overimpressed by the net gain of gold and dollars by countries other than the United States, for this increase hardly kept pace with the growth of their import trade, as can be seen in Table VII. The gold stock of 22 billion dollars owned by the United States constitutes 60 per cent of the total gold reserves in the Free World. Allowing for short-time liabilities to foreign governments and central banks, we find that the net gold reserve of the United States is $14 billion or about 100 per cent of its annual imports. At the end of 1956 the gold and dollar reserve of the Sterling Area ($3.9 billion) was 16 per cent of the annual value of imports, whereas in 1937 the proportion was 56 per cent. The distribution of the gold and dollar holdings outside of the United States has been far from even. Between December 31, 1954, and December 31, 1956, the holdings of the Federal Republic of Germany rose from $1,999 billion to $3,329 billion, while those of the Sterling Area fell from $4,223 billion to $3,934 billion. During the Suez crisis, August-December, 1956, the gold and dollar reserve of the United Kingdom fell by $175 million even after allowing for the receipt of $561 million from the International Monetary Fund, and $175 million from the sale of an oil company in Trinidad.

The events of the second half of 1956 did not seem to diminish the optimism of the monetary authorities in Washington, if one may judge from the following quotation from the *Federal Reserve Bulletin*, March, 1957.

Two aspects of international gold and dollar flows in 1956 give promise of continued stability in international financial relations: First, the international position of major trading countries has apparently become strong enough to withstand political, as well as economic, shocks. The Suez crisis did not precipitate a disruption of the mechanism of international payments, and there was no serious flight into gold. No major industrial country found it necessary to raise further barriers in its international trade and payments relations. Second, the International Monetary Fund, by granting large drawing and standby facilities to the United Kingdom, helped to stem the speculative attack on sterling that developed in the course of the Suez crisis, and helped to halt the decline in the gold reserves and dollar holdings of the United Kingdom. It thus fulfilled its function of preventing international financial disturbances from reversing the trend toward integration of the world economy.[28]

Unfortunately, the "promise of continued stability in international financial relations" was rudely dispelled in a matter of months. The de facto devaluation of the French franc in August, 1957, unleashed forces which induced a heavy flight of funds into Western Germany at the expense of sterling. There was a run on the pound, and the reserves of the Exchange Equalization Account fell from $2,367 million at the end of July, 1957, to $1,850 million at the end of September. The bank rate was raised to 7

[28] *Federal Reserve Bulletin*, March, 1957, 255.

per cent, the highest level since 1920, and stringent curbs on public and private investment were introduced. While it is true that inflationary pressure in the United Kingdom continued to be an aggravating factor, this crisis of 1957 was not due to weakness in the balance of payments of the United Kingdom or the Sterling Area: it was precipitated by Western Germany's persistent export surplus.

6. The Dollar Problem

The future of the Sterling Area will turn largely on whether there is going to be a long-run tendency towards a "dollar shortage." It has been suggested that the real trouble is that productivity in the United States increases faster than in the rest of the world and that this superiority is found in industries producing substitutes for the goods which America imports from abroad.[29] This explanation is not free from theoretical difficulties,[30] and in any case it does not seem to correspond to the empirical facts, since advances in productivity in the United States have if anything been biased on the export and not on the import side. There are grounds for thinking that, apart from war years, productivity grows in the outside world at a rate not much lower than it does in the United States.[31]

The two world wars undoubtedly gave a powerful impetus to the scale and productivity of the American economy and dealt heavy blows to the productive power of Europe. The United States emerged from both wars with a higher consumption of steel than previously, whereas the opposite occurred in Europe. The most striking example is chemicals. The industry was born in the Old World, and in 1913, 59 per cent of world chemical output was produced in Europe, and 34 per cent in the United States. As a result of the First World War the American share

[29] See J. R. Hicks, "An Inaugural Lecture," *Oxford Economic Papers*, vol. 5, no. 2 (June, 1953), 117-135.

[30] For a convincing critique, see Harry G. Johnson, "Increasing Productivity, Income-Price Trends and the Trade Balance," *Economic Journal*, vol. 64 (Sept., 1954), 462-485.

[31] See G. D. A. MacDougall, "Does Productivity Rise Faster in the United States?," *Review of Economics and Statistics*, vol. 38 (May, 1956), 155-176.

by 1927 had grown to 42 per cent and the European share had declined to 48 per cent. By 1938 Europe had recovered and was producing 50 per cent of world output, while the United States was down to 30 per cent. The Second World War again changed the balance; between 1938 and 1951 the American share increased from 30 per cent to 43 per cent and Europe's declined from 50 per cent to 33 per cent.[32] Such differential advantages tend to have a cumulative effect. In the words of an American economist, "What is needed is a partial reversal of the abnormal self-sufficiency forced upon the American economy by war as well as tariff policy in the past. It would not be a painless process. And it would take time. . . ."[33]

The American economy is different in nature from the British economy of the nineteenth century described in the first section of this paper. It has certain characteristics which may well make it difficult to avoid a periodic "dollar shortage." First, there is the volatile character of American consumer preferences. The United States has a high level of real income and it is continually rising; in 1955 personal consumption expenditure was $254 billion out of a gross national product of $391 billion. Although consumption is fairly stable as a proportion of the national product, it is subject to sharp changes in its component parts. The richer people are, the more volatile do their consumption habits become. In the United States this tendency is accentuated by the important part played by advertising in maintaining the propensity to consume. To sustain its rate of expansion this high-consumption economy has to undergo frequent readjustments; as the consumers' favors are swiftly transferred from one commodity to another, rapid relative changes in the outputs of different industries can occur. The system is so dynamic that these internal shifts, although relatively large, do not entail anything like a

[32] Ingvar Svennilson, *Growth and Stagnation in the European Economy*, U. N. Economic Commission for Europe (Geneva, 1954), 156. This work contains evidence from several important industries showing the effect of the two world wars on Europe and the United States.

[33] R. Nurkse, "A New Look at the Dollar Problem and the U. S. Balance of Payments," *Economia Internazionale*, vol. 7. no. 1 (Feb., 1954), 54.

depression. For example, there was the adjustment a few years ago when the output of automobiles fell from 8 million to 6 million—no less than 25 per cent—without having any marked effect on the economy as a whole. This volatility, while essential to the expansion of the American economy, is a source of instability for individual countries exporting to the United States. It takes a great deal of initial investment to establish a strong bridgehead in the American market; but it may be quickly undermined because of a sudden shift in consumer preferences. There is nothing perverse about this; it is part of the mechanism of maintaining full employment in a rapidly growing high-consumption economy. It is true that this growth entails a favorable income effect, but against this there is the burden of uncertainty thrown upon individual foreign sellers.

Much depends in the long run on the movement of wages in relation to productivity in the United States and the outside world. If productivity were to go on rising at the same rate in the two areas while money incomes rose faster in the outside world than in the United States, there would be a chronic tendency to dollar shortage. The evidence available seems to suggest that this kind of development is likely,[34] although it is hazardous to generalize for the heterogeneous collection of countries making up the "outside world." We must also reckon with the fact that the American standard of living sets the pace for other countries and that there is a widespread propensity to adopt American consumption habits. The attempt to do this is undoubtedly one of the factors causing inflationary pressure and difficulties of maintaining equilibrium in the balance of payments.

We must also consider the possibility that in the American economy imports rise more slowly in relation to income than they do in the outside world. Because of America's versatility and high degree of self-sufficiency she tends very easily to produce substitutes for imports and at the same time she is continually putting new products on the world's markets. A growing propor-

[34] See Sir Donald MacDougall, *The World Dollar Problem* (London, 1957), chap. 4.

tion of all that she does buy from abroad consists of the output
of branches and subsidiaries of American companies operating
abroad, and in the long run this direct foreign investment entails
an increasing flow of transfer payments back to the United States.
There are strong reasons for thinking that a structural imbalance
exists, but it is not easy to demonstrate it quantitatively.[35]

It remains to examine the nature of American private foreign
investment. Total net private capital outflow between 1946 and
1955 was $12 billion, and 85 per cent of it was direct investment
by foreign subsidiaries of American companies mainly in petroleum, mining, smelting, and manufacturing, where the product
could be sold in the American market or for dollars in other
markets. About 40 per cent went into petroleum. Already
more than 25 per cent of all the imports into the United States
comprises output produced by American companies operating
abroad. The bulk of American private foreign investment receives its impetus from the growing appetite of American industry
for raw materials from foreign plantations, oil wells, and mines.
A few years ago an American authority pointed out that: "In
sum, United States private investment cannot be considered as
making any appreciable contribution either directly or indirectly
to the alleviation of the dollar shortage. . . . Since 1946, United
States investors have shied away from soft-currency areas, being
guided largely by what might be called the principle of 'risk elimination' in order to safeguard capital values in the long run and
the transfer of earnings in the short."[36]

The key to the role of foreign lending in the years immediately after the war is found in American exports of *public* capital.
The gross movement of public long-term capital and grants
from the United States between 1946 and 1952 was no less than
$40 billion, $25.5 billion of which went to Western Europe. This

[35] Sir Donald MacDougall has made a careful analysis of possible trends on
various hypotheses for the period 1950-53 to 1975 and reaches the conclusion that
the rest of the world's balance is more likely to worsen than to improve. See
ibid., 145-237.
[36] E. Bloch, "United States Foreign Investment and Dollar Shortage," *Review of
Economics and Statistics*, vol. 35 (May, 1953), 159-160.

made a tremendous contribution to the economic recovery of Western Europe. The United Kingdom, which received $10 billion in loans and grants in 1946-50, was thereby herself able to make $3.7 billion of loans and grants and $4 billion of private investment mainly in the Sterling Area. There was thus a triangular mechanism whereby American public capital flowed to Europe and the recipients, e.g., the United Kingdom, France, the Netherlands, and Belgium, exported capital to their own under-developed dependencies.[37]

After 1950 the countries of Western Europe reaped the benefit in a remarkable rate of economic growth. Total aid given by the United States went on increasing—from $4.5 billion to over $6 billion between 1950 and 1953—but in the latter year two-thirds of it was military aid; since then the proportion of military aid has remained about the same while the aggregate has been falling. Meanwhile, however, private foreign investment has been increasing in a striking fashion. The results of a special study of the role of American investments in the Latin American economy were published by the Department of Commerce in January, 1957.[38] The analysis shows that in 1955 the gross amount of goods produced in Latin America by U.S. undertakings for export and home consumption, plus capital flows, came to $4.8 billion. Company income remitted to the United States was $610 million, imports of capital equipment and materials from the United States $515 million, and imports from other countries $150 million. When this foreign exchange outlay of $1.3 billion is subtracted from the total value of output plus capital flows, there remains a sum of no less than $3.5 billion as the net amount of goods accruing to Latin America through U.S. direct investment there in 1955.[39] Taking this study as a basis, it has been calculated, on rough assumptions, that American private foreign investment in all countries in 1956 amounted

[37] See Brinley Thomas, "International Movements of Capital and Labour since 1945," *International Labour Review*, vol. 74 (Sept., 1956), 225-238.
[38] *Survey of Current Business*, Jan., 1957, 6-15.
[39] *Ibid.*, 7.

to \$4,980 million, of which \$3,700 million was direct investment. Total American investment in underdeveloped countries (i.e., all areas outside the United States, Canada, Western Europe, Australia, New Zealand, South Africa, and Japan) is estimated at \$1,760 million, of which \$1,430 million was direct investment. According to these figures 39 per cent of the direct investment is now in underdeveloped areas, excluding those in Europe.[40]

If these estimates are any guide to the future course of American foreign investment, particularly as regards underdeveloped countries, it will have a considerable effect in raising standards in the poorer areas. But there is no reason to qualify the view quoted earlier concerning its bearing on the dollar problem. In the long term the increase in the yield on these investments is highly likely to involve a burdensome transfer problem; the receiving countries, faced with a dollar shortage, may have to resort to restrictions on imports of American goods.

The above review suggests that it is not going to be easy to overcome the problem of imbalance between the United States and the nondollar world.

7. Prospects

According to some recent American studies the outlook for the Sterling Area is not promising.[41]   After a thorough survey Professor Philip W. Bell concludes that the cohesion of the group no longer depends on convenience or even inertia. "The present structure," he asserts, "is built upon bargaining power, and the future course of the Area will depend primarily upon shifts in bargaining strength and upon the utilization of positions of strength by Great Britain and individual OSA members, or OSA members acting in groups."[42]   This seems to suggest that an element of duress has entered the relationship. It would appear

---

[40] Emilio G. Collada and Jack F. Bennett, "Private Investment and Economic Development," *Foreign Affairs*, vol. 35 (July, 1957), 633.

[41] See Philip W. Bell, *op. cit.*, and Judd Polk, *Sterling: Its Meaning in World Finance* (New York, 1956).

[42] Philip W. Bell, *op. cit.*, 399.

that the Sterling Area, like the mule, has neither pride of ancestry nor hope of posterity.

Professor Bell's conclusions are partly the result of his concentration on the *internal* mechanism of the Area, with hardly any attention being given to the interaction between the Sterling and Dollar Areas. It is possible to be misled by appearances. Internal bargaining is necessarily a basic feature of every coalition; in this respect the Sterling Area is not different from the American Democratic party, and no one would say that the latter does not have a fairly respectable expectation of life. There is not a shadow of duress or compulsion in the relations between self-governing Sterling Area members; it darkens counsel to keep alive the legend that the Area is one of the last vestiges of imperialism. Each member has its own independent scale of values and material interests, and the continuance of the union rests on the fact that each participant reaps a balance of advantage by belonging to it. The advantages are not only economic; there are powerful political and cultural considerations intermingled with them.

Between 40 and 50 per cent of the world's international trade is financed through the medium of the pound sterling. The complementary economic nexus between the members is a strong cohesive factor. Professor Bell has to admit that "the United States *could* rival Great Britain as a market for the principal OSA export products, but that such a situation is highly unlikely in view of the import restrictions now existing and the political pressures available to maintain them. Only in metals is the U.S. market sure to expand, and trade in these products forms a relatively small proportion of total OSA exports at present."[43] He concedes that "in a world of uncertainty the combination of preferences, stability, and the known concern and knowledge of the United Kingdom with the problems of OSA members is a difficult one to beat."[44]

The crisis of 1957 threw a sharp light on the forces which

[43] *Ibid.*, 320-321.   [44] *Ibid.*, 407.

threaten the Sterling Area's viability. In the year ended mid-
1957 the United Kingdom had a surplus of over £200 million on
current account, and yet the pound sterling had to face such a
severe speculative attack that the bank rate had to be raised to
7 per cent. Clearly London's position as an international banker
has weakened. Before the war Britain's reserves were about equal
to her short-term liabilities; now her gold and dollar reserves
are under 20 per cent of her liabilities. She is dogged by the
failure to solve the problem of the sterling balances at the end of
the war, and the responsibility for that must be placed on Britain
herself.

Now that external aid has ceased the testing-time has come.
If Great Britain is to function properly as the head of the sterling
system she must generate enough of a surplus to meet three
obligations. First, there are the claims of the holders of sterling
balances. As colonies become independent, e.g., Ghana and
Malaya, they will want to use their London balances for economic
development. In the past it has been usual for some members
of the Sterling Area to be adding to the dollar pool while others
were drawing on it. But when the raw material producing members are facing a fall in prices and wish simultaneously to purchase
capital goods and manufactures for their development programs,
the dollar pool has to face an outflow when hardly any member
is putting anything into it. If the industrial members of the club
are indulging in inflationary expansion while the underdeveloped
primary producing members are busy industrializing by drawing
on their reserves, it will be impossible to go on regarding the
sterling balances strictly as bank deposits. The second obligation
is to pay back loans obtained from North America and the International Monetary Fund and to repay debt to the European
Payments Union. Thirdly, a vital factor binding the sterling
countries together is the free movement of capital; and Great
Britain should be investing at least £150 million a year overseas.
Her achievement in this field since the war has been praiseworthy;
of the £2,370 million of capital received by the Outer Sterling

Area in the years 1946-55, Great Britain supplied no less than £1,650 million, or an average of £165 million a year.[45] During much of that period, however, Britain was herself the recipient of liberal loans and grants from the United States.

The three major claims on British resources mean at least £350 million a year, and this of course does not allow for the necessity to build up her gold and dollar reserves. It is to the interest of Great Britain as well as the underdeveloped nations of the Commonwealth to face the problem of the sterling balances realistically in the light of changed circumstances. Even to secure the short-term advantages of seceding, members of the Outer Sterling Area would have to leave as a group, and they are unlikely to do so. There is no alternative that would do all that the Area now does for its members. It will take more than action by the nondollar countries to solve the problem of dollar shortage. The situation created by the enormous surplus built up by Western Germany is a clear case where the "scarce currency" clause should be invoked. Keynes was surely right when he declared that "the world's trading difficulties in the past have not always been due to the improvidence of debtor countries. They may be caused in a most acute form if a creditor country is constantly withdrawing international money from circulation and hoarding it, instead of putting it back again into circulation, thus refusing to spend its income from abroad either on goods for home consumption or on investment overseas."[46] In an imperfect world where neither debtors nor creditors can be depended upon to play the game, it is hard to see how some countries could manage without certain controls. In addition to the deeply rooted noneconomic forces which give meaning to the British Commonwealth and the economic forces making for community of interest within the Sterling Area, there is the factor of cohesion induced by the towering stature and bewildering dynamism of the American economy.

[45] See A. R. Conan, op. cit., 17.
[46] Lord Keynes, speech delivered in the House of Lords, May 18, 1943, quoted in Seymour E. Harris, ed., The New Economics: Keynes' Influence on Theory and Public Policy (New York, 1948), 362.

To Carolyn,

The CWL Retreat was a delight in Alabama.

May your intimacy increase as you share your love.

Have fun!

Love,..

Catherine

from loneliness to intimacy

Help for the Golf Widow and Other Lonely People

Catherine and Loren Broadus, Jr.

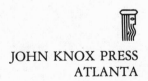

JOHN KNOX PRESS
ATLANTA

Chapter XIII is a revision of a previously-published article by Loren Broadus, Jr. Reprinted by permission of Lexington Theological Seminary, Lexington, KY, © Loren A. Broadus, Jr. "A Gospel of Intimacy," *Lexington Theological Quarterly* 7 (73) 117–127.

DEDICATION

This book is dedicated to two golfers who symbolize the spirit of amateur golf:

Nettie Arnold (Catherine's mother), who, at the age of 72, said, "The doctor's crazy telling me I need more medicine. What I need is a good round of golf every day."

Loren Broadus, Sr., who taught Loren, Jr. to laugh at himself when he misses a golf shot, to head for the practice tee, and to enjoy people.

ACKNOWLEDGMENTS

We are indebted to many people who, directly and indirectly, contributed to this writing. Behavioral scientists and novelists, through their stimulating thoughts, have challenged us to reconsider our ways of living. Insights have unexpectedly emerged while participating in growth groups, counseling with couples, visiting with friends, and playing with children.

Thanks to those special persons who trusted us enough "to speak the truth in love" when they disagreed with what we said and disliked what we did. We have changed because of what they are, did, and said.

Dr. Richard C. White, colleague, friend, and fellow golfer, served as style consultant for the book. LaVerne Barnett and Jo-Ann Whitcomb, both superb secretaries and sensitive persons, typed the manuscript. We are grateful for their assistance.

Our special gratitude to the friend who said to Loren, "It irritates the hell out of me the way you and Catherine get along with each other. You seem so happy . . . I don't believe it. You're faking it."

"No, it's like it shows," replied Loren. "But it wasn't an immaculate conception occurrence. We work to make it good."

Loren's self-righteous response seemed to disgust John.

"If it's so darn good, why don't you write a book?"

So we did.

Finally, we acknowledge our indebtedness to the compulsive golfer and his possessed partners on the fairways, for if golf didn't do so much for the golfer and so little for his family, this book would not have been written in its present form.

Editorial Note

Because the book is written for women, the feminine pronouns have been used when referring to the neuter gender.

CONTENTS

1
THE GOLF WIDOW—
AN ILLUSTRATION

The golf widow is a wife who has been emotionally deserted by her husband. She is called a "widow" because for all significant emotional and practical purposes she has been separated from a loved one. She has the problems of a widow whose husband died and left an adequate estate when he went to the great golf course in the sky. The only support the golf widow receives is financial, and then only if the golfer fails to convince his wife that it is her place to support the family while he devotes full time to practicing putting, correcting slices, and grooving a swing.

The golf widow is a wife who is being upstaged. She is not being upstaged by a cute, seductive secretary or by a mysterious mistress. The golf widow is being upstaged by a set of stylized sticks, a small, round, white pimpled ball, and a large, manicured, green playground.

The golf widow's problem is real. Her husband is in love with a game, or so it seems. He plays golf every chance he gets. He thinks golf. He talks golf. He dreams golf. He is possessed by a demon which drives him to the golf course early in the morning, late in the afternoon, every Saturday and Sunday, and all holidays.

The golf demon is a strange, powerful disease. It causes intelligent men to make irrational decisions. The golfer with a home, wife, and two children may risk losing his job by playing golf when he should be working. He may change jobs so that he can play more golf. A psychologist worked as a night watchman rather than practice his profession so that he could pursue his golfing hobby. A salesman refused a promotion to a managerial position because the new responsibilities would interfere with his golf game. A father chose golf over his family when given the ultimatum by his wife to quit playing golf or move out. The golf demon turns otherwise ethical people into deceptive devils. The golfer may lie to get out of the house to play nine quick holes of golf, and then "forget" to count all of his strokes when he plays.

The golf widow is a prime candidate for the feminist movement. She is trapped in a house with two or three children; she also may work to supplement the family income. She doesn't receive the help she needs from her husband in rearing the children. He doesn't have the time to teach Teresa how to ride a bicycle. His schedule is too tight for him to throw a baseball to Tom. He is not available to his wife when she needs to share her frustrations.

The golfer lacks the interest span to discuss insignificant issues like who will have custody of the children when they get their divorce. When the golf widow does get a few minutes of his time, the golfer talks about the sixteen-foot putt he made on the sixth green, instead of the divorce. Even if he sits with her, she senses he is not listening —his eyes have a dreamlike quality. He smiles when she shares bad news; he frowns when she talks about happy events. When the golfer enters the conversation, he tells stories about his golfing game, and he does so out of conversational context. If the subject is the unpaid family bills, he may suddenly say, "My *new* woods are working beautifully. I hit the ball 250 yards straight down the fairway on the second hole today."

Shortly after the golf demon possesses a man, his wife feels emotionally deserted. She gets that trapped feeling—that cabin fever which engulfs one when confined by children and a home, that loneliness which comes from being taken for granted. The golf widow feels the frustration that accumulates when there is no one with whom to talk. She knows that worthless feeling that creeps up inside when one is treated as a function instead of an important person with feelings. When a woman (or a man) begins to feel this way, the clouds of conflict are in the emotional air.

Whatever else the golf demon does or does not do, it produces a golf widow. A hobby can be a happy, healthy activity, but when it becomes a one-person compulsion, it creates serious family problems. Family problems often erupt into family fights. Family fights have to do with anger, frustration, resentment, and hostility.

Frustrated people and family fights will be described to illustrate the problems and principles. When people are openly hostile they use language which they don't use in less emotional situations. Hostile conflicts between husbands and wives cannot be described with the "clean" clauses of a traditional Sunday school lesson. It would be difficult to believe that persons were hostile if they verbally fought with phrases such as:

"You're a naughty woman."

"Yeah! You're just a pooh-pooh."

"Your mother is a nosey nanny."

"Heck! Your father is a darn devilish thing."

In over twenty years of counseling couples, Loren has never met a couple who displayed such superegos and manifested such self-control when they fought. The vernacular of family fights is used to describe actual incidents, with some censoring.

The names of persons and some of the details of the incidents have been changed to protect the identity of practically everybody.

This book is written for the golf widow, and the fishing widow, and the bowling widow, and all women who have been deserted by their husbands for a hobby, or a profession. It is for wives who want to do something about a dull and/or painful personal relationship. Recognizing that the husband must change for a relationship to grow intimate, the authors focus on procedures which the wife may use to change and to effect change in her family. For a relationship to change, *one* person decides to do something about it and acts to involve the other person.

This is a workbook for frustrated wives. It can help one find freedom in and with the family. By applying the principles one may discover a feeling of personal self worth, and enjoy being who she is, and realize satisfaction from what she does. The authors are not advocating that women have to leave their families to find freedom, as some suggest. On the contrary, they know that two people can be married to each other, and have children, and manage a home, and each enjoy freedom with integrity and intimacy with mutual respect.

An additional editorial note is needed. Reviewers of the manuscript thought that the sub-title may be misleading. Thus, this note:

Golfing is used to illustrate problems; it is not *the* problem, or the theme of this book. As the book progresses, golfing fades into the background and the identity and intimacy program emerges gradually from its sports-like cocoon to enable people to become alive, joyous, and beautifully present to each other.

2
I'VE GOT TO HIT SOMETHING

The golf widow has scores of reasons to be angry. On a typical day, she cleans house and sorts and runs two loads of clothes through the washer and dryer. She cooks two or three meals, scrubs peanut butter off the television set, and picks up toys. Her day is filled with big problems such as sibling rivalry between Joey and Sue. She tries to give equal attention to both children and neglect neither. When she isn't giving her children "rich meaningful experiences" and cooking and cleaning, she is potty training. The golf widow may work outside of the home to supplement the family income, in which case she manages these responsibilities in evenings and on weekends.

These activities are important. If the golf widow has read much child psychology, she feels like an executioner at a teenager's heresy trial when she loses her temper, shouts, and threatens her children with some kind of terrible fate.

When her husband telephones from the clubhouse to tell her that he will be late for dinner because he is going to play nine more holes, the golf widow has just cause to be angry.

Dinner is ready. She has been counting the minutes until she could say, "Children, daddy's home. Go play with daddy." When she learns that her golfer will not be home for two more hours, she may shout obscenities over the telephone, or she may wait until he comes home to vent her feelings.

Venting one's feelings over the telephone, or cursing one's husband when he arrives home, doesn't help a relationship, nor does it solve any problems. There are helpful ways of using anger. When used creatively, anger enhances a relationship, rather than killing the love once shared.

Anger is a normal, healthy emotion. Contrary to much religious propaganda, there is nothing religiously wrong with being angry at someone. Problems occur when anger produces destructive action. The following theory and suggested practices may help one learn to use anger and other emotions creatively.

Displacement

Emotional displacement is expressing the feelings created by one person or situation to a different person or in a different situation. The golf widow may be angry with the children because they fought all day, broke three dishes, and invited four playmates to have lunch without consulting mother. When her husband telephones five minutes before dinner to tell her that he'll be home in two hours, the golf widow may displace the anger she feels towards the children on her husband. He may get the whole emotional impact of the day's irritations.

The golf widow may control her anger when talking to her husband on the telephone. Ten minutes later Joey spills his glass of cherry Kool Aid in the cheese and ham casserole. She unloads the anger she feels towards her husband on Joey. Children often become the objects of displaced anger, sometimes with disastrous emotional and/or physical damage.

Displacement is a common phenomenon. Most of us displace anger on the wrong people. The golfer may displace the anger his game causes on his wife. He claims to play golf as a way of harmlessly displacing his anger created by the employee, or the boss, or the family. He hits the golf ball as hard as he can while imagining that the ball is the irritating employee, or the pompous boss, or possibly his wife. The ball can't strike back like the employee who can cause a strike, or the boss who can fire him, or his wife who can make life miserable for him.

It is better to displace anger on an inanimate object, such as a golf ball, than on one's children, or husband, or wife. Hitting a log with a hammer, or pounding a rug with a broom, or beating a pillow with one's fist may take the edge off the intensity of the feeling. It may feel good to pound an object while imagining all sorts of evil things.

The idea that anger can consciously be ventilated through physical activity is valid. Physical displacement is a way of acting out the anger without hurting other people. It releases some intense feelings, eases the inner pressure, and prepares persons for problem-solving.

A family which was in constant conflict, and in which five of the six people had violent tempers, used this method. The father, a professional person, bullied the family with his six-foot bulky body and deep loud voice. He had an extension cord relationship to the family. Within thirty seconds after arriving home from work, or the golf course, he caught the mood of Mary, his wife. If she was upset or angry he instantly became upset or angry. He didn't just sense that she was upset; he felt angry, and shortly thereafter his voice boomed mouth grenades all over the place.

The electrical current shot through everyone and eventually boomeranged back to father. Mary shouted at Arthur Jr., fourteen years old, or Sally, twelve years old. Arthur Jr. or Sally and/or Al, ten years old, started shouting at each other. Eventually Alex, eight years old, got his punishment from a brother or sister.

Alex was not only the smallest but the smartest of the group. He didn't yell at people when he was angry. He cried, as his mother did when Arthur Sr. fussed at her. Arthur Sr., the protector of the weak, would start with the mouth grenades again, threatening anyone who hurt Alex.

Sometimes Arthur Sr. arrived home with a mouth full of grenades looking for an excuse to start bombarding the helpless victims.

Problems were seldom solved. People were rarely listened to. Tension filled the home atmosphere much of the time. There were quiet periods, but it was the type of quietness that wears on the nerves, the quietness created by fear.

Occasionally, the family had peaceful moments, but these were about as rare as humility at a Howard Cosell-Muhammad Ali interview.

The first task was to help each person recognize how he/she and other family members were acting when angry. The second task was to discover a way for every family member to defuse her anger so that people could hear each other, discover needs, and work out problems.

The family decided to place a large log and a hammer on the back porch of their home. When someone started losing her temper, the other members of the family said, "Beat the log and then we'll talk about it." For people who were used to trying to outshout one another, it was difficult to adjust to this new way of relating; it was especially difficult for the father. Within a few weeks, the phrase "beat the log" communicated to the angry person that she would be ignored until her temper tantrum subsided. Eventually, the log became a family joke. But it served a useful purpose while six people learned to relate to one another in a supportive way.

Physical displacement is a temporary measure. It doesn't solve the basic problem. If one displaces anger on her children, it would be better to find an object or an activity upon which she can pound, beat, slap, or hit. This eases the inner pressure until a better way of managing anger and relating to people can be learned.

Catharsis

Golf is an excellent cathartic for some people. Catharsis is the purification or purgation of an emotion by some activity. Playing golf is a way of expressing and exposing emotions. The assumption is, "If I can perform an activity (golf) different from the one I usually perform (profession), I will feel better. I will feel purged, cleansed, and renewed emotionally and mentally."

One reason golf is a good catharsis is that it demands complete concentration. To ignore this principle is to be punished with hooked drives, sliced irons, missed putts, and double bogie scores. The golfer learns to *think golf.* When playing golf, he blanks out complaining customers, company problems, irritating adolescents, ridiculous wars, and his tendency to play rather than work. The physical activity, cool breeze, warm sun, and total preoccupation with keeping his eye on the ball while swinging often relaxes a person for a pleasant evening at home.

The golf widow knows this is a half-truth, which works half of the time.

Ralph was the sales manager for a food jobber. He often rationalized, "I play golf to escape the constant complaining of salesmen and customers. As a sales manager, one of my major functions is to deal with conflict. The tension I live under is tremendous. When I play golf I forget about mixed-up orders and late shipments. I relax and have fun."

Ralph was waiting on the first tee when George, John, and Loren arrived at the golf course. He was grinning like a mad scientist in a grade B film. "O.K. men, I've got you today! I bought these new woods. I can really hit that ball."

The three men tested Ralph's new woods as he nervously watched them swing the clubs. "They're beautiful," George said. "A limber shaft. My swing is too fast for the shaft."

"They are nice," said John. "The clubhead is a little heavy for me."

"$205!" said Ralph. "But they are worth it. Let's get started." He was ready, laughing, smiling, and swinging his new driver.

Ralph's new woods did not produce the magic he expected. His fast backswing and jerky downswing caused him to fade the ball. However, he didn't slice his drives. On the first few holes a fade was not a problem due to the wide fairways and open rough.

The fifth fairway looked as narrow as an alley in a city ghetto. The right rough was a typical Florida forest with oak and pine trees, small bushes, heavy moss hanging on every limb, and tangled vines tying trees and bushes together. To venture into this rough was to risk a fight with bears, briars, bobcats, rattlesnakes, mocassins, and various other reptiles and animals. If one sliced his ball on this hole he left it in the forest. The left side of the fairway was lined with thick bushes and tangled trees.

Ralph was hitting his woods with some accuracy, but he was putting poorly. He had missed a three-foot putt on the fourth green for a bogie. Sulking, he walked towards the fifth hole.

George, John, and Loren hit their drives in the fairway. A sigh of relief followed each safe drive.

Ralph was nervous and very serious when he teed his ball on the fifth hole. He looked down the fairway and carefully placed his left hand on the driver and moved it a little to the right. He placed his right hand on the club. Moving his left foot three inches to the left, he studied his grip. He firmly planted his right foot to give him a wide stance. He looked at his left foot. He examined his right foot.

He flexed his shoulders. He was operating with the deliberation and caution of a brain surgeon.

Uncharacteristically, Ralph moved the clubhead back slowly, keeping it close to the ground until the arch of his swing began. When he reached the top of his backswing, he jerked his club towards the golf ball with one big yank.

The ball sliced into the woods. Ralph calmly placed another ball on the tee. He carefully repeated the ritual with his feet and hands. He jerked and yanked his club again. Another slice. He placed a third ball on the tee. He sliced again.

During this drama no one spoke, including Ralph. It was like watching a young army recruit study a hand grenade after he had pulled the pin. There was going to be an explosion. Ralph had a temper. He was far too calm for safety. He was suppressing his anger beyond belief. He was the type of golfer who threw his clubs after a missed shot. Ralph had been known to take a divot out of a green after missing a short putt. That indicates a low suppression valve, for divoting a green is the one unpardonable sin in golf.

The four men usually joked about a missed shot, but not this time. The tension was high, and the silence added to the nervous atmosphere.

Ralph teed his fourth ball. He sliced. He watched the ball disappear into the forest. He slowly walked towards the small, green, wooden bench. Ralph raised his driver over his head with both hands. With one big yank, he slammed the club over the bench as hard as he could. (An expensive physical displacement). The new driver snapped into two pieces. He reached into his bag and took out the new two wood. He broke it over the bench. He repeated this act with his three and four woods.

The hand grenade had exploded. Ralph grabbed his golf bag and stalked off towards the clubhouse without looking at or saying a word to anyone.

When Ralph was 100 yards down the fairway, George reached into his pocket, withdrew the scorecard and said, "Let's see . . . he lies eight, doesn't he?" The laughter eased the tension.

Ralph plays golf to escape tension, to have fun, and to relax.

Golf is a cathartic for some people. For others it is a source of frustration and anger. And often the anger is carried home and displaced on the wife and children.

Participating in an interesting activity different from one's usually routine work is a valid way of emotionally refreshing oneself. The daily routine with its irritations and frustrations can cause a severe case of cabin fever and subject one to displacing anger.

The golf widow needs a hobby or some special activity which will enable her to purify her emotions. She needs a different activity outside of the home, *and* away from the children, which will give her a change of scenery. Regardless of how much one loves her children, they can push her to the breaking point. For the children's sake and for her own sake, the golf widow needs to get out of the house and participate spontaneously in some activity such as golf, or tennis, or a bridge club, or a part-time job, or a choral group, or a feminist action group. (Try not to select an activity which will effect one the way golf does Ralph).

Knowing that Tuesday from two P.M. to five P.M. she will play tennis, or golf, or bridge, she can better manage her emotions at home. Knowing that she will have some relief diminishes a touch of that trapped feeling.

The golf widow needs a cathartic activity and such an activity refreshes her for the home scene. The children usually appreciate their mother more and she usually has greater appreciation for them. A cathartic activity relieves immediate tension and diminishes the possibility of displacing anger on the children or the husband or the wife. However, it doesn't solve the basic problem of being emotionally separated from one's spouse.

3
TABLING ANGER

There are those who advocate expressing exactly what one feels and thinks *when* one feels and thinks it. Preoccupation with verbal openness however, can cause havoc in a family. It is an ineffective method of dealing with anger for several reasons.

It is ineffective because when one gets angry and shouts instantly and hostilely, she usually says more than she means and much that she doesn't normally believe or feel. Words can't be retrieved. They shoot like poison arrows into the psyche of an opponent and remain forever in the other's memory. "I'm sorry" doesn't erase the imprint of raucous, rejecting rhetoric.

Martha wanted John to spend all day Saturday with the family. Emotionally and physically she needed him. The week had been hectic. Joey had a cold. He was irritable and demanding of his mother. Joey caused Sue, his two-year-old sister, to cry three times in three hours. Martha had been out of the house once in five days, and that was to go to the grocery store. She felt that if she had to read Dr. Seuss's *Green Eggs and Ham* one more time she would turn green with nausea. By Friday, she was beginning to identify with the big chicken on "Sesame Street." She needed to get out of the house and talk to someone over five years of age.

In her mind, Martha planned to get a baby sitter for early afternoon Saturday. She and John would have lunch at Don Q's restaurant. She imagined a delightful, relaxing two-hour interlude: adult conversation, sipping Sangria, eating a Cavalier sandwich, and looking pretty as she listened to the soft background music.

John planned to play golf Saturday. He was to meet his regular foursome at the clubhouse at one o'clock. At breakfast on Saturday, Martha said, "I thought we might go to Don Q's for lunch today.

I can get a babysitter, and we can have a couple of hours just to be together."

John slowly chewed his toast while he planned a response. "Well . . . that's a good idea. I sure would like that . . . , but . . . I wish you had mentioned it before. I have a golf game at one o'clock. You know that I always play with the same men every Saturday."

"I thought you might cancel today," said Martha.

"I would, but they need me to round out the foursome."

"Couldn't they get someone else?"

"It wouldn't be the same, and I doubt if they could on such short notice," rationalized John.

"I don't see why they couldn't."

"Even if they could get someone it wouldn't be the same. All of us shoot about the same score."

"John, I need to get out of this house. I need to be with you."

"I sure wish I could help. But a commitment is a commitment," replied John.

"Then you won't take me to lunch?" Martha said sharply.

"I can't."

"You are going golfing and will be gone all day long!" Martha said sternly.

"I don't have any choice. I have to keep my appointment."

Pushing her chair back, Martha stood up and stared coldly at John.

"YOU have an appointment," Martha said, jabbing her forefinger at him, stopping it three inches from his nose.

"YOU have a commitment," the forefinger repeated its accusing action.

"YOU feel obligated to the boys," she said a little louder.

"YOU need to get away."

"Keep that finger out of my face," John said hostilely as he stood up.

The more Martha thought about John's insensitivity the madder she got.

"You don't feel any obligation to your family. You don't care at all about me. You don't have a commitment to *us*. You don't care about Sue or Joey. What *is* important to you is to fulfill your commitment to the boys."

"You know that's not true," said John.

"How am I supposed to know it? Tell me that! How can I know it? When was the last time you spent any time at all at home? Every Saturday and Sunday you play golf with the boys. Any afternoon you can get away from the office early, it's nine holes of golf with the boys. How am I supposed to know that you care about us?"

Martha was almost in tears—tears of futility and anger.

"You are getting everything out of proportion," John said sharply.

"Am I? Is it out of proportion? The only time you want me is when we go to bed. You're always too busy or too tired to take me to dinner or to the theatre. You're always too preoccupied with your damn golf to even think about us."

"You're acting childish," said John.

"Childish? You're the one acting childish. Putting a game ahead of your family, running around hitting and chasing a little white ball."

"You're right," said John. "You aren't acting childish. You're acting like a shrew."

"Oh! You lowlife beast. You insensitive animal. Well, go ahead! Play golf with your fairy friends. For that's what you act like, spending all of your time with the boys!"

John's mouth began to quiver with anger. His fists were as hard as rocks. He shook the right fist at Martha, and then slammed it against the kitchen table. The coffee cups bounced up from the saucers, and coffee splashed on the table. John's action startled Martha.

Martha watched the spilled coffee run off the table onto the floor. Smirking triumphantly she glanced up at John and calmly said, "Now, who's acting childish?"

"Oh! You . . . oh! You . . . I'm leaving! I'm getting out of this house and there isn't a thing you can do about it."

"I don't care if you never return," Martha said disgustedly.

Whirling, he picked up his golf cap, slapped it on his head, and stomped out the front door. He went to the golf course to practice and play golf.

Martha went to Sue's bedroom. Sue was crying. Joey was sitting on the floor by her bed. His mouth was open. He was motionless, staring at the floor.

Lifting Sue out of the bed, Martha said, "Joey, what's the matter?"

Joey slowly raised his head. He was frightened.

Martha sat down on the floor beside him and put her left arm around his shoulders.

"Will Daddy be back?" asked Joey.

"Oh yes. Honey, Daddy will be back tonight for dinner." She hugged him. "How would you like for me to read *Green Eggs and Ham* to you?"

Martha was justifiably angry, but she didn't use her anger to help the relationship. Instead of solving the problem, she created an additional one. John's insensitivity to the family will probably continue, and the relationship will deteriorate so long as anger is expressed in this way. His anger and actions were also destructive. By refusing to give her the time and attention she needed, John rejected Martha.

Obviously, there are many other dimensions to this relationship, and to this scene. The destructive expression of anger is apparent. When one expresses anger the instant she feels it she usually says more than she means, and some things she normally doesn't feel or think.

Although at times certain people feel free to express instant anger, it is usually better to postpone the ventilation of angry feelings. In *Robert's Rules of Order* there is an act which enables a group of people to postpone action. It is referred to as "tabling a motion." Tabling some *emotions* is also a good practice. Tabling anger is usually more helpful than instant expression of it.

When a motion is tabled in a meeting, everyone understands that the issue will be discussed at a later date. In postponing an angry outburst, one does so with the assurance that she is going to deal with the issue at a later time. She is going to relate to the anger-producing situation and person, but she is going to do so in a constructive way.

Postponing anger is very difficult. Yet, angry outbursts can be postponed, if one is concerned for her spouse, herself, and their relationship, and if she knows she will be more satisfied by doing so. It is not easy, but it can be learned.

The purposes of tabling anger are (1) to avoid destructive conflict as illustrated by Martha and John (innocent bystanders are also often hurt in the battle), and (2) to discover a solution to the problem creating the anger.

By tabling anger, one has time to examine the facts before responding. She is able to view the situation more objectively. Martha can identify her feelings of trappedness and the part Sue and Joey play in it. She can examine her feelings of loneliness and John's neglect and support of her. She may discover that John is not as neglectful and thoughtless as she felt during the argument. Or she may discover that he is more neglectful than she felt. Martha can examine her own behavior. She may discover that she builds in John's rejection of her by making assumptions about what John should do. She may never tell him what she expects him to do until it's too late for him to respond appropriately. She may discover that she nags John, or caters to him like a child begging for affection.

After she sees the conflict situation as clearly as she can, she determines the action necessary to solve the problem. When she approaches John on the subject, she can do so with facts and feelings. She can tell John how disappointed she was when he refused to take her to Don Q's for lunch. She can share how lonely and frustrated she felt and explain why she needed and wanted to be with John. She can tell him how angry she was, and still is, without displacing her accumulated hostility.

Some women manage to table anger by physical displacement followed by reflection. However, most people need someone with whom they can share their deepest and most damning feelings and thoughts. One needs a person who will listen understandingly without judging, who can assist in clarifying feelings and facts. The confidant should be a person who cares, yet who is not so empathetic as to lose her objectivity. The golf widow doesn't need someone to nurse her hurt; she needs a friend who will enable her to solve a problem.

Some people share problems with a special friend. Others talk to their ministers. There are those who seek professional counseling from a psychiatrist or psychologist. In an intimate marriage, one's spouse is the confidant. The confidant is a great help in tabling anger.

If one knows that she has a person with whom she can express her anger, and if she knows that she has a way of dealing with the anger producing situation, she can more successfully table destructive outbursts of hostility without permanently suppressing her feelings.

4
I NEVER GET MAD

The golf widow may be conditioned to suppress her anger, to refuse to act angry. This is the most destructive, and yet the most common way, of dealing with anger.

Acting angry is a "no-no" for North Americans. The man is supposed to be aggressive and have angry feelings, but he is supposed to keep his anger under control. Occasionally he may express his anger without too much societal punishment. Sometimes he is rewarded for the right kind of angry expression in the right situation. Politicians can express righteous indignation angrily about the popular social injustice and be rewarded with votes.

The woman is taught to be passive, sweet, pleasant, and under no circumstances to express anger publicly. She is conditioned to suppress negative feelings. If she acts angry in a committee meeting, or in a church gathering, or at a political rally, or in a social setting, she is branded as an aggressive malcontent who doesn't know how to act like a "lady." The feminist movement has exposed what every home in the United States knows. Women *do* get angry. Some women are openly aggressive and some men appreciate aggressive women. Women, much more than men, are reprimanded for expressing anger. And for many women the only outlet for anger is in the home with their families.

There are those women (and men) who have been so conditioned in early childhood not to act angry that they automatically suppress the feeling. These people are often referred to as being "even-tempered." They are admired for being so. Nothing seems to arouse them. They always appear in control of themselves and undisturbed by outside events.

What creates the even-tempered person? First, the person may be so secure emotionally, and have her values so firmly established, and be so self-contained and in control of her environment, and understand and accept people so fully, that she is not upset by the normal irritations of life. The totally integrated person is a rare species.

Second, the even-tempered person may present this public position to people outside of the family and act out the anger with the family. The most even-tempered person the authors know is a holy terror in his home. It was shocking to learn that he viciously beats his wife and children with his fist. This man suppresses his anger in public and expresses it to his family.

Third, the even-tempered person may be an expert in suppressing anger. She learned her lesson well from her mother, "It is evil to act angry"; "Ladies do not get mad." When one suppresses anger over a long period of time (years) she loses the capacity to feel any emotion deeply. To suppress anger is to deny that one can feel hurt. The continued denial of angry feelings chips away at the capacity to feel love. One learns to be stoic, to build emotional armor to protect oneself against emotional pain.

After suppressing feelings for several years, it is difficult to identify feelings. "I don't know what I feel. I can't describe it," is a common response to an inquiring counselor.

Suppressing anger is a self-dehumanizing act; the consequences are disastrous.

Resentment

Suppressed anger becomes resentment. All people suppress anger and collect resentments. Resentment occurs when one doesn't get her way and is hurt in the process. Resentment is a matter of control. If one were always treated as she desired, and always got her way, and could control all people all of the time, it is possible that she would never feel any resentment. However, no one controls all people all of the time.

During infancy and childhood one is dependent upon others for emotional and physical survival. She is in what feels like a powerless period of life. During this period she is punished for speaking back to her parents angrily. One learns that to act angry is to be evil, and that one should not try to get one's way. Affection, gifts, and special rewards are given for acting pleasant and accepting the decisions of parents with humble gratitude, whether the decisions are hurtful or helpful to one. "Shut up or I'll slap your jaws," spoken angrily by a parent, usually programs resentment.

Many of the early resentments are repressed. They are recorded and stored in the unconscious, and remain there unless depth therapy retrieves them for reviewing. Specific resentments are stored, but the hostile feeling experienced at the time is readily available for expression. One may not remember her father unjustly spanking her for something her little brother did, but she retains, and can express in a moment's notice, the hostility she felt at the time. That hostility pops out over the most insignificant events, and resentments accumulate during her preschool life.

Elementary school children, and sometimes teachers, are insensitive and unintentionally and unknowingly hurt each other. If one can remember when someone embarrassed her in front of her peers, she can remember a resentment and a person she probably doesn't like. This is a prime time for collecting resentment; some are repressed, others are remembered.

Throughout life one is subject to collecting and storing resentments. The golf widow may patiently accept her homebound state and say nothing about her husband playing golf every free moment. But every time she feels neglected and hurt by his golf playing, she catalogs another resentment.

Resentments have acumulative nature. Resentments are collected unconsciously, especially by suppressors. Every time one feels treated unjustly, she adds one more to all of the rest. She stockpiles resentments, as an army stockpiles ammunition.

The authors have worked with many groups of people in exploring the problem of resentment. The groups have included children, youth, college students, single adults, married couples, and retired persons. The groups have been as small as six people and as large as one hundred.

The method used was simple. The participants were asked to close their eyes and try to relax. The following information and instructions were then given.

"Most of us have resentments. . . . There is some incident in our lives which we resent. . . . For the next few minutes, do a little remembering. Select a resentment. . . . Look at the action taking place. . . . Who did what to you? Remember the feelings."

One minute of silence followed these instructions. Less than a dozen people out of hundreds did not remember a resentment. Resentment is close to consciousness, and near to expression. Underneath the sweet smiles of almost every person is a stockpile of resentment, and usually one very big resentment is waiting to explode on some unsuspecting victim. The specific resentment may not be identified and expressed, but the hostility it generated is available for use on anyone who embarrasses, hurts, or frustrates one.

Following the remembering exercise, the group participants were asked to describe their feelings. They used the following words:

angry—at self	frustration
angry—at others	futility
anxiety	gypped
attacked	grudge
bewilderment	helpless
death-wish	hopeless
("I wish I were dead")	hostility
debased	hurt
deflated	hypocrisy
dehumanized	insecurity
dejection	isolated
despair	"I knew it"
dethroned	jealousy
devalued	loneliness
disillusioned	mad
disappointment	miserable
dumb	misunderstood
ego-deflating	nauseous
embarrassed	outraged
envy	pain
failure	pity (self)
fear	repressed

resentment	tightness
sad	uneasy
separation	withdrawal
stunned	

In a resentment-producing incident one feels powerless. One doesn't have control, and doesn't determine the outcome of events, and can't change the results. For example, when she tried to explain to her father, he said, "Shut up and go to your room." Her husband walked out of the door and said, "There isn't anything you can do to stop me." One was disappointed, disillusioned, and hurt by her husband, or mother, or father, or friend.

In a resentment-producing incident one feels devalued and dehumanized. During the resentment-producing incident one feels and thinks that she is a mere function in the family, valued only for the services she renders as baby sitter, cook, cleaner, sex machine, and, possibly, income producer. She feels more like a maid than a mother, an underpaid prostitute rather than a life partner, a cheap caterer rather than a happy homemaker. She feels way down on her husband's value scale. When he places his income-producing profession ahead of her, she can rationalize that her husband has to work long hours to support the family. But when one's husband ignores her to play golf or anything else continuously, she feels unappreciated and unimportant.

In a resentment-producing incident one feels rejected. The golf widow feels isolated, lonely, and at times, bewildered and stunned by her husband's actions. When she tries to talk to him about the children's need for clothes, or her many frustrations, and he counters with, "We can't afford it. I bought a new set of irons today," the golf widow is bewildered and stunned by his insensitivity. A sigh of futility, helplessness, and hopelessness follows the argument in which she fails to convince him of her position. "I don't know what to do. He isn't rational." (A golfer's logic is not understandable by an outsider. Purchasing a new set of golf clubs on sale when the mortgage payment is two months overdue is perfectly logical to one possessed by the golf demon.)

A specific resentment is unfinished business. One is not satisfied with the way the encounter ended. She wants to change the ending of the incident, to alter the outcome so that she will get what she wants. She cannot forget the incident and let it fade into the past.

Fantasizing the encounter over and over again, she imagines herself coming out the victor. Often the fantasy involves "getting even" with the person. Revenge is the mission. In the make-believe world one can be the heroine, or the controller, or the lover, or the desirable one, and/or the liberated person. The fantasy may include altered actions. "When he said, 'You are just a dull, dumb broad,' I should have said 'You are no substitute for a man with your watermelon stomach, football shaped head, and peanut nose.' " One may fantasize her husband bowing to her rational thinking and natural charm. In the fantasy he dramatically throws away his golf clubs and says, "I would rather stay home with you than play golf any day." (This is a far-out fantasy for a golf widow married to a man possessed by the golf demon.)

Resentment is unfinished business. It imprisons one in the past and prevents living spontaneously in the present moment.

Resentment affects relationships to present people. Past problems are projected onto present people. Fantasizing the resentment situation to a satisfactory conclusion doesn't resolve the feeling, nor does it effect a reconciliation. One often unknowingly attempts to affect the desired outcome with people similar to the person who hurt her. The slang expression for this process is a "hang-up." "She has a *hang-up* with authority figures, or aggressive men, or pollyanna women, or alcoholics." The hang-up expression is appropriate, for it implies that a person is tied up inside and cannot turn loose of the past. It suggests a conditioned reflex. When one encounters such a person the same negative feelings emerge. She often projects the past problem by resolving not to let this encounter come out as did the resented one. This process is often not a conscious response but an emotive reflex.

Unremembered resentments can often be identified by making a list of the people one dislikes and then examining the past for people who are similar in personality to the disliked people. The amusing and sometimes painful insight is to discover that one has the characteristics she despises in others.

Charlie was a middle-aged minister. Rebecca, his wife, was uncomplaining in her role as a "minister's wife," a mother, and a wife. She lived a routine life of attending the ladies' circle meetings, worship services, and performing the tasks of a housewife and mother of two young children. She fulfilled the roles of the submissive, sweet, supportive minister's wife. She endured the petty gossip, and accepted the paternalistic and maternalistic affection that a minister's wife often receives.

Charlie was a successful minister in traditional terms. He was organized, made hospital and pastoral calls regularly, and preached with insight and compassion. Charlie was a smiling, pleasant, paternalistic pastor. The people in the church, and in the small community, were impressed with Charlie's composed, compassionate, person-centered ministry.

What the people of the church and community didn't know was that Charlie had a terrible temper. When the doors of his home were closed to the outside world, Charlie unloaded his hostility on Rebecca. Conditioned to believe that anger is bad, evil, and immoral, Rebecca didn't fight back. When Charlie ranted, raved, cursed, and condemned her for some minor offense, Rebecca remained silent. After each outburst of anger, Charlie was remorseful. He felt guilty. He was confused; he did not know why he acted the way he did. Charlie, too, was conditioned to believe that anger is bad, evil, and immoral.

After such incidents, Rebecca became pensive, acted hurt, and waited for Charlie to apologize. Charlie always apologized, and asked Rebecca to forgive him. He tried to ease his conscience by giving her a gift, or by fulfilling one of her desires. Rebecca got the extra grocery money, or the new clothes for the children, or a trip to the nearby city to visit former college friends.

Rebecca wanted more than her way. She wanted Charlie to quit frightening the children, and to cease cursing her, and to spend more time with her. Although Rebecca eventually got her way most of the time, she still felt lonely, unappreciated, and emotionally isolated from Charlie. Charlie seemed to understand her feelings, and after

each temper tantrum he remorsefully resolved never to have another
one. In Charlie's case his profession affected him the way the golf
demon affects the golfer. He was always thinking, living, and working ministry.

Charlie decided that the pressures of the ministry caused him to
act hostile at home. He didn't feel free to act angry with his laymen
or laywomen when they frustrated him. He projected the posture of
the all-understanding pastor. To act angry would be to disillusion the
people, and thereby to receive criticism. He rationalized that the
only place he could express his hostility was at home with his wife,
who would continue to love him in spite of his rejecting behavior.

Shortly after discovering the preceding insight, Charlie attended
a two-day retreat designed for eight male ministers who were considering leaving the ministry. The retreat began with each person introducing himself by sharing an incident from childhood. When it was
Charlie's turn, he did the unexpected. He moved to the edge of his
chair, clasped his hands between his outstretched legs, and lowered
his head to stare at the floor. Choosing his words carefully, Charlie
spoke softly as he told of an encounter with his mother when he was
ten years old.

When he finished telling the incident, he raised his head to stare
at the other eight men in the small room. His hands became two
steel-like balls of hatred. His cheek bones were accentuated by his
narrow eyes, clenched jaw, and tense, tight lips.

"My mother," he said disgustedly. "My mother never touched
me except to punish me. She shook me. She switched me. She
slapped me. I don't ever remember her rocking me, or holding me,
or hugging me, or kissing me. She never spoke to me except to order
me to do something. I don't remember a single time in my whole
life when she ever told me that she loved me."

For twenty minutes Charlie hostilely condemned his mother. He
opened the door to his feelings and out gushed the resentment of
a stoic mother which had been fermenting for twenty-five years.

Charlie finished his initial ventilation and sat back in his chair.
"The terrible thing about this is that I take it out on my wife and
. . ." Charlie stopped talking. He stared at the wall. His forehead
wrinkled. The inner pain showed in his eyes. "That's it. That's what

I've been doing and didn't know it. I'm taking all of my hostility out on Rebecca. Not only my frustration from the church but my feelings about my mother. It seems like I have to punish Rebecca all of the time. Any time I don't get my way, I take it out on Rebecca. Oh God, what have I been doing to her for the last fourteen years?"

Gazing at the floor, Charlie talked about how patient and loving Rebecca was, and how terrible he treated her. For ten minutes he eulogized Rebecca and castigated himself. Then Charlie made another connection, "You know, I can't stand the older women in my church. I am pleasant to and agreeable with them, but they make me nervous. When they disagree with me, and especially when they criticize me, I feel like slapping them until they can't talk. It's the same way I feel about my mother at times."

Charlie unconsciously punished Rebecca for the hurts his mother had caused him. He continually hit her with the hostility he felt for his mother. No woman was going to tell Charlie what to do, nor was she going to get the upper hand in the relationship. In order not to be defeated again, he aggressively attacked Rebecca. He acted towards Rebecca much as his mother had acted towards him.

The irony of the situation was that Charlie, a thirty-five-year-old man, travelled one hundred sixty miles every week to visit his mother and father. According to him, he hated every minute of the visit. Each time he visited his parents he secretly hoped that his mother would throw her arms around him and tell him that she loved him. Charlie fantasized this scene with himself saying, "You're too late." Revenge! Occasionally, he envisioned himself accepting her affection.

Resentments are unfinished business and thereby affect present relationships. The golfer and the golf widow would be helped by investigating their past resentments. The golfer could be punishing his wife, especially during arguments, for hurts he endured in his first home. The golf widow could be projecting the problems of an absentee father.

Charlie eventually resolved his resentment toward his mother within himself. He learned how to use anger constructively. He ceased using Rebecca as a scapegoat for past resentments and present irritations. Charlie even learned to enjoy the "old ladies" in his congregation. It is questionable whether they enjoyed him as much as when they could control him with minor criticism.

Resentment is a paralyzing disease. It contaminates good feelings. It eats away at the soul and may turn a wonderfully warm woman into a terrifying tyrant. Resentment can cause a potentially sensitive, supportive husband and father to become a sadistic slave driver to the people in HIS household. Resentment blocks the spontaneous, free, exciting flow of affirming feelings. It encases one in a scarred, calloused casket of conditioned reflexes. One expends unnecessary energy on past problems and projects old hostile feelings to present people.

5

YOU ARE NO GOOD

Resentment is a feeling created by specific events. The expression of resentment is hostility clothed in wrong words and destructive deeds. Hostility is the urge to hurt. It knows no rules; it has no boundaries; it feels no mercy. Hostility is the result of nursed hurts, and stockpiled resentments increase hostility. The simmering inner feelings wait for an excuse to attack the nearest enemy.

When the resentment stockpile is unloaded, the accumulated feelings burst forth. Although specific hurtful incidents from childhood and/or adolescence may not be remembered, the psyche feels every hurt, and stores hostility for instant attack.

Hostility stimulates memory. When the golfer and golf widow start fighting, past hurts are recalled to hurt one's spouse.

Martin was a typical person possessed by the golf demon and encountered a typical problem of the golfer. While watching television, Martin glanced towards June, his wife, and said, "Oh yes! I forgot to tell you. I've been changed to the night shift at the plant."

"What did you say?" asked June.

"I've been changed to the night shift." Instead of facing June, Martin stared at the television set.

"Oh, no!" said June. "That's terrible."

Martin ignored June's response as he kept his eyes fixed on the television screen.

"Martin, I don't understand. You have seniority. I didn't think they could do that."

"It's done," Martin replied. "I start Monday."

"MONDAY!" exclaimed June. "That's just three days off." Images flashed into June's mind; keeping the children quiet in the mornings; preparing meals at irregular times; sleeping alone at night, with noises awakening her at two A.M.

"I thought we were through with that horrible night shift," June said dejectedly. "You told me three years ago that with your new promotion and your seniority that you could stay on the day shift until you retired. It's unfair. I'd like to give those big shots a piece of mind."

"Well . . . they didn't exactly do it," said Martin.

"What do you mean?" asked June.

"I asked for the night shift."

"WHAT? . . . You asked for it? Why? Martin, for God's sake, *why* did you ask for it?"

Martin glanced towards June. Her startled expression caught him by surprise. He turned his head away from her while he explained.

"The city golf tournament is coming up in a couple of months. By working the night shift I'll be able to play golf every day, and have extra time to practice my pitching and putting."

June didn't say anything. Her mouth was open. Her arms were limp. She was stunned; she couldn't believe what she had just heard.

Martin moved to the edge of his chair. He turned to face June. Matching the enthusiasm of a hungry Edsel automobile salesman he said, "With a little practice I think I can get good enough to win the first flight. I need to work on my putting and. . . ."

"I don't believe it," interrupted June.

"Yes. I think I can win the first flight," Martin quickly replied.

"I don't believe it. You changed to the night shift to play more golf. You already play every Saturday and Sunday. On your way home from work, you stop at the golf course almost every afternoon to practice. You're late for dinner half of the time because you're either practicing or playing golf."

"I know, and I'm sorry for that," Martin said. "But with a little more time to practice I can win. I know it. I know I can win the first flight."

June wanted to discuss this calmly, but she was getting angrier with every stupid statement about golf.

"You didn't even discuss it with me," said June. "You did it without considering the problems this will cause me and the children."

"I thought about it," said Martin. "When I worked the night shift before, we got by."

"We got by, all right," said June. "We got by because we HAD to. I went through hell. If you remember, you would try to sleep in the mornings. The kids would wake you up. You shouted and cussed and screamed at all of us. . . . How about those times you charged out of the bedroom like a madman and spanked Marty? And those times you shook Jane until she became almost hysterical?"

"I acted that way only a few times," Martin said defensively.

"A FEW TIMES!" June said angrily. "You have a short memory. I don't know how many times you scared the children out of their wits. They're half neurotic right now."

His face turned red. His hands became fists. The hostility showed in his eyes, and jaw, and hands as he tried to control his anger. Standing up, Martin turned to walk out of the room.

June continued, "I don't know how many times you called me a bitch, and accused me of being a no-good mother."

"Calm down," said Martin, through gritted teeth. "And don't blame me for our children's nervous condition. They caught any neurosis they have from their paranoid mother."

"PARANOID! A paranoid is a person who *thinks* she is persecuted. I am persecuted by an insensitive slob, who never helps around the house, never helps with the children, and never takes me to a movie or out for dinner. I married a man who is set on making me a houseplant."

"You're exaggerating. We didn't go out much when I was on the night shift, but we've done better in the last few years."

"Exaggerating, huh!" June said. "You forgot my thirty-second birthday. And your excuse was, 'I was so exhausted that I couldn't think straight.' When was the last time you played with Marty for over ten minutes?"

"STOP IT! You're getting everything out of proportion."

"When you were on the night shift you didn't have time to watch Marty play little league baseball because you were too tired. You needed your beauty rest. I've noticed that you've always had time to play golf. You haven't missed a Saturday in over three years."

"SHUT UP!" shouted Martin.

"But you missed our tenth anniversary to play in a weekend golf tournament in Daytona Beach."

"STOP GRIPING!"

"I have a right to gripe. You treat me like someone you dragged into the house out of the gutters, who doesn't have any feelings or brains."

"By God, I don't believe you do have any brains. Any middle-aged woman who would get drunk at a plant party and start jerking and bumping like a go-go dancer in a cheap bar can't have much in the head."

"That was five years ago," said June. "And I can't help it if I married a tired old man, who is hung up on the fox trot. You were no angel that night yourself. You danced cheek to cheek with that cute little office girl. Remember, she had on a low-necked red dress."

"I don't remember any such thing."

"You should. You danced with her three times. Her name was Janell, and you eyed her bosom like you were going to perform heart surgery."

Martin and June continued to remember and to remind each other of past hurts as they tried to hurt each other. Their language got rougher and the barbs more cutting.

When the resentment stockpile is unloaded, the hostility that has accumulated through the years is vented and many conscious memories of hurtful incidents are graphically described. Not only is behavior attacked, but also the core character of the opponent. With the accuracy of a guided missile, one seeks out and strikes the vulnerable traits. The intent is to hurt, and to hurt deeply, because she has been hurt in the past, and is hurting at the moment.

Resentment and the resulting hostility causes one to depersonalize one's spouse. The feelings and thoughts of the spouse are not considered. Characteristics about which the other person has little control are attacked. Past actions which cannot be changed, and about which there are guilt feelings, are often the target. The unconscious intent is to humiliate, to hurt, and to harass the opponent—to drive him to his knees.

How is *hostility* different from *anger?*

A. *Hostility is a feeling created by a past event.* It is a feeling out of the past. It has the emotional intensity of accumulated hurts; the revengeful feelings ferment as resentments stockpile and feed on each other. When one begins to feel sorry for herself, she doesn't remember just one incident in which she was mistreated, she thinks of the many times when she was neglected, or embarrassed, or insulted.

Anger is a feeling created by the present person and the contemporary situation. There is one incident with which a person must deal. The feeling is related to one problem, and usually one person, or a group of people, or one organization, i.e., church, social club, political organization.

B. *Hostility projects past problems onto present people.* Hostility uses past events to hurt the person present. The person present may have caused some past hurts, but it is unlikely that she/he caused all of the hurts. The past problems are too removed from the fighters for them to agree on the specific dynamics involved. Each person remembers the past differently. The resolution of past hurts is extremely difficult because of the different perceptions and the various people fused into the resentment stockpile.

Anger relates to the person present and the contemporary situation. Anger does not attempt to hurt. The intent of anger is to solve a problem, not punish a person. People are close enough to the specific actions of the incident to agree on what happened and, thereby, possibly to resolve the conflict.

C. *Hostility damages a relationship because the words, actions, and intonations of the hurt person attack the character of the opponent.* The person being attacked feels hated; she feels totally rejected. The tone of the words communicate a clear message, "You are no damn good."

Anger enhances a relationship because two people share feelings and thoughts as they work together to solve a problem. Behavior and feelings are the subject, not the character of persons. Words are rarely spoken that are later regretted and need retrieving. The tone of voice is clear, "I am angry at you because of what you did or did not do." After the angry incident is over, one may feel remorseful for what she did or said, but she is left with her integrity.

By knowing the difference between hostility and anger, and by identifying emotions before the confrontation gets out of hand, feelings can be used creatively to grow an intimate relationship.

When anger and/or hurt feelings emerge, there are four questions which can be asked which will assist in distinguishing the difference between anger and hostility. (Tabling anger is a prerequisite to asking these questions.)

1. Am I thinking about the present situation, or am I remembering past hurts? In remembering past hurts one is fanning the simmering coals of hostility, preparing to punish the person present for his and other people's past offenses.

2. Are my feelings appropriate to this incident? Am I about to over react? The golfer being ten minutes late for dinner may not be just cause for the golf widow to break her husband's golf clubs. An overcooked TV dinner may not be just cause for her husband to join a weekend monastery for golfers. (Some motels and hotels have golf courses as special attractions for such people. Any golfer worth his putter would use any excuse to escape to one of these playgrounds.)

3. What am I feeling? Anger? Yes. What else? Hurt? Unappreciated? Ignored? Undesirable? Self-pitying? Insecure? Afraid?

When one identifies feelings which indicate a sense of low self-worth, she knows that she is primed to unload the resentment stockpile.

4. How do I usually act when I feel this way? Do I attack and attempt to hurt the person present? Do I sulk and try to punish people with the silent treatment? By examining usual behavior, one has a choice in how she will respond to the person present.

The person who is subject to fits of hostility is at the disposal of anyone who can make her angry. The hope is to *use* anger and to choose behavior, rather than to be a conditioned reflex who is controlled by unresolved resentments, unhealthy hostility, and fermenting feelings.

This is a high ideal, one worthy of a herculean effort. But for one who is easily frustrated, the ideal seems almost too difficult, for frustration is the trigger which often unloads the resentment stockpile's stored hostility on the wrong person, much to the dismay of all concerned.

An understanding of frustration in this process, and of frustrating factors in a marriage, may enable one to move closer toward this ideal.

6
THE TRIGGER: FRUSTRATION

Frustration is caused by the blockage or delay of a desire or a goal. One becomes frustrated when she wants something and doesn't get it when she wants it.

The golf widow wants and needs her husband to assist in the Saturday morning tasks. She needs him to drive their son to the little league baseball game, and to take their daughter to dancing school. She wants him to baby sit with their infant child, while she grocery shops for their dinner party that evening.

For George to consult his calendar and to agree to perform these tasks three weeks from Sunday is frustrating. When George walks out of the door carrying his golf clubs, the golf widow feels trapped, powerless, and angry.

Frustration is the trigger which releases hostility. The difference between people is not that some get frustrated and some do not. Rather, some people constructively confront frustration, while some become its victims by reacting hostilely or by suppressing their feelings.

Frustration is related to personal goals. Goals are desires and expectations. Expectations of oneself come from two sources—self and others. The golf widow's self-expectations, via her roles, are determined by what she thinks she should do, say, and be. Her roles constitute her self-image and determine to a great extent her self-expectations.

Traditional Roles

Self-images are caught from parents and peers during childhood. A girl learns how a woman acts. She discovers the roles she is expected to fill and the functions she is supposed to perform.

The traditional role of the female is homemaker. In the traditional family, the girl is expected to believe that all women should have the "family" dream for the future, and to function as a homemaker in society. She is to be a mother and to rear her children patiently and wisely, according to her mother's example and the latest child development books.

She is to be domestically skilled in cooking and cleaning and scrubbing and serving everyone's needs. The girl learns that she is supposed to dream of being the woman behind the successful man, supporting him emotionally, entertaining his vocational associates and supervisors, and boosting his ego. She is programmed to cook three meals per day, clean clothes and kids, wash dishes, handle sibling rivalry, transport children to and from special activities, and to look like Doris Day when her husband arrives home from work.

As she matures, the girl learns that she is supposed to look like the Madonna in the morning and to perform like Aphrodite in the evening. She is to become the lover for one person, and to feel sexy without being too aggressive.

The women who have these expectations of themselves cannot avoid getting frustrated as they fail to live up to their impossible standards. There aren't many women who can cook like Betty Crocker suggests, rear children as Ginott and Spock say they should, be as humorous as Phyllis Diller, appear as beautifully seductive as Racquel Welch, and perform with the skill of Aphrodite, and live to tell it.

Tradition Roles vs. New Roles

Add to the traditional roles the new roles which are being suggested by the exponents of the Feminist Movement. Suggestions range from abandoning the family and establishing lesbian relationships to adopting interesting hobbies with which to earn extra money. Women are urged to join the revolution so that all women will be treated as persons and not as functions. "Enter a vocation and don't be dependent upon anyone" is a resounding theme. Women are seeking recognition of their intelligence, abilities, and individuality. They are urged not to suppress their feelings, nor deny their integrity, or conceal their abilities. The traditional role of the silent, sweet, supportive, sexy, home-bound woman is constantly attacked.

Many women are experiencing a new freedom. Others are caught in what appears to be an impossible bind. The caught woman loves her husband and children, yet she feels trapped in the home. She wants a fulfilling life in which she can

—use her dormant abilities and receive the satisfaction of achieving new goals,

—express her opinions in open forum and be acknowledged as an intelligent person,

—be appreciated for who she is as a person and not be confined to the image of a homemaker.

The caught woman appreciates the respect and affection she receives from her family. She recognizes the importance of her presence to her family. She knows that she makes a positive difference in the lives of her children and husband. Yet, caught in the traditional female family roles, she yearns for some of the idealized dreams of her feminist friends.

The old roles clash with the new ones. She is frustrated by the expectations she is programmed to fulfill, and the new ones she is urged to adopt. When she does not live up to these expectations, or realize her hopes, hostility emerges to create conflict within her, and between her and those people nearest to her.

How she perceives herself and functions in relation to these images is directly related to frustration. When an electrical current overloads, it blows a fuse. When a woman has unrealizable expectations of herself, acquired through traditional and new roles, she blows a fuse and the sparks fly everywhere.

Choosing Roles and Reducing Frustrations

There are ways to reduce destructive frustration. The following suggestions can assist in establishing realistic, reachable roles and self-expectations.

I. Identify Role Expectations

A. *List every role one expects to fulfill*—mother, wife, daughter, lover, employee, employer, income provider, etc. List every function re-

quired of each role. Complete the following types of sentences for
each role.

    1.) A mother is . . .

    2.) A mother performs the following functions:

      a. Plans meals

      b. Nurses children

      c. Plays with the children

      d.

      e.

    B. *Beginning with the most important ones, rank roles according to their importance.* This is difficult because many roles are interdependent, i.e., wife and lover, mother and dietician.

    In ranking roles one discovers the built-in conflicts within her value system. The professional person may discover that she is defensive about her role as a mother. When she is criticized for being a working mother, she feels her role as a mother is being attacked.

    The professional mother, commonly called a housewife in our society, may discover that she is upset when someone says, "Oh! You're just a housewife." Her role as a creative person, who expresses her creativity with the family and/or through hobbies and volunteer organizations, may be a source of inner tension for her.

    In ranking roles one may discover that she can't be a perfect mother, gourmet chef, immaculate housekeeper, editor of a magazine, and a desirable lover seven days per week. She doesn't have the time or energy to fulfill all of these roles. Yet, she may be conditioned to expect the impossible from herself.

    Ranking roles enables one to make objective decisions prior to frustrating events.

    When six-year-old Sally hurts herself and needs medical attention, the dinner for the guests can be late without the hostess-mother feeling guilty. Emotional crises are less obvious, but usually affect Sally more than the physical hurts.

    Dinner guests are arriving in three hours. Dinner preparation has been delayed one hour by an unexpected home visit by the pastor. ("Darn him!" No one is exempt from secret resentment when he frustrates others.) Sally arrives home red-eyed and pensive. Instead of asking for a piece of cake and a glass of milk, she silently goes to her room. The pressure is on; the choice is difficult. Either spend thirty minutes with Sally to comfort her, or be on time with the dinner; disappoint Sally or inconvenience guests.

Having decided that her most important role is to be a sensitive, supportive mother, she sacrifices her self-image as a prompt hostess. She knows that it is more important for her daughter to think well of her than it is for casual acquaintances to do so.

The golf widow probably will be frustrated regardless of which decision she makes, especially when Junior grabs the linen table cloth with his fudgecicle hands. When Junior commits this unpardonable sin, he will be the unsuspecting victim of suppressed anger; that is, unless the principle of tabling feelings is used.

In ranking roles, the kind of person one wants to be is objectively decided. She determines her priorities before the frustrating events force her to choose between two role expectations. By deciding in favor of the most important role expectation she fulfills her highest self-image and lives more comfortably with her decisions. She eliminates feelings of guilt and incompetency, and, thereby, is enabled to control more easily hostile reactions in frustrating situations.

II. Examine Feelings About Role Expectations

Identifying feelings about role expectations is more difficult for some than others. There is a subtle difference between what one *thinks* she ought to feel and what she feels. There is subversive moral and ethical invasion into feelings. One is conditioned to feel good about some feelings and bad about others. Some feelings are "supposed" to be morally correct, and others morally corrupt.

According to parental programming, it is evil to dislike one's mother or to dislike being a mother. One is supposed to like and to feel good about being a full-time mother, which includes everything from scrubbing floors to chauffering the children. She is to anticipate with equal joy burping the baby and changing her diaper. If one secretly despises feeding her baby, she may be conditioned to feel guilty about it.

One may enjoy her job as a secretary, or an architect, or a nurse, and enjoy being away from home eight hours a day, but she may be conditioned to act as though she dislikes being a "working mother."

The feelings about role expectations may range from intense dislike of cooking to extreme pleasure in the sex act, or the opposite may be so; one may enjoy cooking and dislike making love.

One may decide on a new self-image, but the programmed feelings don't follow immediately. The woman who has been programmed to feel that the only way to be a good mother is to be on instant call to her family twenty-four hours per day, and who enters a career in law, may discover that she feels guilty about her professional activities which keep her away from home. And every time her husband criticizes the condition of the house or the children, she may react hostilely, for the usual reaction when feeling guilty is to attack the person who reminds one of guilt-feelings.

Negative feelings about roles cause growing resentment, unless the task involved is accepted as a necessary routine serving a greater good. One may dislike changing the babies' diapers, but she performs the task without feeling resentful because she is aware of the comfort it gives the baby. The less altruistic person may change the diaper to stop the baby from the nerve-wrecking crying. Most people do it for both reasons—the baby's comfort and the mother's peace of mind.

In identifying feelings about the roles, some of the causes for the unreasonable outburst of hostility are discovered. Feelings are managed more effectively when exposed to the light of reason.

III. Identify Who Is Responsible for These Roles and the Resulting Tasks.

One may assume that she has to perform all of the distasteful tasks because no one else will. She may perform the boring jobs without asking for help. She *assumes* that she is the person in the family who performs these functions. Her mission in life is to make life easier for all people. And if golfing weekends and afternoons make her husband happy, she performs routine family and household tasks with a sense of mission. In this situation, the woman is not a golf widow, she is a woman who dutifully does dull chores. She chooses and is responsible for these tasks, and the frustration she experiences is minimal.

One may perform the distasteful tasks without asking for help, and silently resent every task every day. She secretly suffers, and yet masochistically enjoys every minute of it. She protects her hurting tasks with the dedication of a lioness protecting her cubs. When someone volunteers to cook, clean, or care for the children she responds, "No! I'll do it. It's too much to ask of you." Her self-image is one of a suffering servant to her family. Anyone who threatens that role is in danger of attack. She chooses and is responsible for these tasks. She programs her life for frustration with the skill of a double agent living in Paul Harvey's home.

One may perform distasteful tasks without asking for help and gripe about every little one. She blames world conditions, the failure of the Pill, the school system, and her husband's excessive golfing for her fate. Complaining is her programmed response to life. She needs a reason or an excuse to express her basic temperament, and to fulfill her self-image as one who is mistreated. If necessary, she can turn a wedding into a wake to meet this need. The griper chooses and is responsible for the distasteful tasks. Frustration is not only the griper's fate but her fulfillment.

One may perform distasteful tasks and request assistance from family members and not get the desired distribution of undesirable duties. She is trapped with an insensitive spouse. In this relationship the resentment gradually grows, and the eventual result is disastrous. Homelife becomes hell. Individual energy is consumed in conflict instead of creative causes; the relationship is riddled with ridiculous wars which culminate in a divorce court.

Many couples are attempting to resolve this problem by writing a marriage ceremony and contract which includes not only property rights but human rights. The menial, distasteful home tasks are included in such contracts. This procedure is helpful because it clarifies roles and functions.

However, if the couple doesn't have an intimate relationship, resentment emerges over contracted role functions. Even in an intimate relationship, frustration arises in the most clearly conceived marriage contract. So whether or not a couple has a marriage contract which includes clarification of roles, roles and functions need to be evaluated periodically. People grow and change, and with the growth personal needs change.

There are distasteful, "unfun" tasks which serve a greater cause.

Every person performs her share of such tasks. In an intimate relationship distasteful tasks and joyous ones are shared by both persons.

IV. Eliminate the Unnecessary Tasks.

It is unusual for a person to fulfill all of her expectations. The accumulated expectations cause inner conflict which causes interpersonal conflict. One needs to decide which tasks do not have to be done. Some old worn-out ideas and images may need to be discarded. The family will not suffer greatly if the linen closet is not straight. The health department will not condemn the house if the breakfast dishes are left in the sink all day. The children will not get scurvy if they do not eat garden fresh vegetables every day.

An hour in the morning to sit, read, and relax rather than wash another load of clothes may be the best thing one can do for the family. A spotless house, the work of which creates an exhausted, nervous woman, may not be the trait of a good mother or a sensitive wife; a littered home sustained by a second income may be healthier than a spotless, stoic, solemn house.

By using the preceding suggestions, some tasks which are not necessary can be objectively discarded. Then, one can decide how she will use her time and abilities to fulfill her highest self-image. After convincing herself that all tasks are not of equal importance, one eliminates the unnecessary tasks. The eventual result should be a more likable, liveable, loveable, joyous person who is frustrated occasionally, but who doesn't use frustrating situations as an excuse to ventilate hostility.

This would be the result except for one fact—one's spouse has a mass of expectations he projects onto his wife.

7
I've Got to Be Me

When two people get married and decide to live together "for so long as they both shall live" (some people still make such a commitment), there are thousands of potential problems. In reality, the blending of two lives into an intimate relationship is a miracle. When marriage is viewed objectively, it is not so startling that one out of three marriages does not last, but that two out of three do. For a person not only has scores of self-expectations programmed into her, but she has to try to mesh her inner network with another complex personality in such a way that both are satisfied. She has to try to reconcile the differences between her programmed expectations of herself and her husband's expectations of her.

In childhood the husband learned what a wife and mother should be, do, and say. The wife learned what a husband and father should be, do, and say. The tragedy of most marriages is that these expectations are not explored before marriage; they are argued afterwards.

Areas of conflicting expectations are limitless. An examination of a few of the most common areas demonstrates why so much frustration and hostility erupt in many homes. The following checklist will enable the reader to identify some causes of family fights and, in fact, may cause a few more. It would be helpful for the wife and husband to check the appropriate item for herself/himself and spouse, and then compare and discuss the individual perceptions.

The categories are popularly phrased. A much more complicated personality structure than is described is evident in each category. The categories are not to be considered good or bad, merely descriptive. The way two people compliment or conflict in their roles and expectations is important.

House Cleanliness	*Antiseptic*	*Health Hazard*	*Liveable*
Wife			
Husband			

Antiseptic: The house is expected to be as clean as a hospital operating room. It is boastfully said of such housekeepers, "You can eat off her floors."

Health Hazard: One can eat off the floors—stale bread, wilted lettuce, baked beans, etc.

Liveable: Any condition in which both people feel comfortable.

House cleanliness is evaluated by the amount of litter, dust, and dirty dishes that accumulate before someone gets frustrated. The issue may appear trivial, but it is a major obstacle for many couples.

It is one of the least discussed areas, *until* the frustration reaches explosive proportions and the truth emerges through a hail of hostility.

Conversation	*Talkative*	*Close-Lipped*	*Listener*	*Dialoguer*
Wife				
Husband				

Talkative: One who begins talking before she turns off the A.M. alarm clock and continues to talk uninterrupted until she falls asleep at night. She interrupts conversations and changes subjects without motive or transition.

Close-lipped: One who never volunteers information or opinions until she becomes angry, and then tells more than she knows. The close-lipped person is noted for short responses to questions. Question: "Where is Junior? I haven't seen him since I came home."

Close-lipped: "Hospital."
  "What!"
  "Hospital."
  "What happened?"
  "Car wreck."
  "My Gosh! Was he hurt badly?"
  "No!"

"Thank God! Why is he at the hospital?"

"To see a friend."

"You could get laryngitis, and I wouldn't know it for three weeks."

"Yep!"

Listener: One who is interested in people and listens to what they say. The listener doesn't need to talk, but usually enjoys other people talking. The comment most often spoken about a listener is, "She is a terrific conversationalist."

Dialoguer: One who shares thoughts and feelings freely and listens sensitively. The dialoguer is interested in people and in being known by people. She is excited when exchanging ideas and feelings. The dialoguer listens when others speak and speaks when others are ready to listen.

Money	*Spender*	*Miser*	*Economist*
Wife			
Husband			

Spender: One who acts as though items purchased with a credit card don't cost money. The spender uses all of the money available, and stretches the credit system to its seams.

Miser: One who acts as though food were a luxury item.

Economist: One who believes that living within one's income is a reasonable idea.

The conflict possibilities over money are unlimited. The income provider(s) often inflicts guilt on the purchaser and/or budget keeper for not making the income purchase more. The budgeter or purchaser often blames the income provider(s) for not producing more income. When both persons are employed, the issue of who purchases what with whose income is a potentially explosive topic. When the wife wants to contribute to the basic living cost, and the husband is programmed to be THE provider, the issue may get hot. When the wife thinks her income is *her* income, and is programmed to believe that the husband should be the only provider of family income, and the husband thinks otherwise, the barbs begin.

When the wife makes more money than her husband, and the husband is programmed to believe that his manhood is gauged by his ability to provide financially for his "dependent" wife, war breaks out in the home.

Time Consciousness	*Habitually Late*	*Time Is Money*	*Respecter*
Wife			
Husband			

Habitually Late: One who begins to dress for the theatre at curtain time. This behavior is often reinforced by people giving special attention to the late arriver. Almost all prompt people resent habitually late people. Prompt people often feel insulted because they interpret lateness as a lack of respect and consideration for them. The spouse is the only one who tells her, tells her, tells her.

Time Is Money: One who is programmed for promptness, and who feels guilty when she is unavoidably late. This person feels guilty when not using time constructively. The time saver proudly proclaims, "I haven't been late for an appointment in ten years."

"And look where it has gotten you," replies Mr. Habitually Late. "An ulcer and three kids."

"No. That didn't do it. Waiting on you gave me the ulcers."

Respecter: One who respects people and their time, and who uses time wisely without being controlled by it. The respecter understands time as a way of measuring meaningful events, and not as an enemy which requires constant consciousness.

A difference in time perception varies greatly with cultures, subcultures, families, and individuals. It needs special attention in a marriage relationship *before* someone's suppression cap pops off.

Religion	*Have to*	*Ought to*	*Never Want to*
Wife			
Husband			

A description of these categories is too complex for a brief explanation. Instead of categorical description, conversation starters follow.

How people think of, feel about, and act in relation to God, people, and self is their religion. When one believes that God will burn her spouse in hell forever if he doesn't believe a particular doctrine or behave a particular way, anxiety is the inevitable results. The love one holds for her spouse and the fear she feels for him often produces harmful behavior in the relationship. When one's spouse believes that God is an opium for the masses, he becomes frustrated by the spouse's nagging and pleading about church attendance, tithing, and his fallen state. And when he plays golf Sunday morning instead of attending church worship services, the golf widow feels guilty for her failure to convert him, embarrassed by her minister's and friends' inquiries about her husband's absence, and frustrated by her inability to solve a big problem.

When programmed for a legalistic religion and conditioned to respond to fear and guilt, while one's spouse is reared to believe that "a person does what he has to to get ahead," conflict arises in a thousand subtle ways. And when the couple agrees never to talk about religion again, the resentment builds up and the persons use other frustrating events as an excuse to ventilate the hostility created over religion, without ever "bringing up the subject of religion."

Conflicting expectations of religious beliefs and behavior is not resolved by avoiding the issue.

Sex	*Ugh*	*O.K.*	*Whee!*
Wife			
Husband			

Ugh: One feels that sexual intercourse is ugly, evil, dirty, and/or feels guilty when she copulates. "Sex is disgusting" is the feeling, if not the thought. If one feels "Ugh" about sexual intercourse, professional counseling is needed.

O.K.: One responds sexually to the spouse out of a sense of duty. For this person, sexual intercourse is neither good nor bad, it is something one does to satisfy one's spouse, much as one prepares breakfast or mows the lawn.

Whee!: One who experiences the joy, excitement, and serene satisfaction of making love with one's spouse.

To be frustrated sexually is to be frustrated all over. The resulting hostility uses any excuse—lateness, untidy housekeeping, children's behavior, personal appearance—to express the inner tension.

There are scores of other causes of frustration growing out of the expectations couples have of themselves and their spouses. When frustration mounts, either suppression stores the resentment or hostility spews all over the home.

Frustration is an inner signal that things are not as one wants them; one is not controlling some person or situation.

It is satisfying to identify the causes of frustration, whether the cause is from self-expectations or other's expectations, and then to act to improve oneself and one's immediate environment.

After examining her programmed personality and her husband's expectations, she chooses the roles and functions she wills to fulfill.

8
DOING GOOD FEELS GOOD

Every person needs to feel good about who she is. She needs to derive fulfillment from what she does. The ways people try to find this feeling of personal worth are unlimited.

Most people in Western culture are conditioned to feel good about themselves when they achieve a special goal. A child who gets good grades in school receives praise, affection, and sometimes prizes from teachers and parents. The child who performs poorly is often criticized, condemned, and sometimes punished physically by teachers and parents. The maturation process is accompanied by the reward-punishment system through such activities as little league baseball, dance recitals, thespian clubs, and learning table manners.

One learns that worthfulness as a person is directly related to performance, the accomplishing of goals chosen by and for one. One is conditioned to feel worthful when she is working towards or accomplishing a goal. The golfing dynamic offers an outline for exploring the characteristics of people who seek a feeling of personal worth through achieving.

Achievement-motivated people need goals. One of the reasons golf is so satisfying and frustrating is that the goals are endless. Golfing goals are limited only by one's imagination. A partial list of goals follows:
—Par for each of the eighteen holes
—Birdie for each of the eighteen holes (better than par)
—Eagle (better than Birdie)
—Bettering one's lowest score
—Hitting one's longest drive
—Sinking one's longest putt
—Par for the course (the weekend golfers' glorious fantasy)

—The golfer has a goal with each shot on every hole.

If the golfer is an assemblyline worker, or an office worker, or if his job has become routine, he gets that good feeling from playing golf which comes from accomplishing. The average weekend golfer hits so many shots, that the law of averages enables him to make one or two good shots to remember and to talk about, talk about, talk about.

The golf widow is an achiever. She needs goals that give that good feeling. Many of the tasks she performs are often routine and boring, and don't feel good as goals should.

The enculturating process produces a special dynamic in achievement-motivated women. In early life the woman is encouraged to succeed. It is acceptable for her to make excellent grades the first twelve to fourteen years of formal education. She is encouraged and rewarded for excelling in the arts and in education and in home economics. But when she enters what has been considered a traditionally male profession, people often withdraw their approval, and, in some situations, attack the woman hostilely for violating male squatter's rights.

Recent research has shown that many women suppress their achievement needs when they near the "marrying age." They feel that, if they want to get married, they must not threaten the men. This is sad for the women and sad for the weak-egoed men. The women who suppress their need to achieve deny themselves the satisfaction of fulfilling their potential as persons. Even if they succeed in suppressing their need to achieve, it is not many months or years after marriage that these women yearn for ways to express their intelligence and abilities. Yet, they often continue to hide their talents and intelligence, and that causes much frustration. In moments of hostility the truth emerges.

Fortunately this situation is changing for some women. However, there are millions of wives caught in a routine of living who are not receiving that good feeling from achieving goals.

Achievement-motivated people need goals which can be measured. Loren has been playing golf for twenty-five years. He has never met a golfer who did not keep score.

One of the problems of the golf widow is that some of her most important goals seem vague and distant; they are not immediately measurable. She has the goal of enabling her children to become healthy, happy, free, spontaneous adults. Or she may want them to be successful surgeons to fulfill her unrealized dream. The goal is so far in the future that she receives little goal satisfaction in the present.

The golf widow can measure her routine tasks. She knows when she cooks a meal and redecorates a room. She may feel good about her accomplishment when she calls the family to dinner, or displays her redecorated family room to her friends and family. This type of achieving may be very satisfying to some women.

If frustrated with her roles as mother, wife, and homemaker, one may need to seek other measurable goals which will satisfy her need to achieve. Hobbies (golf, tennis, bridge, etc.), volunteer service organizations, local politics, and being an adjunct social worker meet this need for millions of women.

Achievement-motivated people need reachable, reasonable goals. Achievement-motivated people do not respond to impossible goals. The golfer sets his own goals in addition to the goals set by the golf course. He may have a long-range goal of shooting par for the course. He sets immediate subgoals which hopefully will enable him to reach eventually his big goal. His first goal may be to "break a hundred." Later, when he shoots an eighty-nine to break the ninety score barrier, he struts into the clubhouse with the pride of a Master's Golf Tournament champion.

The golf widow has the long range goal of rearing her children to *be* something special. It is difficult for her to see the relationship between her big goal and the tasks of changing diapers, cooking meals, refereeing fights, transporting children, and vacuuming the living room.

The people who grasp, emotionally and intellectually, the significance of subgoals to their ultimate goals maintain a good emotional balance and manage routine tasks with a minimum of irritation.

Suppose one's goal is to be a sensitive, supportive mother. There are subgoals which characterize a sensitive mother: She acts with rational love. She doesn't react hostilely toward the children when they act like children by getting their new clothes dirty or by leaving their room cluttered and bed unmade.

Just as the golfer doesn't par every hole, the golf widow does not consistently fulfill all of her subgoals. But, if she can envision the big goal and work on the subgoals, there can be satisfaction. After deciding to cease displaying hostility on her children when they frustrate her, she receives great satisfaction when she acts sensitively in a tense situation. Instead of shouting and screaming in a situation where she usually loses control, she says, "I'm mad. We need to talk. We need to solve this problem now." Self-respect grows rapidly as she acts to improve herself, whether the goal be emotional control or becoming a lawyer.

Goals need to be reasonable and reachable. It is not reasonable to assume that a person who has been sexually frustrated, nervous, and irritable for twenty years will suddenly become a calm, controlled, happy individual just because she decides to. For this person to decide *never* to lose her temper again is an unreasonable goal, which can cause additional guilt feelings rather than improve one's self-image.

There are two steps in setting reasonable, reachable goals. First, assess the facts before setting goals and subgoals. Questions to ask in setting goals:

—Do *I* want to accomplish this goal?

—Which needs do I expect to meet through this goal?

—What will I gain when I reach this goal?

—What will it require in time, energy, ability, and intelligence?

—What will I have to give up to reach the goal?

—Am I willing to pay the price?

—Whom will it affect? (children, husband, friends, etc.)

—How will it affect them? (less or more time with the children, threaten or support the husband, etc.)

—Can I accomplish this goal?

The second step, after careful analysis, is to devise a plan for accomplishing the goal. Subgoals serve as a road map to the desired destination. It is relatively simple to establish subgoals for becoming a lawyer. The road map is furnished and one merely chooses from the alternate routes and adjusts life accordingly. It is more difficult to establish subgoals for becoming a more relaxed, joyous person. However, the procedure is the same. One devises a plan for doing so and measures the results as she works toward her goal. She receives that good feeling from achieving each subgoal.

Continual failure in the same activity ultimately produces a loss of interest in that activity. Warren developed a duck hook in his golf game. He practiced daily to correct the hook. He took lessons from the golf pro. Nothing worked. Warren lived golf for seventeen years, but six months of frustration was too much for him. He said sadly, "I'm going to quit playing. I've practiced for hours. I've taken lessons and read books, and I still hook the ball. I used to shoot seventy-five to eighty. Now I'm lucky to break ninety. I can't stand the frustration."

Gripping the handle of his putter, Warren took a few practice putts at the imaginary ball on the floor of the clubhouse. He said nostalgically, "It's like getting a divorce from a woman you love. You know what's causing the trouble, but you don't know how to correct it. You can't live with her, and you don't want to live without her." Warren chuckled as if he were embarrassed about his nostalgia and asked, "Anyone want to buy a set of clubs?" The incident appears melodramatic and even ridiculous to the nongolfer, yet it is real. Warren had to find a new lifestyle after seventeen years, for until this day his family and work had been scheduled around his golf.

One who tries to create a laughing, loving home for seventeen years without much success feels as Warren felt. She may know what's causing the trouble, but she can't correct it. She may have tried everything she knows, yet the situation has not improved; the family continues to erupt into a horror of hostility, or resemble the wake of a despised, deceased relative.

People react differently when faced with this situation. Some women give up and accept the emotional life of a zombie. Others get out of the relationship as soon as the children are grown. Many women seek an outside affair with a man.

Continual failure in the same activity produces a loss of interest in the activity whether it be sex, or water skiing, or cooking, or comforting a child. Continual failure also dents away at one's sense of self-worth.

Continual success in an activity eventually produces a loss of interest in the activity for a high achiever. Golf can be a lifelong hobby because it is rare for a person to have continual success in it. Even the professional golfers have slumps when they cannot play consistently good golf.

A high achiever does not receive much satisfaction from preparing the same gourmet meal month after month. She may enjoy the compliments from her guest, but she doesn't receive the inner satisfaction which comes from accomplishing a difficult task. She may be bored because she can do what she does without using any of her creativity or imagination. Of course, the potential for creative imagination in establishing new difficult goals in the family setting is unlimited, especially if one has children.

Summary

"Achieving equals a feeling of self-worth" is the theme of American culture. Most people are conditioned to feel good about themselves when they achieve. Men are programmed to expect to assume the major achievement roles in society, such as the professions, i.e., lawyer, doctor, politician, and business executive. They are programmed to expect the professional plums and to receive satisfaction from such activities. The plums are roles which are clothed with prestige, prosperous pay, and popular power.

The women have been programmed for the societal subordinate goals. They are supposed to withdraw from the competition of prestigious, prosperous positions, and to find satisfaction as homemakers, secretaries, sales clerks, and school teachers. Whereas the elementary school teacher has one of the most influential and important professional positions in society, she is not given the prestige or pay commensurate with her position. The roles assigned to women in the past have offered little opportunity to satisfy the achievement needs of highly motivated people.

A major frustration for the high achievement-motivated homemaker is the lack of challenging, measurable goals to conquer when she gets bored with the routine tasks. It is not impossible to find such goals in a family, but it requires consistent creativity.

One needs measurable goals through which she may receive the good feeling that comes from doing a difficult job well. When the goals are not present, she is subject to a contagious case of stockpiling resentment. And any home furnishes more than enough frustration to trigger the stockpile and unload the hostility.

That achievement equals a feeling of personal self-worth is a valid concept. It works. Achieving feels good. But after the goals have been conquered and the citations tacked on the wall, or the presidency of the firm become a daily job, or the children successfully seen through college and in profitable positions, there is still something missing.

Very often after accomplishing the "big" goal of life, one feels an inner emptiness. At each step of the way towards the goal, one thought that there would be some kind of salvation in this special accomplishment. Each time a new goal was set, and a new plan devised, and each time the satisfaction was short-lived.

To reiterate: Achieving is good. It feels good. It is necessary in a society. It helps to build strong egos and boost budgets. But achieving is not the answer to the basic question of life—it does not enable one to feel personally worthful in a continuous, creative, caring way. The ultimate goal of life is not reached through achievement.

9
IT FEELS GOOD TO HAVE FRIENDS

Some people are programmed to feel worthful through friendships. Their sense of self-worth is determined by the people who enable them to feel good about being a Friend. (The affiliation-motivated person will be referred to as Friend in this writing.)

There is much misunderstanding about the Friend, as contrasted to the high achiever. Many people assume that the Achiever is a ruthless villain who destroys people as she compulsively collects and counts her victories on her symbolic rosary. The Friend is seen as a selfless, benevolent, non-threatening, soothing saint who is interested only in people. This is not the case.

A difference between the Friend and the Achiever is in the means by which they identify themselves in order to get that good feeling about who they are. The Achiever identifies herself by accomplishments: She is president of the Woman's Club, vice-president of the Garden Club, chairman of the United Fund Campaign, champion bridge player, editor of I.Q. Press, and vice-chairman of the League of Women Voters. The Friend identifies herself by the people with whom she associates: she is the mother of Sue, Jamie, and John, the friend of Mary, Donna, and Harvey, and the lover to Max, her husband.

The Friend knows who she is primarily through the people with whom she associates, and not through the projects she completes. She defines herself in terms of personal relationships, not deeds done nor victories won. She is not necessarily more compassionate, sensitive to, or concerned about people than the Achiever. The Achiever usually has friends and the Friend usually has some accomplishments to her credit. The Achiever gets that special feeling of personal self-worth when achieving. The Friend gets that special feeling of personal self-worth through people.

Playing golf affords one the opportunity to meet both the achievement and affiliation need. Some men play golf more for the fraternal value than the achievement satisfaction (and their score indicates it). This is the continuation of early life patterns. The male child is reared in a culture which promotes team sports, boy's clubs, and scores of other activities that foster friendships or bonds between male and male. During the pre-teen years, most boys who are not overly organized in little league baseball, pee wee football, swimming teams, and elementary school basketball leagues gravitate to other boys to create games and activities to occupy their time.

Even when boys begin to notice the positive differences between girls and boys, they continue to have special male companions, and to participate in exclusively male activities. They hunt, fish, play team sports, or room with a gang of boys.

Adult males continue the pattern through the Rotary Club, Lions' Club, Kiwanis Club, and the Shriners' Organization. There are hunting clubs, fishing companions, bowling teams, and even country clubs where women are not permitted to play golf.

Playing golf is a fraternal activity for men. This "night out with the boys" syndrome confuses some wives. The golf widow often assumes that her golfer wants to be with the boys because he is bored with her. The time away from home is interpreted and experienced as personal rejection. This may not be the case. One's husband may need this kind of friendship. At least part of the resistance to the "Feminist Movement" is an attempt to protect exclusive male fraternalization.

Playing golf with the men is not necessarily a rejection of the wife, or a sign of boredom with the home scene, or a lack of love for the children. It is a way men meet their need to establish, express, and enjoy friendships with men.

The golf widow needs female friends and the time to sustain the friendships. She needs women with whom she can share her thoughts, activities, and feelings. She needs someone she can talk to about Sue's dance recital, John Jr.'s school problem, and the irritating person in the P.T.A., or the incompetent employee at the office. She needs relief from the pressure and routine of her family duties and/or her profession.

The golf widow who realizes her self-worth through being a Friend can find satisfaction as a homemaker. She doesn't need to achieve the public goals which give prestige, power, and pay. She has her goals with her family. She receives prestige from her family and realizes the power of her presence in their midst. She accepts the emotional pay of their esteem and affection.

A closer look at the Friend (affiliation-motivated people) explains why this fulfillment is realized by some women.

The Friend needs people to endorse, affirm, and enhance her sense of personal worth. This need is felt early in life. The Friend is taught that people are more important than projects or property. Her family stressed the importance of friendship and affection rather than routine, works, and rewards. The Friend did not live in an atmosphere of the double bind which is illustrated by the parent who says, "I wouldn't take a million dollars for you," and who ten minutes later spanks the child for tearing a two-dollar blouse while playing. The Friend's parents may have punished her when she was a child, but it was for being rude to an adult, or failing to thank her grandmother for the gift of Amy Vanderbilt's book on etiquette.

The Friend learns that there are certain ways to act to receive affection and win friends. The script reads: (1) do not openly disagree with people, (2) do not express negative feelings ("If you don't like the food, person, or program, keep quiet"), and (3) be friendly. This way of acting *may* be the way the Achiever acts to accomplish her goal, but her behavior is designed to win the cooperation of people in order to accomplish the goal. It is a means to an end. The Friend "behaves" to win the friendship as an end in itself.

The Friend needs affection. The Friend's sense of self-worth is felt in direct relationship to the affection she receives. When the housewife Friend is confined to the house fourteen hours a day without any adult conversation or affection, she usually feels lonely and may get hostile. The lack of affirmation causes her to feel personally worthless.

The Friend fears conflict. The Friend often acquiesces in the conflict situation. She suppresses her hostile feelings because she does not want to risk losing the affection she is already receiving. She avoids conflict because saving a friendship or keeping a family together is more important to her than winning a point of view in a discussion, or getting her way. The Friend opts for peaceful coexistence, which is an unhealthy practice, for one who consistently compromises in the name of peaceful coexistence stockpiles resentments, and eventually erupts inside with a psychomatic illness, or explodes outside with the cannon shooting balls of hostility.

The Friend seeks people and groups of people who think as she does. Because of the fear of conflict the Friend needs people who agree with her. She seeks people who will make her feel good by endorsing her prejudices, affirming her political positions, and pleading her case. The Friend identifies more with the people of an organization than the purpose of the organization. The purpose of the organization may be important, but the people who belong to the organization are more important. The Friend attends meetings, supports programs, and serves on committees, for through her attendance and support she is with the right people.

Because her basic need is affection and friends, the Friend can find much satisfaction as a homemaker. She does not need to conquer high measurable goals to get that good feeling about herself. She realizes her sense of personal worth through friendships. She needs a friend with whom she can share her thoughts and feelings and feel accepted while doing so. This friendship enables her to ventilate and thereby to avoid displacing hostility.

This kind of friendship is based on sameness. It is maintained so long as two people agree with each other, avoid serious conflict, and make each other feel good with compliments, mutual gripes, and soothing emotional support. This friendship feels good. It is important for it gives one fleeting feelings of personal worth.

This type of friendship does not solve the basic problems of life. One needs more than a few agreeable friends in order to discover the deeper satisfaction which comes from feeling like *Somebody* who makes a big difference in the world.

Everyone needs an intimate relationship.

10
AN INTIMATE RELATIONSHIP

An intimate relationship enables one to feel good about who she is. Intimacy is feeling good about me, you, and us. Before exploring the intimate relationship, the principles of intimacy will be described briefly.

Intimacy

Intimacy is the emotional nourishment needed for growth in infancy. One cannot become a healthy, happy functioning person without the support of at least one person who cares deeply for her. The absence of intimacy scars one emotionally and physically.

During infancy one absorbs affection passively. One is totally dependent upon others not only for a relatively normal life, but for the propensity to establish intimate relations.

Intimacy is directly related to a sense of personal worth. The way one thinks of, feels about, and perceives herself is related to the intimacy (or lack of it) she received in infancy and childhood. If in infancy and childhood she was loved for who she was, and not for what she did or how she behaved, she feels a worthy part of creation. Although it may be held unconsciously, the life position is, "I am worthy because I am loved," which is to feel, "I am worthy of love."

Intimacy is experienced as a gift. It is not something one does for herself. It is not a reward for a good performance. It is a gift received from another person. The gift is given in infancy and childhood by parents or parental substitutes. The gift may be given by one's spouse or friends later in life.

Whereas it begins with a passive position in infancy, intimacy becomes an active attitude towards oneself, people, and God and/or the Universe.

Intimacy is the will to relate. Intimacy is the innate drive to establish intimate relations. There is within each person, sometimes buried deep within, the need to be in intimate relations; it is a created part of one's nature.

Very often the tendency to establish intimate relations is repressed or suppressed under a mountain of enculturated crust. One is conditioned not to risk intimacy. Programmed for fear, one hears and often believes the calloused cliches: "You can't trust people; they will hurt you," "Winning is all that counts, whether it be a race or an argument," "People will not like you if you act angry," "Everyone must like me," "Don't let anyone know how you feel," "Sex is evil," "Men are superior to women," "Women are superior to men," "All men are beasts," and "All women are shrews."

The role expectations and the programmed patterns of getting one's way often block the establishing of intimate relationships. It is possible to break programmed patterns and to redefine roles and, thereby, to establish a redeeming relationship with one's spouse.

An Intimate Relationship

In an intimate relationship openness is encouraged. In the current popularity of "openness" there are many misconceptions. Openness is not a preoccupation with feelings, nor the shoving of thoughts down other people's throats. It is not the advertising of sensuous sensations to casual acquaintances. The destructive consequences of the spontaneous expression of hostility prove this.

Openness is being aware of oneself. It is being aware of one's feelings. As previously noted, extensive suppression of feelings causes one to lose the capacity to identify particular feelings. Consider again the feeling of anger. The popular "Christian" belief that anger is evil encourages suppression. When this thought is drummed into one's head, and when one is repeatedly punished for expressing anger, she suppresses her anger until she no longer recognizes it. Instead of identifying the feeling of anger and expressing it she feels guilty and evil. She feels worthless without being able to identify the cause of the worthless feeling.

In an intimate relationship one is encouraged to identify and express anger and affection, apathy and love, hate and compassion, and sadness and joy. She can have feelings and own them without feeling guilty about them. She rediscovers a new depth of aliveness through her feelings in an intimate relationship.

Openness is being aware of the thoughts which keep racing through the mind. It is being receptive to the conceptual presuppositions as they emerge. The "AHA!" experience surprises one. "AHA! I assume that men don't feel as deeply as women do," or "I assume if I treat Fred nicely he will take advantage of me," or "I assume that women are not as smart as men," or "I assume that God is a man." Openness enables one to discover the conceptual presuppositions, prejudices, and resentments which have accumulated within her, and which cause her to suppress the drive for intimacy.

Openness is being aware of the effects of one's behavior. The small irritating mannerisms and the big ways one tries to win are identified, examined, and evaluated. It is often surprising to a couple to discover the patterns of winning each uses with the other. It is a shattering experience for an adult to discover that she uses motherly guilt-producing words to win with her husband. It is embarrassing for the husband to admit that he uses the child's sulking pattern to win with his wife. In an intimate relationship the behavior of each is identified, examined, and evaluated. The irritating mannerisms are either accepted or eliminated.

Openness is an attitude towards and relationship with another person. It is not a solo activity. Openness is being aware of and sensitive to a spouse's feelings, thoughts, behavior, and presuppositions about life. Openness exists in an intimate relationship because each thinks and feels that the other is important. One is as concerned about the other's happiness as about one's own. Openness is an invitation by each for the other to be herself without public posturing to receive praise and approval. Each wants and expects the other to bring her own brand of being to the relationship—to be as open as possible so that together they may grow in and through intimacy.

In an intimate relationship people trust each other. If one trusts her spouse, and if she feels that he trusts her, there is a minimum of suppression. Each person is free to express what is felt and thought about herself and her spouse without fear of rejection. Feedback is given and received. Problems are confronted. Conflict arises. Insights emerge. Feedback is given in a special way, with a concern for the other person as well as for oneself. Seeing or feeling something which is hurtful to either, she speaks and acts. One confronts her husband about the effects of his golfing habit, and expresses her feelings, and solicits his help in resolving the problem. She cares about and trusts herself and her husband, and because she does she takes the risk of expressing happy and angry feelings, clear and confusing concepts, and bizarre and beautiful behavior.

In an intimate relationship the revealed and concealed differences between self and spouse are excitedly, and sometimes painfully, explored. This shared, mutual exploration occurs because the trust which exists is deeper than the expectations each has of the other. The relationship is not founded upon or grounded in role playing, public relating, agreeing with each other, or becoming like the other. It is grounded in intimacy. When intimacy exists between two people, the hope is that each will find her own brand of being. The traditional and the new role expectations are tossed up for grabs. The wife may enter a profession, or take up a hobby, or become a homebound, happy family maker. The irritating tasks are examined and distributed, the exciting ones shared. There is no such thing as women's work, or men's work; there are simply tasks which must be accomplished.

In an intimate relationship people accept each other. The enculturating process often creates a tendency to hide that which hurts, or embarrasses, or frightens. One is often programmed to share successes modestly, and to hide failure cleverly. She is taught to stress strength and to conceal weakness. She is encouraged to anticipate what is acceptable to others, and then to perform accordingly so that she will receive praise and approval. This behavior stockpiles resentment, and hinders expression of intimacy.

These tendencies hinder the experience of acceptance when one shares *only* that part of herself which she considers to be worthy of praise and approval; the acceptance she receives feels fraudulent. She must pretend to be happy when she is sad, to act pleasant when she is angry, and to appear naïve when she is engrossed in the erotic.

When a spouse or friend responds positively to this artificial projection, one feels phoney. She lives with the fear of being found out and the pressure to produce the pretty picture. As the pressure mounts, she often feels resentment towards her spouse for not helping her reveal more of herself, and for not making her happier. She often blames her spouse for her nervousness, headaches, and hostility.

Acceptance is only experienced when one shares those acts and feelings and thoughts which make her feel unacceptable. Openness in a trust relationship enables each to reveal *gradually* (sometimes explosively) that aspect of her personage which she has learned to fear, or to be ashamed of, or to feel guilty about. When this occurs one experiences acceptance where she needs it—with that part of her personage which causes her to feel worthless.

It is important to note that every act and feeling and thought doesn't have to be shared with one's spouse. There are some situations which may be better resolved with a professional counselor.

Marie did not enjoy sex. She was highly nervous and irritable. She was unresponsive in and out of the bed to her husband. She felt worthless. According to Marie no one could love her; she was too evil. Through counseling Marie resolved her problem of guilt feelings about an affair she had had twenty-two years before, at the age of sixteen. After she resolved the problem of guilt, she became a "fantastic lover and intimate friend," according to her husband. Marie's guilt feelings had blocked her capacity for intimacy with her husband and with her children.

Until one resolves that something which causes her to feel unacceptable, she cannot believe the acceptance she receives. And until she feels acceptable, she cannot experience intimacy.

Acceptance is different from approval and praise. Approval and praise are the results of a satisfactory or superior performance according to another's standards. When one prepares her family's favorite dessert, or writes a best-selling book, she receives praise and approval. The praise and approval feels good, but the good feeling doesn't last. Acceptance is the affirmation of another's innate worth. Acceptance is, "I love you because you are worth loving," and not, "I love you because you are a good chef and an excellent writer."

With this kind of acceptance, routine roles often lose some of their irritating effects.

In an intimate relationship each is encouraged to share wonderfulness and weirdness, and to accept acceptance. This does not imply an absence of judgment. Rather, it suggests that each person is free to challenge and to criticize the other's behavior, thoughts, and feelings without fear of *person*al rejection.

In an intimate relationship one gradually presents to another pieces of the enculturating crust which cover her intimate nature, and she is accepted with her "imperfections."

Intimacy enables each person in the relationship to discover a free, spontaneous, creative, joyous, fulfilling way of living. This is what marriage should do for every member of the family. The issue is not women's rights or men's rights; it is person's rights and responsibilities, and privileges and potential. The intimate relationship enables one to grow towards her created potential, for the feeling of personal worth is based on intimacy. One is known and is loved as she is. The basic problem of life is solved. An intimate relationship is a high ideal for two people. It is possible. Though not always comfortable, or peaceful, or happy, the relationship is satisfying and exciting for one is becoming who she chooses to be *with* someone whom she loves and who loves her deeply.

11
WE CAN WIN
Preparing for and Growing Through Problems

It takes time to grow and maintain an intimate relationship. The problem in most troubled marriages is that the wife and the husband don't spend enough time together. They become so occupied with the business of making a living, and rearing a family, and fulfilling their many roles, and possibly participating in a hobby, that they seldom take time to be together—to be physically, intellectually, and emotionally present to one another. Even when there is mutual free time they watch television, or work in the yard, or displace hostility.

Couples who do not spend time together enter into the crisis periods of marriage unprepared to work through their problems. The three major crisis periods in a marriage produce enough of a challenge without encountering them with a stranger.

Trapped Feeling

The first major crisis period occurs the first three to seven years of marriage. Children have become a part of the family. Both the wife and the husband get a trapped feeling. The wife feels trapped by children, cleaning, cooking, and sometimes a salaried job. The husband feels trapped by the confining boundaries and heavy responsibilities of a family. During this time in a marriage, persons either grow closer together by working through their problems, or they begin to become strangers who meet at meals to eat, and in the bed to have an almost impersonal affair, which often results in extramarital affairs or preoccupying hobbies. During this period people need to be together to share their frustrating and fun feelings and the disturbing and exciting incidents in their lives. If the couple ignores their problems during this period, the second major crisis in marriage is devastating to them.

What's the Meaning of It All?

The couple enters middlessence with little to hold them together as they ask the question, "What's the meaning of it all?" During middlessence the children leave home for college or marriage. If one has devoted all of her time and emotional energy to her children to the neglect of her husband's emotional needs, she is lost in the lovely house which used to pass for a home. If her spouse devoted all of his time and emotional energy to his profession and/or hobby, he awakens beside a stranger. When the only person one has to talk to in the evenings is that stranger she married twenty-five years before, she may become very lonely and disillusioned with life. She may discover that this stranger who partially paid the bills doesn't fill the emotional vacuum left by the departure of the real "love people," her children. Buying new clothes, building the dream house, eating strawberry cheesecake, and drinking martinis doesn't seem to help with this problem.

The husband also has an emotional upheaval during this time. This is the period in life when men realize that their youthful dreams may not be fulfilled. The promising young executive awakens to discover that he is the middle-aged office manager, and will probably always be just that, and not president of the firm. He may realize that he is not going to be the head of the physics department at the university, or chief engineer for the city government, or a famous surgeon, or foreman at the plant. It is disillusioning for a man in an achievement-oriented society to discover that he is "average." With this feeling reinforced with grey hair, or no hair at all, this man enters the toupee-sports car-mod dress syndrome fighting to hold back time. Even becoming president of the firm doesn't stop the aging process nor does it necessarily cause the crisis of values to vanish.

What seemed so important twenty years before, once attained, may appear trivial. Gazing at trophies may trigger fond memories, but the present and future demand a worthy reason for living now.

After one has played the game of collecting honors and possessions, the demand for purpose peeks out to tease and torment the complacent collector.

During this crisis people need emotional support. They need to feel they count big in the life of another person. They need to be needed and to feel it. They need to be wanted and to hear it. They need to talk honestly about their fears, frustration, and fantasies. They need to feel understood and accepted with their fears and failures, and with their loves and victories.

A stranger cannot fill this role; even a stranger to whom one has been married for twenty-five years.

What Now?

The third major crisis period in a marriage occurs when the man and/or wife retires. For the first time in his life, the husband hears his wife say, "For goodness sake, go golfing! Go hunting! Go fishing! Do something, but do it some place else." The man feels useless because his culture has taught him that he is worthless unless he is actively achieving some great and glorious goal. During the years since the children left home the wife has discovered a new lifestyle, often without her husband, and his constant presence irritates her. An hour a day of the right kind of time could bring some mutual understanding, support, and romance to two people who will live many more years together.

These periods do not have to be crisis-centered. If two people grow an intimate relationship they meet personal crisis together, and give and receive emotional and intellectual support. The wife shares her feelings of lostness when the children leave home. The husband ventilates his hostility about being passed up on the promotion at the office. Instead of blaming each other for each personal crisis and making the marriage the focal point of every individual crisis, two people enable each other to grow through the adjustment phases of life.

An intimate relationship is not something which can be postponed until the crisis occurs. Very often, by the time a crisis occurs in a marriage, two people have become strangers to one another. The love they once felt has diminished; the hurts they have endured control the consciousness of both. They remember all that is hurtful and have forgotten much that was helpful about their relationship.

It takes time to grow and maintain an intimate relationship.

Me—You—We

When two people blend their lives in marriage a new entity comes into existence. The woman brings her programmed feelings, thoughts, behavior, and needs to the marriage. The man brings his programmed feelings, thoughts, behavior, and needs to the marriage. Thus two unique persons create a relationship. Although it cannot exist without both, the relationship is different from each person; it is an entity in itself. The relationship has characteristics as does each person.

The characteristics are determined by the ingredients each brings to the relationship, and how these ingredients blend to meet, or fail to meet each person's needs. The relationship has needs which must be met for each person to be nurtured in it. These needs are met through intimacy skills which each performs.

The relationship is the WE of the marriage. Thus, there are three entities with which to deal.

ME—One wants to discover and to share who she is and how she is doing. "I feel lonely and unappreciated." "I am frustrated about the unpaid bills." "I need more time with you." "I've been thinking about going back to college." "I enjoyed the dinner at Don Q's last night. I relaxed and felt loved."

YOU—One wants to know how her spouse is doing. "What is frustrating you?" "How were things at work today?" "Did you enjoy the dinner at Don Q's?" "How do you feel about my new job?" One wants to know what her spouse is thinking, hoping, feeling, and fantasying.

WE—One wants to know how WE are doing. "Are you feeling good about us?" "Do you think we are meeting each other's needs?" "What can WE do to solve this estranged feeling which exists between us?" "How can I help us?" "How can you help us?"

Obviously, the WE is enabled to grow in intimacy by giving special attention to each person's needs through the application of intimacy skills.

Intimacy Skills In a Marriage

Listening

Many people are too preoccupied with *their* feelings, needs, wants, and ideas to give undivided attention to another person. They prepare their responses while the other is speaking. It is difficult to listen when hurting. Yet giving undivided attention is a necessary skill in a marriage.

Listening is focusing on the speaker's words, thoughts, and feelings. It is watching to catch the non-verbal messages and intonational tips. Listening makes the other person the subject of the universe, the center of all thoughts and activities, and the person needs to know that someone thinks so. What one's spouse says and thinks and feels and does is important. Listening communicates respect and concern.

Talking Straight

Many people have difficulty verbalizing thoughts and feelings clearly. Some people have been programmed to make small talk. Small talk is safe; no one will get hurt talking about grocery lists, the high cost of living, the children's health, and flowers. Everyone makes some small talk. But the person who only makes small talk with her spouse never reveals her deepest thoughts and feelings and wants and needs. Yet, she expects and wants her spouse to know and to respond to her helpfully. The "guess what I expect you to do . . . and you had better do it" behavior saps a relationship. It can be overcome with increased skill in discovering and revealing hidden hurts and hopes.

Some people have been programmed to complain. Complaining is a normal response when feeling treated unjustly. All people complain occasionally. However, the programmed complainer is preoccupied with the practice. When she speaks, it is to gripe. Disguising her needs, the complainer says, "You are an inconsiderate slob," instead of saying, "I am lonely and need you." Instead of confessing and requesting, she insults and attacks, making the other person the subject; the subject switches from *my* needs to *your* devilish deeds. Rather than focus on her feelings and needs, she nitpicks her spouse's behavior and character.

Talking straight is sharing thoughts and feelings clearly. She can learn to share her deepest desires, her greatest fears, and her happiest moments. She can learn to let herself be the subject—openly, trustingly, and acceptingly.

Giving Feedback Supportively

Feedback is not helpful when given with a saintly superior attitude which says, "I am telling you this for your own good . . . You're repulsive." Anyone who enjoys telling people what is wrong with them, shouldn't.

Supportive feedback is given for the benefit of the other person; it is given to help the person solve a problem.

Until the need for help is felt a person can't accept and use feedback. Pointing out the causes of another's nervousness will not help unless she can't tolerate her inner feelings. She has to want and need to feel differently. Discovering that hostile outbursts are creating neurotic children may furnish the motivation to change. Feedback will be used when the need for it is seen and felt and not before. So hostile criticisms do more damage than good.

Accepting criticism from people who do not respect or care for one is difficult. Thus, feedback is given because one emphathizes with her spouse. She hurts because he hurts. Only people who care deeply about people acquire the skill and sensitivity to enable others to grow through their problems. So, "If you don't respect and love her, don't tell her what's wrong with her." It will not help either person.

People must be emotionally ready for feedback. They can use feedback when they feel loved and respected. There is a problem with this theory. When people are feeling loved, and when WE are getting along well, there is a hesitancy to disrupt the peaceful atmosphere with a critical note. When people are not feeling loved, and when WE are in trouble, feedback is usually given with a hostile tone. And feedback given with a hostile tone is destructive to me, you, and WE.

Giving feedback supportively is a skill used to express love. Everyone needs the support of someone who cares enough to help her grow, change, and find her own brand of being and sense of personal worth. Negative feedback is given when one feels loving, and her spouse feels loved. Positive feedback is given when one's spouse needs to feel loved and when one wants to express love and *any time* it feels right (given even to those people who are uncomfortable with compliments).

When two people learn to listen with undivided attention, and to talk straight, and to give and receive feedback supportively, the WE of "you" and "me" is sustained through intimacy.

12
AN HOUR A DAY
A Plan for Growing
an Intimate Marriage

"An hour a day!" Mac exclaimed. "You must be kidding, Loren."

"No, I'm not. If I am going to work with you and Jane, the two of you will have to work on the relationship, too. I can't solve your problems for you. I can only help you identify the nature of the problems, and possibly help you discover some methods by which you can solve them."

"But an hour a day just sitting and talking to one another. That's a long time," Jane said.

"Yes, what will we talk about?" Mac asked. "We love each other . . . I think . . . but we don't have that much to discuss."

"Mac is right. I don't have the time to sit around and talk."

Loren waited, watched, and listened as they tried to convince him that an hour a day visiting with one another was a waste of time.

Finally, Loren said, "Those are my terms. If you don't want to do it, I suggest that you try to find a counselor who will agree to solve your problems without bothering you with each other."

"That's not fair, Loren," Mac said.

"Yes it is fair, because that's what you're asking me to do—to solve your problems for you. I can't do it."

Mac and Jane looked at each other and then nodded their agreement which was the first important thing they had agreed upon in two years.

The following week they entered Loren's office with solemn, hostile expressions on their faces. Loren greeted them. They sat down.

After two minutes of silence, Loren asked, "How did the hour go?"

"It was hell," said Mac. "After the first fifteen minutes we were shocked to discover that we didn't have anything to talk about."

"What do you mean?"

"What I mean is that we didn't have anything to talk about. . . . We don't know each other."

"Yes," said Jane. "We tried to talk to each other but . . . uh . . . after I told Mac about the kids' activities there wasn't anything to say."

"Your scheme is artificial," Mac angrily said.

They described an hour of awkwardness and tension which ended in an argument. They tried the hour a second day that week. It ended in another argument. Except for the thirty minutes Jane and Mac joined together to condemn Loren for suggesting such a ridiculous plan, they avoided each other for the next five days.

Much to their consternation Loren insisted on the hour a day. He re-emphasized the suggested guidelines for using the hour. He reminded them that they had agreed to try this approach for three months.

Mac and Jane's experience is most common. It is unusual for a couple who uses this plan not to be shocked by their apparent strangeness to one another. The first few weeks are usually filled with silence and sarcasm, much conflict and little comfort. Only those people dedicated to making a marriage what it should and could be use this plan.

The "one hour a day" plan can be an effective way of working through problems, and meeting individual needs, and growing an intimate relationship. It is not a panacea; it is not a cureall for every marriage. People emotionally estranged encountering a crisis in their marriage need professional counseling to assist them in learning to confront and to comfort constructively, and to support and to sustain each other sensitively. People who love each other can create an intimate relationship. But loving each other doesn't guarantee an intimate marriage.

Couples who love each other and who apply intimacy skills have an exciting, joyous marriage. Couples who use this "one hour" program for three to six months usually discover a process for managing problems and for fulfilling each's goals of living. The need to formally structure time gradually diminishes. The couple spontaneously creates the time when it is needed, and applies intimacy skills as a natural response to each other. Each person listens when the spouse speaks, and talks straight when her mate is listening. Individual needs are sensed and appropriate responses made.

The WE supports, sustains, and satisfies each person as both grow towards their chosen goals.

The "one hour a day" principles apply to those marriages in which a person's profession involves days away from home. The equivalent in time is needed to grow an intimate relationship.

Objectives

The hour is approached with agreed upon objectives. Suggested objectives should include the following.

1. To identify feelings about me, you, and WE.
2. To identify thoughts about me, you, and WE.
3. To identify specific behavior and explore the ways it affects me, you, and WE.
4. To identify life presupposition which affects me, you, and WE.
5. To explore and to accept, or to reject, or to compromise the roles each person is fulfilling.
6. To fantasize and plan for the future.
7. To share and work through frustrating situations.
8. To learn to use anger constructively.
9. To resolve old resentments which affect the relationship.
10. To express appreciation for one's spouse.

Me—You—We Time

The hour is divided into four phases. The suggested time for each phase is approximate.

"Me" Time—15 Minutes

During the first fifteen minutes person A is the subject. She uses the skill of talking straight. (The person who needs to ventilate the most usually takes the first "me" time.) She shares her feelings and thoughts as clearly as possible. The intent of "me" time is to reveal as much as is needed. Frustrations about the children or a secret hope for the future or the impossible deadline at the office may be the topic.

Person B practices the skill of listening. B asks questions for clarification so that he will understand what A is saying. He refrains from leading the conversation. He tries not to judge A. A condemning gesture such as a frown or arms crossed tightly about the chest, or a calloused comment such as "You sure were dumb to do that," communicates rejection. It suggests that A censor her sharing. B attempts to create an accepting emotional tone.

A is the subject. B enables A to feel the importance of being THE subject.

"You" Time—15 Minutes

During "you" time the subject changes. A and B reverse roles. A becomes the listener; B the straight talker. The perspective is, "I want to know how *you* are feeling, and what *you* are thinking, and what *you* hope will happen."

"We" Time—25 Minutes

During "we" time the couple works on particular problems. The problems may focus on excessive golfing or too seldom sex. A couple may explore a particular life presupposition, or try to understand and to resolve the problems revealed in their last fight. "WE" help each other.

Conclusion—5 Minutes

Conclude each session by telling one's spouse something about her/him which is appreciated, liked, or respected. Focus attention on the positive aspects of each other. Close with an affirmation of each person.

The Resulting Relationship: A Joyous Process

The one hour a day plan ideally:

—Assures each person that she will have time with her spouse, which eliminates the need to use deceptive devices to get special attention.

—Prevents people from drifting apart and gradually becoming

strangers. They change and grow together, instead of aimlessly wandering down different identity highways.

—Furnishes a setting in which disappointment and anger may be expressed, which reduces the tendency to suppress anger.

—Enables each person to deal with hurts, thus preventing the stockpiling of resentment.

—Reduces the displacing of hostility, and thereby eliminates the depersonalizing, devaluing of the spouse; the hostile rhetoric which cuts at the sense of personal worth vanishes from the vocabulary.

—Enables each person to work on frustrating situations and to deal with the need to control, thus learning that sharing responsibilities is more important than always winning.

—Validates concern for oneself, thereby eliminating the need to pretend to be unselfish.

—Establishes a fantasy factory in which dreams and plans for the future are unashamedly shared.

—Creates a *process* for growing together as me, you, and "WE" problems are resolved.

—Affirms each person's sense of personal worth as both give and receive love.

By increasing their skills of listening, talking straight, and giving feedback supportively, two people create a relationship which encourages openness, builds trust, and demonstrates acceptance. Each person discovers her/his brand of Being. She feels good about who she is and what she does. She feels good and enables her spouse, her children, and her friends to feel good about who they are. She affects others positively because she feels respected, fulfills her chosen self-image, and shares her affirmation of life openly.

Where there has been a deficit of intimacy in childhood it is found in marriage. One discovers and affirms her and her spouse's personal worth, which is to feel "I am worthy of the love I receive and joyously give the love I have."

The basic problem of life is solved. One is saved from the fruitless, frantic fighting to prove her worth. She relaxes and enjoys her family and friends, most of the time. She pursues her achievement goals for the satisfaction she receives in accomplishing.

She works and plays. She feels and thinks. She laughs and cries. She fights and loves. She is alive, because someone has awakened within her the gift of life—her potential to give herself intimately and to accept the intimacy of another.

13
THE PRESENCE OF GOD IN PERSONAL INTIMACY[1]

Have you ever felt the mystery of personal intimacy with someone and wondered about its larger meaning? Many people have had this experience. Our experience of personal intimacy seems to have an echo of something more about it. You could say that it is one of the most meaningful ways in which God makes his presence known to us.

Thus, it will be very natural if your growth in an intimate relation begins to reawaken a sense of the presence of God within your life. This does not happen immediately in all cases, but it does happen many times. You may want to read or think more about the presence of God when this begins to happen.

As our experience of intimacy begins to grow, we often begin to appreciate the value that we have as individuals. We are becoming more aware of our own unique characteristics. This too is quite natural, for in very realistic ways, the birth of each person is a wonderful and unique event in history. Biologically, psychologically, socially, and even chemically our creation is something special. It never happened in quite the same way before and it never will again. It is, even at this elementary stage, an intimate and personal adventure. Each of us is, as a result, a unique creation. The particulars of each person are never repeated. In all of its mystery, one's birth represents the holy order of the universe. Theologically interpreted, one's miraculous birth and life is an event which God co-creates with a man and a woman.

The principle of intimacy is also inherent in the continued growth in human relations of each person. One is created with inborn need to be in intimate relationships. This becomes a crucial matter for an infant.

Intimacy is the emotional nourishment needed for growth in infancy. Through extensive research René Spitz discovered that

> infants deprived of handling over a long period will tend at length to sink into ireversible decline and are prone to succumb eventually to intercurrent disease. In effect, this means that what he calls emotional deprivation can have a fatal outcome.[2]

Petirim A. Sorokin, drawing upon the research of René Spitz, Ashley Montagu,[3] and other social scientists, concluded that the absence of intimacy in infancy not only retards emotional and physical growth, it also causes emotionally disabling conditions and may result in the loss of the will to live, thus death. Sorokin wrote,

> The therapeutic power of love is especially important in preventing and healing mental and moral disturbances. . . . The grace of love—in both forms of loving and being loved—is the most important condition for newly born babies to grow into morally and mentally sound human beings.[4]

With her breakthrough in a cure for schizophrenics, Jacqui Lee Schiff reinforces the intimacy thesis. In *All My Children* she describes her method. She re-Parents patients with parental love. Schiff writes,

> Intimacy, love, are the keys to a sick child's [of any age from one to one hundred] recovery, infinitely more powerful than medication and theory. Overwhelmed with unmet needs, the child must have the feel of love.[5]

Intimacy is the emotional nourishment needed to grow in infancy; it is in the order of creation; it is a principle of life.

The principle of intimacy thus has several characteristics.

1. Although intimacy is an inborn need of all people, it must be received in infancy for one to realize her created potential as a human being. In infancy this is a passive position—affection is absorbed. Thus, one is totally dependent upon others not only for a relatively normal life but for the propensity to establish intimate relations.

2. Intimacy is directly related to uniqueness. The way one thinks of, feels about, and perceives herself is related to the intimacy (or lack of it) she receives in infancy and childhood. If in infancy and childhood one is loved for who she is—her innate worth—and not for what she does or how she behaves, she feels that she is a worthy

part of creation. Through intimacy people affirm her created, innate worthfulness. Philosophers have called this an ontological issue, for one experiences *being* in relationship to Being. One belongs to and is a part of the universe and God. The life position, though it may be held unconsciously, is "I am worthy because I am loved," which is to feel "I am worthy of love."

3. Intimacy is experienced as a gift of Grace. It is not something one does for herself; it is something which another gives to her. Intimacy is God's gift of love through people.

4. Whereas it begins with a passive position in infancy, intimacy becomes an active attitude towards self, people, and God. Intimacy is the will to relate, the innate drive to establish intimate relations. One needs to be loved and to love in order to realize her created potential, and her tendency to express love is related to the intimacy received early in life.

Created uniqueness is a principle of creation which includes not only the qualities of personage that make one unique, but one's likeness to all persons in her need to receive and to give intimacy. Intimacy is a principle of God's creation which is integral to the physical, emotional, and spiritual health of infants, children, and adults. Received passively, intimacy becomes an active attitude towards self, people, and God through the will to relate.

Developing Uniqueness and Intimacy

One's developing uniqueness is who she becomes as the physical, psychological, social, and religious forces affect her.

If all parents or parental substitutes were spontaneously intimate, totally integrated within themselves and with each other, and if one's social environment was intimately integrated, one would grow into her created potential. If reared in an ideally friendly, affectionate environment free from hostility, fear, and guilt, one would become a spontaneously loving person who would accept love openly and give it trustingly. She would enjoy the company of people and moments of solitude. She would express and suppress feelings appropriately and helpfully. Living by her beliefs she would experience her and other's holiness, feel a worthy part of creation, and celebrate life as the holy order of the universe.

One enters a less than perfect world, however, and the forces of the world affect her. Feelings and thoughts about self, people, and God are caught which form who one is at any particular moment. One's developing uniqueness includes everything from hunches about heaven to feelings about husbands. It covers everything from what little girls should do to what big girls should not do. Ideas about appropriate behavior and God's nature cuddle together in one's mind. Resentments accummulate which add a special flavor to living as feelings are suppressed or expressed. Self-expectations and other expectations complicatedly compound to produce one of a kind in all of creation.

During the maturation period the enculturating process produces conflicting messages which are internalized; and many of the messages order a suppression of intimacy and a denial of one's innate worthfulness.

The popularly preached concept of original sin is such a message. It enforces the feeling of worthlessness while trying to solve the problem of relationships to self, people, and God. "You are a born sinner. You are basically evil and must be saved from the curse of creation," shouts the pulpit-pounding preacher. This position implies that God created the curse of sin so that he may be a sacrificing hero by sending His son to reverse the order of creation. It implies that one must overcome the curse of creation to be acceptable to, loved by, and in communion with God. Add to the problem such sophisticated phrases as, "God loves you, and if you do not enter into a meaningful relationship with Him He will permit you to suffer existential dread until you are dead; then who knows beyond that?"

Original sin is not a Being problem. It is a result of the enculturating process. One feels the conflicts within herself. She feels alienated from people and God because she has caught the feeling that she and people are basically worthless, that creation itself is evil, unloving, and untrustworthy. The feeling is caught that love is an illusion, people are unfriendly, and God (or "Fate") is out to punish her. The traditional original sin message frustrates the search for self-worth and distorts the vision of the nature of God and the intended order of creation.

An achievement-oriented society communicates a message which often hinders the intimacy principle. One is conditioned to believe that her innate worthfulness depends on achieving some great goal. The hope is that life's basic problem of feeling worthless and alienated from God and people can be solved with actions and abilities. Whereas achieving goals has its own reward and value, it does not solve life's basic problem, which is to feel innately worthful, to be integrally related to people, and to feel a unique, important part of and in communion with God and creation.

The enculturating process often buries one's intimate nature under a crust of conflicting, counter-productive concepts, feelings, and behavior. Life's determinative forces blend to produce one's developing uniqueness, which is everything one is now. *From Loneliness to Intimacy* is an attempt to help people break through these forces by growing an intimate relationship with one's spouse.

The characteristics and dynamics of an intimate relationship—openness, trust, and acceptance—are the conditions which enable two people to experience the affirming Presence of God through each other.

Thus, in an intimate relationship one gradually presents to another pieces of the enculturating crust which cover her intimate nature, and she is accepted with her imperfections. She shares her developing uniqueness in its many-sidedness and eventually experiences intimacy.

God is experienced when intimacy is present between two people, because, "No man has ever seen God; if we love one another, God abides in us and his love is perfected in us." (1 John 4:12)

How is God in this process? The authors are writing another book which will describe the process in detail and suggest specific ways parents may enable their children to know God through both reason and experience. Yet some of the most basic dimensions of God's involvement with us are surely relevant here.

God's Creative Acts

God is the Personalizing Presence who prods people to discover their created uniqueness and worthfulness through intimacy with other persons.

God is personal. He is in His creation. God is not outside of the

situation pushing buttons to produce cause and effect; he is within
the human scene. The principle of created uniqueness and the principle of intimacy are God's creative acts. God is in these acts. He is
immanent; He is within people as the principle of intimacy. The
created intimacy within every individual is God's Presence.

God is the Presence who prods. The drive to relate, to establish
intimate relations is God prodding one to reach toward others. The
sex drive is the most aggressive form of the prodding principle.[6]
God prods one to look inward at herself. He prods one to look
outside of herself to others.

When one is entrusted with the intimacy of another this is experienced as a gift. The gift is the Grace of God expressed through
the principle of intimacy. Through intimacy, that is, through God,
one grows in appreciation of who she is, who other people are, and
what God has done for her through His creation. God is immanent,
within the human scene through His Graceful Presence.

God is also transcendent. He is more than the principle of intimacy within each person or the total intimacy in all people. God is
the transcendent Presence who unites a person with another in an
intimate relationship. He is within each person and between two
people, uniting them with the power of His intimacy. The intimate
relationship has the feel that "there is something in us and between
us which is bigger than both of us."

God is the Personalizing Presence who:
—enables one to accept love openly and to give love spontaneously,
—to enjoy the company of people and moments of solitude,
—to express and suppress feelings appropriately and helpfully,
—to live by one's beliefs,
—to experience the holiness of life in herself, and in her spouse,
   and in her friends,
—to feel a worthy part of creation, and,
—to celebrate the holy order of a graceful creation with one's
   family and friends.

The Grace of God is inherent in human life through God's intimate nature and creation. Thanks be to God who created us with the capacity and urge to be intimate.

"God is love, and he who abides in love abides in God, and God abides in him." (1 John 4:16[2])

APPENDIX—
Topical Notes

Anger

In controlled situations, such as many encounter groups, angry outbursts are encouraged and rewarded; expressing anger is usually praised and personal acceptance follows in the form of comforting clichés and wholesome hugs. Often after a week of training in expressing emotions, the "free spirit" returns home to her husband (or his wife) and lets the anger explode only to discover that, instead of a reward, she receives a one-way ticket to the street. It is unlikely that angry explosions will be rewarded with warm hugs and frilly fuzzies on the uninitiated homefront.

Dr. George R. Bach and Peter Wyden in *The Intimate Enemy* (New York: Avon Books, 1968) describe how couples are taught to fight fair. And we add that two skilled people with sufficient insight, timely training, high self-esteem, mutual respect, and forgiving intimacy can express anger instantly and probably benefit from the exchange. However, for us mortal souls it is usually more helpful to table it.

See also: *The Angry Book,* Theodore I. Rubin (New York: Macmillan, 1969).

Resentment

Although the authors had studied Gestalt Therapy before, the dynamic potential of resentment in personal growth and interpersonal relations surfaced through reading Fritz Perls' *Gestalt Therapy Verbatim* (New York: Bantam Books, 1969). An additional insight Perls offered was in the relationship between resentment and guilt. He wrote, "In Gestalt Therapy, the guilt thing is much simpler [than in Freudian psychology]. We see guilt as projected *resentment.* Whenever you feel guilty, find out what you resent, and the guilt will vanish and you will try to make the other person feel guilty" (p. 51). Obviously, this is an oversimplification of the problem, but it is a fascinating thought. Try it and write us.

The Gestalt Therapy enthusiast will benefit from *Gestalt Therapy Integrated,* Erving and Miriam Polster (New York: Brunner-Mazel, 1973.)

Innocent Bystanders—Children

In an interview a ten-year-old child described the problem of the innocent bystander: "They [parents] build up so much anger that they see you walking through, and all of a sudden they remember everything they've ever been angry at you about. So they say something stupid and sarcastic to you, and all of a sudden you're in the middle. When my mother gets mad, she'll take it out on anybody."

The above quote appeared in "How Children Feel When Parents Fight" by Sam Blum, an article in *Redbook* (November, 1974), p. 148. Mr. Blum described the children's feelings, which is a concern of parents who fight.

In the situation children feel:
1. Afraid the parents will hurt each other,
2. Afraid the parents will hurt them physically,
3. Afraid they caused the fight, which also produces guilt feelings,
4. Afraid of being abandoned by one or both parents,
5. Afraid they will have to choose between parents if one leaves, and,
6. A desire to stop the fight.

A child wants and needs to know (a) that she did not cause the fight, (b) where she stands with her parents, and (c) that the "fight" has been resolved and things are back to normal.

Basically, a child needs to know that her protecting parents love each other and her.

Achievement—Women

Vivian Gornick in "Why Women Fear Success" writes of the tendency in many women to avoid success because of their fear of the consequences in a patriarchal society. She quotes Dr. Matina Horner, a psychologist researching the relationship between motivation and achievement: "Unusual excellence in women was clearly associated for them with the loss of femininity, social rejection, personal and societal destruction or a combination of the above."

The article may enable some women to identify causes for their suppressed anger and resulting resentment. The article appeared in *The First Ms Reader* (New York: Warner Paperback Library, 1973).

The Natural Superiority of Women (New York: Macmillan, rev. ed., 1968) by Ashley Montagu is a must for women seeking a clearer understanding of themselves and a boast in self-esteem. After reading the book it will be weeks before the mysterious smirk vanishes.

Low Self-Esteem Creates Conflict

Virginia Satir in *Peoplemaking* (Palo, California: Science and Behavior Books, Inc., 1972) describes the family as a system. Her unique way of describing the interpersonal dynamics of a family system is not only easy reading, but helpful. While using the term "low-pot" to identify low self-esteem, she graphically grasps the probable behavior and resulting conflict caused by one who feels unappreciated.

Marriage Contracts

The First Ms Reader includes advice on and examples of marriage contracts. As stated both in that book and in this writing, a marriage contract enables people to discuss and to resolve some issues prior to the ceremony. But a marriage based on *law* instead of *grace* doesn't have much chance of growing in intimacy. A marriage contract can be used as a weapon to control rather than a tool by which to grow. In such situations, the wife and husband act like parents to one another, trying to control with guilt or fear, and the home becomes a courtroom for prosecuting attorneys.

Reference: "How to Write a Marriage Contract," Susan Edminston in *The First Ms Reader* (New York: Warner Paperback Library, 1973).

Affiliation—Men

To gain insights into why some men play golf, "go out with the boys," and form exclusive male organizations, see *Men In Groups,* Lionel Tiger (New York: Vintage Books, 1970).

Intimacy

Ashley Montagu in *Touching* (New York: Harper and Row, Publishers, 1971) presents a comprehensive view of the relationship between intimacy and touching. For the person who experiences continuous low self-esteem and/or who is afraid to be touched affectionately this is a helpful book.

The Intimate Marriage by Howard L. and Charlotte H. Clinebell (New York: Harper and Row, 1970) offers suggestions for developing an intimate marriage. The book is most helpful when both persons read it together.

NOTES

1. The basic thoughts of this chapter appeared in an article by the same title in the *Lexington Theological Quarterly,* October, 1973.

2. René A. Spitz, "Hospitalism: Genesis of Psychiatric Conditions in Early Childhood" in "Psychoanalytic Study of the Child," 1:53–74, 1945. As quoted by Eric Berne in his book *Games People Play* (New York: Grove Press, Inc., 1964).

3. Ashley Montagu's most recent research is recorded in his book *Touching* (New York: Harper and Row, 1971). See especially chapter four.

4. Petirim A. Sorokin, *The Ways and Powers of Love* (Boston: Beacon Press, 1954), p. 62.

5. Jacqui Lee Schiff, *All My Children* (New York: Pyramid Publications, 1972), p. 83.

6. The sex drive is God's prodding one to enter into an intimate relationship. *Intimate sex* is much more than the satisfaction of a biological urge; it is the celebration of each person's worthfulness and the intimacy which unites them. With intimate sex one breaks through the great skin barrier to become one with another in an eternal relationship which regularly renews both. Intimate sex is a beautifully intimate life-renewing experience because one meets another in an act which symbolizes the sensitive forces of creation and two people affirm each other's worthfulness in all of their created and developing uniqueness.